PHOEBE PALMER

Her Life and Thought

Harold E. Raser

Studies in Women and Religion
Volume 22

The Edwin Mellen Press
Lewiston/Queenston

Library of Congress Cataloging-in-Publication Data

Raser, Harold E., 1947-
   Phoebe Palmer, her life and thought.

   (Studies in women & religion ; v. 22)
   Bibliography: p.
   1. Palmer, Phoebe, 1807-1874. I. Title. II. Series:
Studies in women and religion ; v. 22
BX8495.P26R37 1987   287'.6'0924 [B]   86-31251
ISBN 0-88946-527-4 (alk. paper)

This is volume 22 in the continuing series
Studies in Women and Religion
Volume 22 ISBN 0-88946-527-4
SWR Series ISBN 0-88946-549-5

The Edwin Mellen Press   The Edwin Mellen Press
Box 450   Box 67
Lewiston, New York   Queenston, Ontario
USA 14092   CANADA L0S 1L0

Printed in the United States of America

For my parents --
in gratitude for lives well lived
in "the way of holiness."

ACKNOWLEDGEMENTS

Thanks is due C. Conrad Cherry who helped to launch this study and Ernest B. Lowrie who guided it to completion. I am also grateful to colleagues and students at Nazarene Theological Seminary whose encouragement kept it from being aborted at many points along the way. Most of all, I must thank Joy, Erika, and Derren without whom this simply could not have been written.

TABLE OF CONTENTS

CHAPTER I
INTRODUCTION

When Phoebe Palmer died, thousands of persons mourned her. A bishop of the Methodist Episcopal Church delivered her funeral oration. Magazines carried black-bordered obituaries. Memorial services were held in several American cities. At one of these T. DeWitt Talmage, well known minister of the Brooklyn Tabernacle, eulogized her as the "Columbus of the Higher Life," who "showed to the Church of God that there were mountain peaks of Christian satisfaction that it had never attained." Her guidance, he declared, had resulted in persons from the "Presbyterian Church and the Baptist Church, and the Methodist Church and the Episcopal Church, and all the churches, coming and kneeling down...bemoaning their unbelief and their coldness, and then rising up and saying: 'I have got it--the blessing.'" Though she had gone, reflected Talmage, "she lived long enough to see the whole Christian Church waking up to this doctrine (of Christian holiness), and thousands and tens of thousands coming on the high table-land where she once stood...." "Glorious soul of Phoebe Palmer!" he exclaimed, "Synonym of holiness unto the Lord!"[1] Another clergyman doubted "whether any minister or layman of our times has been so influential for good" as Phoebe Palmer while a colleague announced, "I cannot think of any woman in all the history of the church who has been more useful...."[2]

Allowing for considerable "eulogistic license," these words of profuse praise are important indicators of the impact made by Phoebe Palmer on the religious world of the nineteenth century. Mrs. Palmer (1807-1874) was indeed a significant--perhaps the most significant --catalyst in the movement to promote Christian holiness, or entire sanctification, or the "higher Christian life" which swept through North American Christianity in the nineteenth century, spilling over into Britain and Europe as well. Records indicate that tens of thousands of persons did respond to her invitations to "repent" and "believe" and find release in divine forgiveness and the impartation of "Perfect Love" toward God and humankind. And in certain respects her name is "synonymous with holiness unto the Lord" as this concept was conceived, taught, and lived out in the context of nineteenth-century American religion.

Owing, however, to the fact that the movement in which she figured so largely eventually produced a host of schismatic "holiness" sects and denominations, sometimes perceived as being on the perimeter of American Christianity, Palmer has been subjected to considerable scholarly neglect. Despite this she was no sect maker, playing out a minor role in some side street of history. She was a woman to whom thousands of people looked for leadership, and by whom thousands were instructed, in a time when women were not generally accorded positions of leadership or authority in American culture. She lived and died a pious Methodist at a time in American history when that denomination had become the largest, and in many ways quintessential, American church body, dominating what has been called "The Methodist Age in America."[3] She gained a national and international reputation as a revivalist (and not only among Methodists)

during the middle years of the nineteenth century, a
time in which religious life was very nearly defined by
the themes and practices of revivalism. Her popularity
took her across the Atlantic in the select company of
Charles Finney, D. L. Moody, James Caughey, and a handful of other influential itinerants, a group which one
recent writer has dubbed the "Transatlantic
Revivalists."[4] She conducted a weekly religious
gathering for some thirty-five years which was attended
by persons representing nearly all major Protestant
churches in America, ministers of these churches making
up not a small part of the number.[5] Her religious
writings, beginning with The Way of Holiness published
in 1843, and followed by such titles as Entire Devotion
to God (1845), Faith and Its Effects (1848), and The
Promise of the Father (1859) sold well in America and
Britain, and some were translated into several
languages. She also edited a religious periodical, The
Guide to Holiness, which under her editorship between
1864 and 1874 reached a circulation of nearly 40,000.

The neglect of Phoebe Palmer needs to be corrected.
Her story, while important to the history of the modern
"holiness" churches, is also one that bears upon the
history of revivalism in American religion, nineteenth-
century religious thought, the role of women in American
religion, and some of the dynamics of American culture
generally in an age hugely taken with religion and
religious issues. Yet, Palmer's only "biography" to date
is the 1876 Life and Letters, a compilation of some of
her letters and papers interspersed with pious comments
by an admiring minister.[6] No scholarly examination of
her life and work has appeared in the century since her
death.

This present study seeks to help recover Phoebe Palmer from the historical attic. Her influence, both in her own day and upon the ongoing holiness movement, demands that we know her better. Clearly this opinion is not an isolated one, for during the time that this work has been in preparation, several monographs have appeared investigating aspects of her career, and chapters in several books have looked at her role in various dimensions of American life and religion in the nineteenth century. Still, however, no one has attempted what is attempted here--a comprehensive examination of Phoebe Palmer's life experience, her system of religious thought, and her role as a religious leader in nine-teenth-century America.

A. Antecedent Palmer Scholarship

To the degree that it has been kept alive, the memory of Phoebe Palmer has been conserved mostly by a small group of scholars devoted to understanding the "holiness movement" in American religion, that revival of interest in what John Wesley (1703-1791), the founder of Methodism, had called "Christian Perfection" or "Perfect Love," which arose in the nineteenth century and led to the formation of a number of rather robust Protestant denominations, among these the Church of the Nazarene, the Pilgrim Holiness Church, the Church of God (Anderson, Indiana), and the Wesleyan and Free Methodist Churches (the latter two emerging in connection with other issues in addition to "holiness"), as well as affecting a broad segment of the religious life of the nation in the nineteenth and early twentieth centuries.

From the work of these few, others have picked up clues to the existence and importance of Palmer, and have given her at least passing notice in the appropriate

context. So, for example, Sydney Ahlstrom, in his
Religious History of the American People, cites Palmer
briefly as "the greatest among countless other Methodist
propagandists for the doctrine (of Christian Perfection)
in nineteenth-century America," and directs the reader
to the work of the "holiness" scholar Timothy L. Smith.[7]
Similarly, Winthrop Hudson notes Palmer's influence in
generating "the holiness revival," drawing attention to
the work of Smith and John L. Peters.[8]

The initial interest in Palmer appears to have
been generated by a spin-off of scholarly activity from
the renaissance of Wesley studies which occurred in the
1930s and 1940s.[9] This activity led eventually to a
reconsideration of the history of John Wesley's heirs in
America, the people of the Methodist Episcopal Church,
and the important transfer of Wesley's teachings from
Britain to America, and their propagation and elabora-
tion here. The three volume History of American
Methodism may be seen as the culmination of this
process.[10] A part of it, however, involved the special-
ized work of two or three students of American religion
who had been steeped in the contention of the various
"holiness" churches that they, rather than the American
Methodist Church, have most faithfully perpetuated the
concerns and views of John Wesley, particularly his
doctrine of Christian Perfection.[11] In the 1950s these
students examined the career of that doctrine in
America, and opened up some new vistas in religious
history in doing so. Phoebe Palmer appeared in several
of those.

This effort to some extent built upon, but to an
even greater extent departed from, the "standard" treatments of "perfectionism" in America authored in the
1920s by Merrill E. Gaddis and Benjamin B. Warfield.[12]

Warfield, while not concerned exclusively with American developments, did give a major portion of the second of his two volumes to "perfectionist" concerns in America. He wrote, however, from the perspective of Reformed Protestantism with a major concern for "perfectionist" tendencies and currents in that branch of Christianity. Because of this he largely ignored Wesleyanism or Methodism except to recognize it as a major conservator of perfectionist teaching within the Christian tradition and to occasionally note its influence on American Reformed "perfectionists" such as Charles Finney, Asa Mahan and William Boardman."[13]

In one instance this leads Warfield to refer specifically to Phoebe Palmer as a prominent Methodist teacher of "perfectionism" and as one who influenced the nineteenth-century American philosopher of some note, Thomas Cogswell Upham, a Congregationalist, to embrace perfectionist beliefs. Warfield's concern there is not with Palmer herself, but rather with the "Methodist connection" in Upham's teaching, a connection which throughout the book automatically damns the theories of the one so tainted.[14]

Beyond this, however, Warfield's interest did not extend much to significant individuals or events connected with the Methodist propagation of "perfectionism." Even so his work did establish via its limited focus that "perfectionism" has been an important preoccupation of considerable segments of American Christianity, a fact which was not lost on "holiness" folks.

It is strange that the work of Merril E. Gaddis never saw publication, for his 1929 thesis painted the story of "perfectionism" in American Christianity with a much broader brush than Warfield, providing in the process the most comprehensive account of perfectionist concerns and activities available prior to the work of younger scholars in the 1970s and since. Gaddis about equally balanced his work between Methodist and non-Methodist representatives of perfectionism. He was perhaps the first scholar to call attention to the noticeable decline in perfectionist fervor among American Methodists in the early decades of the nineteenth century, and to take a close look at the "revival" occasioned by the work of the National Campmeeting Association for the Promotion of Holiness in the years immediately following the Civil War.[15] These views found endorsement in the work of his mentor, William Warren Sweet.[16]

Gaddis noted a considerable flurry of perfectionist activity in the decades just prior to the Civil War, but he did not consider this to be a major movement. Rather, he characterized it as a defense of a decaying old order at a time "when the doctrine [of Christian Perfection] was declining in vitality and use."[17] He admitted the existence of a large pre-Civil war holiness literature and even the fact that "this literature appears to have enjoyed a wide reading," but hesitated to say more. In this connection there is reference to The Guide to Holiness "conducted by Dr. and Mrs. W. C. Palmer" and even to its intention of being the "means of creating a movement among Methodist elements of the population for the restoration of the doctrine of Christian Perfection to its former popularity," but that is very nearly the extent of Gaddis' concern with the Palmers or the pre-Civil War " holiness movement."[18] Neither The Guide to Holiness nor any of Phoebe Palmer's books appear in his bibliography.

The first to trace the path of the doctrine of the Christian Perfection in America in the wake of the renewal of Wesley studies in the 1930s and '40s was John L. Peters, a graduate of a "holiness" college, who did his work for a Yale Ph.D. Published in 1956 as Christian Perfection and American Methodism, Peters' thesis went all the way back to the sources behind Wesley's doctrine, but focused primarily on the transplanting, development, and modification of the doctrine in America. Peters found the contention of earlier scholars (notably Gaddis and Sweet) that the doctrine of Christian Perfection had quickly become little more than a creedal matter among American Methodists to be valid, but he also discovered a significant revival of interest in the doctrine occurring much earlier than generally supposed.[19] A key figure in this revival he identified as Methodist layperson Phoebe Palmer. Working primarily with Wheatley's The Life and Letters of Mrs. Phoebe Palmer, and some issues of The Guide of Holiness, a monthly "holiness" periodical which Phoebe Palmer edited for a decade, Peters concluded that she and her husband had done more than any others to spark a renewed interest in the doctrine of Christian Perfection in America, prior to the Civil War, calling them "the outstanding exponents of Christian perfection in American Methodism during the third and fourth decades of the nineteenth century."[20] Though including Phoebe's husband, Dr. Walter C. Palmer, in this assessment, it is clear that Peters considered him a minor player to his wife.

Peters focused on the Tuesday Meeting for the Promotion of Holiness, over which Phoebe Palmer presided for thirty-five years, a weekly religious meeting attended by clergymen and laypeople from many denominations-- sometimes swelling to over 300 in number--as the most significant agency for promoting the "holiness revival."

He briefly sketches Mrs. Palmer's role as writer and "evangelist," but notes that the Tuesday meeting was "her most continuous medium of promotion."[21]

Though Peters does not develop it much, one of the most important aspects of his examination of Phoebe Palmer, in my estimation, has to do with her unique conceptualizations of the doctrine she so ardently propagated. He identifies six emphases of Palmer which "tended to deviate from the Wesleyan mean," but quickly concludes that these "were not major emphases in Mrs. Palmer's teachings."[22] Some later investigators have disagreed with Peters at this point. The whole matter will be analyzed in subsequent chapters, for it figures largely in any final evaluation of Mrs. Palmer as a religious thinker and leader. Peters does allow that many of these emphases became "distinguishing marks" of segments of what eventually came to be called the "holiness movement."[23]

Peter's work was quickly followed up by the work of two others who published almost simultaneously in 1957. The longer work was the notable study of nineteenth-century revivalism as a social phenomenon by Timothy L. Smith, Revivalism and Social Reform In Mid-Nineteenth-Century America, while the shorter was an article entitled "I Commend Unto You Phoebe," which appeared in the summer issue of Religion and Life, and which was authored by Ernest A. Wall.[24] Both called attention to Phoebe Palmer as playing a significant role in nineteenth-century American religious life.

Of the two it may be said that it was Smith who opened the door the widest for later students of American religion through his repeated references to Phoebe Palmer in several important connections.[25] Whereas Peters had seen Palmer as important in Methodism and that primarily through the agency of her "Tuesday Meetings," Smith uncovered evidence of a far wider role, numbering her among a select group of American revivalists and social reformers who dominated American religious life on the eve of the Civil War and who "seemed to their contemporaries the most distinguished spiritual leaders of the age."[26] Smith decried the tendency of historians who preceded him to often ignore revivalism as "but a half-breed child of the Protestant faith" and so to consign its practitioners to the small print of religious histories, if to notice them at all.[27] It was Smith's contention that because of this bias the Bushnells, Theodore Parkers, and Gladdens of the nineteenth century have received ample attention from researchers, while the A. B. Barneses, Edward Norris Kirks--and Phoebe Palmers--have remained in relative obscurity. Even Charles Finney has not received his due, according to Smith, a contention less supportable now than in 1957, though the biography Smith longed for then has still not been written!

Of the neglected religious figures of the mid-nineteenth century, Smith rejoiced that at least Phoebe Palmer had recently "escaped anonymity," referring in a footnote to the work of John L. Peters. Smith attempted to ensure that this escape would be permanent. On page after page Palmer appears in significant, and previously unchronicled, roles as best-selling religious author, itinerant revivalist "preacher" in the U.S., Canada, and Britain, editor of an important "perfectionist" journal, innovative religious thinker, ecumenist, and most importantly for Smith in this particular book, leader of the Christian social movement which he argues had its roots in this period and was integrally bound up with revivalism and the perfectionist coloring that it bore in the

1840s and '50s, especially.[28] The thesis that "the power
which earliest opposed the organized evils of urban
society and stretched out hands of mercy to help the
poor was sanctified compassion" is central to Smith's
book and Phoebe Palmer is central to the substantiation
of this thesis.[29] We will need to return to this in a
subsequent chapter of the present study. In summary, it
may be said that it was really Smith who "rescued"
Phoebe Palmer from anonymity by virtue of the wide
ranging research which he did and the broad context with
which he concerned himself in contrast to the more
limited, narrowly focused concerns of John Peters before
him.

The sketch by Ernest Wall in Religion and Life
drew additional attention to Phoebe Palmer and helped to
further strengthen her nascent reputation. Wall worked
mainly from Richard Wheatley's 1876 "biography" and was
able to illuminate some biographical material neglected
by Peters and Smith in their larger concerns. Appearing
as one of a series on woman "saints," Wall's article in
part attempted to relate Palmer to the mystical tradition of Christianity, specifically as embodied by
Catherine of Siena.[30] This was sufficiently suggestive,
it would seem, to further strengthen Palmer's claim to
significance beyond the context of nineteenth-century
American Methodism and its intramural goings on. In
addition to this, Wall also critically (much more so
than either Peters or Smith) assessed her contributions
to social amelioration ("her help was of a limited
kind"),[31] ethics ("her strict ideas of worldliness must
have been a great trial to her less devoted friends"),[32]
and theology ("a stabilizing mixture of realism and
idealism").[33]

The next treatment of Palmer, important more for its context than its length, appeared in 1964 as part of the three-volume "official" history of American Methodism. In a chapter on "The Holiness Crusade," Timothy L. Smith sketched out a part of Methodist history long neglected by the standards treatments.[34] Beginning with its roots in the 1830s, Smith traced a revival of interest in the doctrine of Christian Perfection among American Methodists through the 1860s and '70s when special "holiness" organizations were created, down to the end of the nineteenth century by which time the "revival" had become the occasion for disruption and even schism. Prominent in the first four decades of this revival was Phoebe Palmer, and though Smith did not refer to her at length, he did refer to her often.[35] It would seem that inclusion in this significant comprehensive history of American Methodism signalled a growing acceptance of the findings of Peters, Smith himself, and Wall as to the importance and yet heretofore neglect of Palmer as a religious leader.

Following the work of the scholars in the 1950s, with the exception of the chapter in The History of American Methodism, there was a hiatus of nearly ten years before another historian published important material on Phoebe Palmer. Ironically, this material had originally been part of a dissertation completed in 1952, long before Peters, Smith or Wall published, and yet none of them showed any awareness of it. Over nearly eighteen pages Delbert R. Rose more thoroughly than anyone in print before him sketched out the contours of Phoebe Palmer's life and public career.[36] Rose drew mainly from Wheatley's Life and Letters of Mrs. Phoebe Palmer and contemporary secondary sources dealing with her activities. There is no attempt to analyze the several books Phoebe Palmer wrote, or to survey her contributions to The Guide to Holiness. This is well in keeping with Rose's purposes, however, which were not to examine Palmer's career and thought in detail, but rather to trace briefly the genesis of the National Holiness Association, an organization of which Rose was the official historian at the time A Theology of Christian Experience was published, and the life experience of one of its prominent leaders, the Rev. Joseph H. Smith (1855-1946).[37]

From his study of the background to the period when Smith was active, Rose concluded that Phoebe Palmer, more than any other, led the revival of interest in "Perfectionism" which culminated in the founding of the National Campmeeting Association for the Promotion of Holiness, even though Palmer was never a member of this group. Rose thus highlighted those activities occupying Mrs. Palmer which he saw as most crucial to the success of the revival, these being her Tuesday Meeting for the Promotion of Holiness, editorial oversight of The Guide to Holiness, her extensive contacts by letter (a veritable "soul clinic by mail"), her books, and her traveling evangelistic endeavors.

Neither Rose nor any of the other students publishing to this point made much of the theological innovations attributable to Phoebe Palmer's influence. Peters had mentioned certain emphases which "tended to deviate from the Wesleyan mean," but had concluded that these were minor aspects of Mrs. Palmer's teachings.[38] Wall, while noting certain characteristic themes, had tended to evaluate these as not particularly palatable to twentieth-century sensibilities, but gave no notice of the fact that they may also have been unique and distinctive even in Palmer's nineteenth-century

milieu.[39] Smith was so taken with Palmer's revivalistic
leadership and social action projects that he hardly
noticed her distinctive stamp on doctrine.

This all changed, however, with the publication of
a relatively brief article in the official organ of the
Wesleyan Theological Society in the spring of 1971.[40] In
this article, Ivan Howard drew attention to Phoebe
Palmer's teaching regarding the doctrine of assurance of
salvation--more specifically assurance of Christian
Perfection--a doctrine central to John Wesley's theological system, and one which clearly distinguished it
from the usual "Calvinist" systems of doctrine. Palmer
is found to diverge from Wesley, and from many of her
Methodist contemporaries, in her understanding and
articulation of this teaching. There is little analysis
of the functional role of Palmer's innovative expression
of this one doctrine in her overall system of thought,
or of its possible derivation, but rather concern for
documenting of differences between Palmer and Wesley,
and others, and the venturing of opinion that perhaps
Palmer's view is more consistent and "biblical" than
that of Wesley.[41] The differences are, however, clearly
drawn and carefully illustrated.

This somewhat tentative exploration into Palmer's
theological innovations set an important precedent for
later researchers, almost all of whom have given considerable attention to this aspect of Palmer's life and
work. In a book which is in many ways a complement to
John Peters' effort in the 1950s, Charles E. Jones
attempted to interpret the American holiness movement
as a social phenomenon, understandable in terms of the
urbanizing process of the nineteenth century. He argued
that holiness religion "aided . . . country folk in
adjustment to urban life in much the same way that

religion had assisted various foreign immigrant groups in accommodating to the New World."[42] Whereas Peters had been concerned exclusively with theological and doctrinal developments, Jones was much more interested in the play of social forces which might account for the emergence of a significant new religious movement and its offspring, the holiness "sects." This interest did not inure Jones to the importance of religious ideas, however. One of the main claims made in the book was that new ideas were propagated in connection with the rise of a "holiness revival" in American Christianity, and further that Phoebe Palmer was behind most of these. While not delving deeply into the nature of these new ideas, Jones drew a conclusion that went beyond anything earlier researchers had been willing to say. He declared that "While the holiness movement always regarded John Wesley as its greatest authority, the movement owed many of its distinctive ideas and practices to Phoebe Palmer."[43] He also found that Palmer "permanently modified American Methodist teaching on perfection. . . ."[44] It was left to others to further delineate the nature and extent of these "modifications."

In the most thorough examination of the American holiness movement to date, Melvin E. Dieter picked up where Charles Jones left off and gave extended treatment to Phoebe Palmer as a creative religious thinker as well as organizer and revivalistic promoter.[45] With Jones, Dieter took Palmer's "special emphases" much more seriously than had Peters or Wall before him, and found them to be major rather than minor components of her system. Echoing Jones, he argued that the nineteenth-century revival represented a "new blend of religious forces," and that Palmer's theological formulations both reflected and contributed to that blend.[46] Dieter explicated with some thoroughness her "altar theology," her insistence on the necessity of public testimony to the attainment of Christian Perfection, her apology for the right of women to minister in the churches and her "Biblicism," among other characteristic emphases, as elements which distinguished her from many of her Methodist contemporaries and from the Methodist theological tradition going back to John Wesley.[47] He concluded concerning Palmer that "The practice, promotion and teaching of holiness, as developed . . . at her home and in her ministry, became normative for the (holiness) movement."[48] In addition, wrote Dieter, "It is difficult to overestimate the importance of a proper understanding of the nature of that incipient history to all further efforts to interpret the ensuing movement, or its proper place in the history of revivalism."[49]

There is an unmistakable challenge in Dieter's work to carry the study of Phoebe Palmer to still greater lengths if one would understand the American holiness movement more fully. Some in the tradition of that movement have taken some further steps in that direction, while others within the scholarly community have "discovered" Phoebe Palmer within their own quite different purviews, and have added interesting facets to our growing understanding of this very notable woman. An example of the former is Donald Dayton who has produced monographs which focus largely, though not exclusively, on Palmer, as well as giving her prominent attention in his book, Discovering An Evangelical Heritage.[50] Examples of the latter would include several women scholars who, picking up threads from earlier studies, have woven considerable fabric of Phoebe Palmer's "feminist" convictions. So, Amanda Porterfield touched on Palmer in her Feminine Spirituality in America.[51]

Rosemary Radford Ruether and Rosemary Skinner Keller included a selection from Palmer's book, The Promise of the Father (1859), in their collection of documents illustrative of women's role in American religious life.[52] And so, too, the editors of Women in New Worlds: Historical Perspectives on the Wesleyan Tradition included an essay by Nancy Hardesty which compares Palmer's rationale for women in ministry to that of Frances Willard.[53] Another example of interest in Palmer for reasons other than her involvement in the holiness movement is the work of Richard Carwardine who has investigated the interrelationship between the evangelical Protestant Christian communities in Britain and America between the years 1790 and 1865, finding considerable influence in Britain of American "new measures revivalism" transmitted there by a group of American itinerants active on both sides of the Atlantic during these years.[54] Phoebe Palmer appears in this study as one of the more significant practitioners of American revivalism on British soil, Carwardine judging the number of speaking engagements filled and religious conversions recorded by her and her husband to be "enormously impressive."[55]

B. Design of the Present Study

From the preceding discussion it should be clear that the reputation Phoebe Palmer enjoyed among her contemporaries in mid-nineteenth-century America as one of the more widely known and respected religious leaders of the time has been gradually rehabilitated over the past twenty-five years or so by students of American religious history. Somehow overlooked in the annals of nineteenth-century history for a time, her story is once again beginning to be told and her importance and

influence evaluated. Standard reference works like The
Encyclopedia of World Methodism now routinely include
entries on her, typically describing her as "an outstanding leader in the holiness movement both in and
outside Methodism, in this country and abroad," and as
"one of the moving spirits in one of the important
theological and doctrinal crusades of the nineteenth
century," as well as noting her role in crusades for
such as the "liberation of women in the church and in
society," the establishment of just wages for domestic
help, and curtailment of the "liquor traffic and its
degrading effects upon human life and the community."[56]

Nevertheless, given the deserved attention Phoebe
Palmer and her work have been attracting, there has
still not appeared a study comprehensive in its scope
and interest. All of the Palmer scholarship so far has
taken the form of brief monographs or has been woven
into the fabric of a study concerned with some broad
theme or movement in which Palmer plays one part. The
present study seeks to go beyond these limitations to
bring Phoebe Palmer to center stage and to delegate the
other issues and concerns to supporting roles. The
following chapters are about Phoebe Palmer--her life
experience spanning the first three-quarters of the
nineteenth century, her public career as a religious
spokesperson and leader, and the central ideas she
embraced and propagated. Issues relating to nineteenth-
century American religion generally, the role of women
inside and outside the churches, developments within
Methodism, the holiness movement, and other relevant
concerns are appropriate, and necessary, dimensions of
this study, but they are taken up in connection with
Phoebe Palmer and not the reverse.

Because knowing and understanding Palmer is the major objective, her own writings have been utilized extensively; they constitute her public testimony and yet they have remained largely untapped. Secondary sources are of course necessary and appear throughout. The work of previous researchers has been acknowledged already; it has been appreciatively consulted and appropriated in the preparation of these pages. Still, it is Palmer and her work which is our main concern. She deserves careful study. Only when all the facts are known can valid assessment and interpretation of her role in nineteenth-century American religious life take place. It is hoped this effort will contribute substantially to this end.

CHAPTER II
LIFE SKETCH: WHO IS PHOEBE PALMER?

A. Early Life

When Phoebe Worrall was born in New York City on 18 December 1807 less than twenty-five years had elapsed since the occupation of the area by British troops during the Revolutionary War. America's third president, Thomas Jefferson, was nearing the end of his second term in office. Ohio, the first state to be carved out of the Northwest Territories, was less than five years old. The War of 1812 was still in the making. The Methodist Episcopal Church, which influenced Phoebe so largely, was still in its bare infancy as an American religious body, only just approaching its twenty-third anniversary. Already, however, it was giving signs of vitality and a promising future, having grown from about 14,000 members in 1784 to almost 120,000 members in 1805.[1] By the time Phoebe reached middle life it would be the largest denomination in the United States.

Phoebe was born to Henry and Dorthea Wade Worrall, the fourth of sixteen children born to the couple, only nine of whom survived to adulthood.[2] Information on the family's background is not plentiful, but what there is suggests a degree of material prosperity and most certainly a commitment to a strict Methodist piety. Both parents were active members of the Methodist Episcopal Church in New York City, and inculcated religious values in the home with great solemnity. Their view would certainly have echoed that of the celebrated Rev. Billy

Hibbard into whose family one of the Worrall sons, Isaac, married.[3] Hibbard took it to be his duty

> not only to exhort people to quit their sins
> and pray to God to convert their souls; but
> also to reprove whatever I heard or saw that
> was sinful, in all company, at home or abroad.
> Some said in this I did wrong . . . But I
> quoted--"Thou shalt not suffer sin upon thy
> brother or neighbor, but thou shalt rebuke
> him."[4]

The Worralls considered religious conversion and holy living to be peerless priorities for their children. To this end they conducted twice-daily family worship, the commencement of which was signalled by the ringing of a bell throughout the household. "The law of the family was that all earthly considerations should be subservient to the duties of the hour devoted to family worship."[5] Most of the Worrall children soon internalized the religious values of their parents. "Trained in the nurture and admonitions of the Lord. The most of that large family . . . became members of the household of faith, in early life."[6]

Phoebe's mother was American born and of "pious parentage." Her father was British born and had emigrated to America in his early twenties.[7] The son of loyal Yorkshire Anglicans who "attended to the ordinances of piety" and were "instructed in the things of the Kingdom," young Henry Worrall had become curious about the "Methodist" followers of John Wesley and had stolen away from home on occasion to hear the famous Wesley preach in the pre-dawn hours at Bradford.[8] He became a regular attender of these "sunrise services" and eventually joined the Methodist society. Worrall was only fourteen at the time, but he would proudly recall to his children years later that he had received his ticket of membership from the hand of Wesley himself.[9]

Not long after the War of Independence Worrall set sail for America "of whose institutions he was an ardent admirer."[10] En route he found the weather sometimes threatening both above and below deck. A group of ship-board "skeptics" flying the popular intellectual banner of the day challenged his Wesleyan-style Christian convictions to the point that he took up reading Voltaire, Rousseau, and Tom Paine. "It was a dangerous voyage, and the soul of the voyager was greatly imperilled...."[11] The young man survived the trip with both body and soul intact, however, perhaps wavering for a time. Worrall clearly never fully embraced the skeptical critiques of Christianity to which he was exposed, for his arrival in New York found him entering into a time of "testing the truth of the Christian faith experimentally" to see if it could answer to the rationalist challenge.[12] The nature of this "test" is not known, but it appears that Worrall's intellectual struggle was not great (the test was to be for two weeks) and that the outcome was never really in doubt. Almost immediately he "happened" upon a church where Methodist hymns were being sung which "conspired to remind him of the scenes and sentiments of early days in his fatherland." Under the influence of these familiar surroundings, "strangely was his heart touched by the finger of the Almighty," bringing to his mind a powerful realization of what he had "lost by the evil communications of subtle companions and bad books ...." Within two weeks, now back in familiar and comfortable territory, Worrall abandoned his brief fling with rationalism and underwent a Methodist religious conversion in which he "cast his helpless soul on the Saviour, and was saved! He was born of the Spirit and old things passed away."[13]

The "near apostasy" was apparently never fully forgotten by Henry Worrall, however, nor were the "culprits" involved, for many years later his daughter Phoebe would rail against the "pernicious tendency" of "Voltaire, Tom Paine, Rousseau, or any other of those infidel writers," and lament the thousands "now writhing in endless misery" who had been "poisoned" by them.[14] She would also take special delight in the conversion of "free-thinkers" and "deists."[15]

Sometime after his conversion, Henry Worrall met and married Dorthea Wade. In all likelihood their meeting took place in the Methodist Church, which was fitting as so much of their lives and the lives of their children were to be bound up with that organization. The Worralls were energetic Methodists throughout their lives, Henry holding various official positions in the Church and Dorthea serving it in ways appropriate to her "meek and quiet spirit."[16] That meant that Henry gained considerable reputation among New York City Methodists, his name revered as "ointment poured faith," while Dorthea wielded less public influence, but no doubt fully as much familial influence, as a matriarch "distinguished in her house by domestic discipline" and as one who "presided with dignity" over her household.[17]

The household over which Dorthea presided, while certainly marked by piety, was also marked by a good degree of material prosperity. It is impossible to be too specific about this for lack of information, but what evidence there is suggests a comfortable style of life. The Worrall home was comfortable enough, and Henry Worrall a prominent enough "son of England" that British diplomats were occasionally entertained there.[18] Apparently servants were employed, for the daughters of the family never seem to have known "domestic labor" other than the supervision of hired help. The biographer of one of Phoebe's sisters thought it "doubtful whether she ever prepared a meal in her life."[19] Phoebe at one point confessed to having inherited "aristocratic feelings" which governed her actions until intense religious experience changed these.[20] Though the father's business is never identified, it is likely it involved the production and sales of machinery to the multiplying number of factories in the Northeastern United States. It may also have involved financing manufacturing ventures.[21] Characterized as "a man of mental vigor, of mechanical genius," he had "by skill and success in business secured ample means for the culture and comfort of his hospitable home."[22] It was in an atmosphere of comfortable gentility, then, that Phoebe Worrall and her eight brothers and sisters grew up.

It is difficult to tell much about the quality of family life in the Worrall family for the simple reason that it is never a concern of any of the writers who give us a glimpse into the home. Most write as "spiritual biographers" seeking to tell how these "souls" lived well, coming early to God and ever after glorifying Him. Incidents and remembrances which illustrate the theme are the stuff of their books; ordinary intrafamily relationships are not. Still one may gather some impressions from what is told, and from the quality of the family life which the Worrall children established in their own homes. The emphasis on piety is of course a clear note which sounds throughout. Family life was structured around periods of Bible reading, prayer, and religious instruction as well as church activities like class meetings, "Love Feasts," revival meetings, and regular weekly Sunday worship. The children of the family were pressed from early childhood to "repent" and "be saved." Much common family activity seems to have been directed to this end. The grown Phoebe very possibly reflected the training of childhood when she described the practice in her own household of "redeeming the time" of dinner and conversation by requiring each person around the dinner table to quote a Bible verse from memory, the first choosing one beginning with "A", the second with "B", the third with "C", until the whole alphabet had been covered.[23] Also revealing is her comment, "I love a cheerful piety--but we need wisdom. Cheerfulness must not degenerate into levity."[24] The Worrall home was probably not a place of much laughter or humor. All indicators point to a disciplined, sober environment.

The picture of solemnity and piety ought not to be overdrawn, however. The Worrall children seem to have developed normal attachments to parents and to one another, and the atmosphere, while intense, seems to have been a supportive and nurturing one as well. All of the Worrall children married well and several distinguished themselves in public careers. In all, there were sixteen Worrall children, nine of whom survived to adulthood. Along with Phoebe, the fourth of the nine, there were Henry C., Caroline, Sarah, Noah, Mary Jane, Wade, Hannah, and Isaac.[25]

It is not surprising that Phoebe Worrall should have developed a sensitive conscience and rather precocious religious sensibilities, given the no-nonsense environment of her childhood. Allowing her some poetic license perhaps (yet given her total life one suspects she may be accurate), she wrote at age nineteen, "I do not remember ever to have been willfully disobedient to any parental command."[26] Her "biographer" supports this:

"Her filial devotion was faultless. She regarded the expressed wish of her parents as binding upon her conduct as a direct command."[27] So sensitive was Phoebe, in fact, that her childish fear of lying became a standing joke. She would hesitate to state all but the most obvious or verifiable facts to be true, on the outside chance that she might inadvertently "lie" about something. Phoebe recalled of her childhood that "this extreme sensitiveness, as to moral . . . obligation, grew up with me; so much so, that I was sometimes smiled at for my well-intentioned scrupulousness, and at other times almost censured for carrying it to a troublesome excess."[28] "Phoebe <u>knows</u> nothing," it came to be said, "she only <u>thinks</u>."[29]

Phoebe's sensitivity to matters of truthfulness and obedience to authority was matched by a keen receptivity to the expressions of piety modeled and taught by her parents. Though she could not recall ever having had a definite conversion experience in the Methodist fashion, in her religious acts and sentiments she was clearly her parents', and her church's, child.[30] Phoebe noted that "early instructed in experimental religion, I was in the morning of my existence aware of the necessity of its affecting my life, and even in minute things inducing a change of conduct."[31] This led her to be a "careful attendant on the ordinances of the sanctuary," as well as motivating her to live "above the frivolities of the day. Neither in appearance nor practice did she conform to the world."[32]

Nursing an interest as a child in writing, Phoebe naturally turned this into religious channels, producing religious poetry. Reflecting her considerable literary ability, and her rather precocious piety at age eleven is this surviving poem which she etched on the fly leaf of her New Testament:

> This revelation--holy, just, and true--
> Though oft I read, it seems forever new;
> While light from heaven upon its pages rest,
> I feel its power, and with it I am blest.
>
> Within its leaves, its grace divine displays,
> Makes known the Almighty's will in various ways;
> Justice, it speaks, to those who heaven defy,
> And with ungracious lips its truths deny.
>
> 'Tis here the wearied one, in sin's rough road,
> May find the path mark'd out that leads to God.
> And when oppressed by earth, all may here find
> Sweet promises of peace to cheer the mind.
>
> To this blest treasure, O my soul, attend,
> Here find a firm and everlasting friend--
> A friend in all life's varied changes sure,
> Which shall to all eternity endure.
>
> Henceforth, I take thee as my future guide,
> Let naught from thee my youthful heart divide.
> And then, if late or early death be mine,
> All will be well, since I, O Lord, am Thine![33]

One of the most perplexing gaps in the record of Phoebe Worrall's childhood concerns her education. Neither she nor others make any reference to it whatsoever. One would love to know the ways in which a prominent religious teacher and writer was taught in childhood, the intellectual influences to which she was exposed and the level of formal instruction she had known. In Phoebe's case, however, this is a closed book. One can only infer that she received the typical schooling of early nineteenth-century America, either in the so-called "public" schools (which would have required tuition from a family such as hers) or at home. There is no hint of her ever having attended a "female seminary," "academy," or college. There were in fact no colleges in America admitting women until 1833, by which time Phoebe was twenty-six years old.[34] Her level of formal instruction then was probably roughly equivalent to an elementary or grammar school education.

Whatever the case, Phoebe was clearly the possessor of a bright intellect which, given even rudimentary training, was able to achieve a degree of sophistication. True, she was not well versed in philosophy, classical literature, and the like, but within the limits of her experience she demonstrates an ability to think and express herself clearly, and a mastery of the sources considered important in her environment, e.g. the Bible, pious Bible commentators, and the religious "classics" of the Methodism of her day, including the Works of John Wesley.[35] This is reflected in all of her writings and Wheatley is quite correct when he observes that "Her pen flowed freely, and thought expressed itself in perspicuous, forcible, and graceful style...."[36] Especially impressive among the writings is The Promise of the Father, a work of her maturity which gives fuller play to her intellectual powers than any of her other works. There she moves through difficult questions of biblical interpretation with considerable facility, drawing easily from a variety of sources, and building a sustained and cogent argument for the right of women to "minister" in the Christian churches from the Bible, history, logic, and practical experience.[37]

B. Marriage and Preparation for the Public Career

Just short of her twentieth birthday, Phoebe
Worrall married a young physician, Dr. Walter Clarke
Palmer; the date was September 28, 1827.[38] Palmer was
not Phoebe's only suitor, but it appears he was the only
one to gain the approval of her parents, a matter of
great consequence to her. Their disapproval would have
signalled divine disapproval of the match to her, or
nearly so, while their approval signalled divine
approbation.

The reason for the parents' endorsement of Dr.
Palmer is not hard to find. Phoebe reveals it clearly in
an entry in her journal only weeks before the wedding.
"In religious, moral, and intellectual endowments he
stands approved. The best of all is, that he is a
servant of the Lord. On his thirteenth birthday he was
powerfully converted, and now, in his twenty-fourth
year, he is still holding on his way."[39] Palmer was,
like Phoebe, an exemplary child of early nineteenth-
century Methodism. In their understanding of religious
life and in their commitment to the Methodist Episcopal
Church, Phoebe and Walter were kindred spirits. Given
the criteria of earnest piety it is easily understood
why Phoebe thought that their union was "ordered by
Divine Providence."[40] As we shall see, their person-
alities were also ideally complementary, a fact which
helped them to build a mutually satisfying, and
immensely successful, joint "evangelistic" career in
later years.

Walter was born near Middletown, New Jersey, on
February 9, 1804. His parents, Miles and Deborah Clarke
Palmer, had moved to New York City when he was only
three months old.[41] Thus he, like Phoebe, was raised and
lived out his life in the environment of a vital urban

center, one which happened to be a major stronghold of American Methodism and which may very well in fact have been the scene of Methodism's earliest activities on the North American continent.[42] The Palmers were earnest Methodists who along with the Worrall family and others of like mind did much to establish and promote their church in the city. For years the Palmers hosted weekly "class meetings" in their home, a model which must have influenced Walter's unflagging support of the Tuesday Meeting for the Promotion of Holiness when it began to meet in his home in the 1830s.

The environment of the Palmer home was no doubt comparable to that in other Methodist households. Early religious instruction aimed toward a childhood conversion experience was the norm, and Walter gives indication of the usual early preoccupation with sin and salvation and the need for subjective "assurance" of one's acceptance by God. The quest for assurance was especially critical within Methodism because of John Wesley's distinctive teaching on the "witness of the Spirit" which held that "there is an inward impression on the soul of believers, whereby the Spirit of God directly testifies to their spirit that they are children of God."[43] Earnest Methodists always sought, but not always successfully, for this "witness." It was a problem-plagued area for Wesley's heirs as will be seen in subsequent chapters. Walter's youthful religious quest appears to be very much bound up with the problem. Early urged to "seek and find the blessed Jesus," he did so but somehow lost the "joys of salvation" which were not recovered until his thirteenth birthday. The matter of assurance was central, for Palmer had "said all along through his early childhood" that he "had one standing wish, and that was that he might <u>know</u> that he was truly born of the Spirit, and that his sins were blotted out. This happy privilege was awarded him on his thirteenth birthday."[44] This attainment was paralleled by his appointment as a teacher in the "Sabbath School."[45]

Palmer's upbringing and early religious activities led him to consider a career as a clergyman, but he also harbored an interest in medicine. The latter won out when he became convinced that medicine afforded opportunities for a kind of "ministry" in some ways superior to that of the clergyman. He concluded that "no calling on earth could be more Christlike, in its aims and purposes, than that of the pious physician," and that "to possess a correct knowledge of the healing art, so as to know how to go about doing good, not only to the souls of the redeemed race, but to their bodies also," would be to follow in the "footsteps of the heavenly Healer when on earth."[46] With this exalted view of the medical profession in hand, Walter entered the College of Physicians and Surgeons of New York. The religious motive continued strong, for upon the completion of his training Palmer did indeed seek to make his career serve religious ends. On occasion patients were converted as a result of the doctor's overt "Christian witness."[47] He acted in less direct ways too, giving free medical attention to the indigent and even sometimes helping them from his own pocket, giving of his means to support numerous charitable and evangelistic projects, and serving in important church-related leadership roles. Eventually he would use the financial gains from his successful practice to take an early retirement and give his later years to a second career as a travelling revivalist and publisher of religious books.[48]

In every way Phoebe Worrall and Walter Palmer were well matched. "They were one in sympathy, in tastes, in church fellowship, and in Christian profession."[49] In a reflection on their marriage on the occasion of their eleventh anniversary, Phoebe revealed her own sense of the quality of their relationship:

MY DEAREST EARTHLY TREASURE:

Can we ever cease to be grateful, or ever withhold the undivided sacrifice of our hearts and lives from Him who has made us of one heart and mind? Oh, how my soul melts in view of such a precious gift, such a companion. I need not say it was beyond my deserts. It came, as does all my mercies, from the hand of Infinite Beneficence.

Did you think, on Friday last, of the circumstances of that day eleven years ago? It was then, beloved companion, that we were given to the embrace of each other, to journey on together through the pilgrimage of life. And thus far we are on our way! May we not say from the retrospect--"Goodness and mercy have followed us."

The sweets derived from mere earthly friendship, where twin hearts are cemented in love, are insignificant, in comparison with the happiness possessed by those, whom heaven in the plentitude of its goodness, in every sense has made ONE. It is not in the power of time to place a limit to the felicities of those thus circumstanced.[50]

While these words might seem to suggest a trouble-free eleven years of marital bliss, in fact the first decade of marriage for Phoebe and Walter was difficult and even tragic. It was marked by three events of profound consequence for their lives together. These were the death of three of their first four children, Phoebe's prolonged religious struggle and its resolution, and the decision to share a home with Phoebe's sister, Sarah, and her husband. All three were interrelated.

The religious struggle is the peg on which the other two events may best be hung. The struggle began before Phoebe's marriage and continued with intermittent intensity for over a decade. In fact, the struggle may be traced to her childhood and the fact that she could not identify a definite conversion experience in the usual Methodist fashion. The problem centered on two areas crucial to Methodist orthodoxy, assurance of one's salvation and Christian Perfection. The first was noted as a problem area already in connection with Walter Palmer's childhood religious disposition and the second is no less significant. Along with teaching that the Christian believer could be "assured" of the efficacy of "saving faith" by an "inward impression on the soul" created by the Spirit of God, John Wesley also taught that it was possible for the sincere Christian to attain a level of spirituality in which one lived without habitual sin, one's thoughts and actions being "governed by pure love." Wesley gave this many names, among them Christian perfection, perfect love, holiness, entire sanctification, heart purity, and full salvation. He described it as "a total death to sin, and an entire renewal in the love and image of God" causing the one "perfected" to "rejoice evermore, to pray without ceasing, and in everything to give thanks."[51] He called this concept "the grand depositum which God has lodged with the people called Methodists."[52] Methodism as a religious movement had grown up within the Church of England in the eighteenth century as an association of

those "seeking after holiness" under Wesley's guidance.
Early American Methodism, true to its roots, gave prominence to the teaching of the possibility and the necessity of "perfect love." The Discipline urged the
Methodist minister in instructing believers to "not
spare the remaining man of sin" but to "anatomize the
human heart, and follow self-will and self-love through
all their windings." He must "hold forth Christ as an
all sufficient Saviour" and "describe to them, in all
its richest views, the blessing of perfect love."[53] The
conscientious minister did this, and the conscientious
believer responded by seeking "the blessing."

Phoebe Palmer was nothing if not conscientious, and
she naturally sought after "heart purity" as a prescribed part of Methodist spirituality. Her religious
quest, however, ran into roadblocks right away because
she had not undergone a "powerful conversion" after the
Methodist fashion, and hence had no definite assurance
of her standing with God, which was a necessary pre-
requisite to going on "to perfection." The difficulty
was with the emotional or affective dimension of
religious conversion so highly regarded by Methodism.
This was implicit in Wesley's stress on the necessity of
the "warmed heart" to a genuine conversion, and it was
further heightened in American Methodism under the influence of revivalism and the "frontier experience"
which played such a large part in Methodist history.[54]
Methodist conversion was an emotional experience as
Methodist spirituality generally was emotionally laden.
Phoebe Palmer struggled from childhood with her emotions
and their role in religious life.

The psychologist could no doubt find much to
account for Phoebe's "block" and her resulting near
obsession with emotion--or its absence--in religious

experience. Suffice it to say that Phoebe never could seem to feel as deeply the motions of God in her soul as others did, and as they told her she should. As a child she had longed to live in biblical days when one's relationship to God seemed more "objective" and less problematic. Considering the animal sacrifice of the Hebrews, she thought, "...had I lived in that day, how gladly would I have parted with everything...and have purchased the best possible offering. All I would have to do, would be to lay it upon the altar and know that it was accepted."[55] Not having the benefit she imagined ancient Hebrews to have, she did the next best thing which was to visit the Methodist "altar" or "mourner's bench" seeking assurance of God's favor among those who "seemed to be the subjects of exciting influences."[56] Yet nothing happened to her though she believed herself sincerely devoted to God. Years later she recounted the times in childhood when she toiled to bring herself into a state of "extreme anguish before God, and wept because of the failure!" seeking to feel "to the degree which I have heard others express."[57] Her failure was "a fruitful source of temptation, resulting in years of painful solicitude."[58]

Phoebe's anxiety is palpable in her various jottings as she neared adulthood. Just after her eighteenth birthday she recorded her desire to "be more conformed to [Jesus'] image," but also noted her fear that she was unworthy of God's acceptance and that His grace was not at work within her. "I long for the full assurance of faith," she wrote.[59] Newly married in 1827 with every reason to rejoice, she instead scorns her religious life: "O, what I lack in my religious experience! I...am wanting in courage, faith and fervor."[60] Another place she reports, "I am getting on feebly in the divine life...."[61] In retrospect she concluded of this period in her life that she "continued to rise and fall, and consequently made but little progress in the way to heaven...."[62]

This matter of assurance was only resolved as it became bound up with Phoebe's desire to manifest the highest degree of Methodist spirituality, that being Christian perfection or "heart purity." No doubt instructed in the "grand depositum" of Methodism from her youth, her concern over the matter seemed to be quickened by a remarkable religious revival in 1832-33 which grew out of a four-day "protracted meeting" at the Allen Street Methodist Episcopal Church in New York City where Phoebe and Walter Palmer were members. The revival continued for two years, a major theme of it being the "deeper work of grace" of Christian perfection.[63] Significantly, the year the revival began was also the year that the "Pastoral Address" from the Methodist bishops to the General Conference decried a loss of distinctive Methodist stress on "entire sanctification" or "perfect love" and urged upon Methodists renewed zeal in seeking "this high attainment in religion." "Is it not time for us," asked the bishops, "to return to first principles?"[64] In a parallel move, 1832 was also the year that the editor of the New York Christian Advocate, John P. Durbin, urged special promotion of "holiness" through the institution of meetings "expressly for this subject."[65] The Allen Street meetings were a response to this high level concern about the health of the church.

As a loyal and conscientious child of Methodism, Phoebe Palmer sought the "high attainment" of perfect love during the course of the meetings. In April of 1832 she answered an invitation to all desiring a "deeper work of grace" to kneel at the mourner's bench in

typical revivalistic fashion. As a result, she reported,
"I was quickened in the divine life, and trust that I
have since been living nearer to the Lord."[66] Still, the
"quickening" was not sufficient as her "longing desire
for purity" continued unabated and unfulfilled. "I am
sure I would not knowingly keep back anything from God,"
she wrote. "But alas! There must be some hindrance
...."[67] The hindrance was the old bugaboo of assurance.
Palmer, never having gotten clear on this matter with
regard to her initial conversion experience, was now
struggling again with it in connection with the "deeper
work of grace" she felt compelled to seek. The whole of
Methodist spirituality seemed to her so subjective and
so much dependent upon emotions which somehow eluded
her. "Not unfrequently she felt like weeping because she
could not weep."[68]

The critical nature of Phoebe's religious quest was
heightened by the second major event of her first decade
of marriage, the death of three of the first four
children born to her and her husband. The significance
of these deaths can hardly be exaggerated. The first
child, Alexander, was born one day short of Phoebe and
Walter's first anniversary, September 27, 1828. He died
nine months later. A second child, a son, was born in
1830, but lived only seven weeks. Phoebe came to understand these losses as more than just random occurrences:
they were acts of God which had a purpose, a purpose
relative to the religious struggle she was undergoing.
She did not comment on the first loss in writing, but
linked the two experiences together following the death
of the second son when she wrote:

> I will not attempt to describe the pres-
> sure of the last crushing trial. Surely I
> needed it, or it would not have been given.

God <u>takes</u> our treasure to heaven, that our hearts may be there also. The Lord had declared himself a jealous God, he will have no other Gods before him. After my loved ones were snatched away, I saw that I had <u>concentrated</u> my time and attentions far too <u>exclusively</u>, to the <u>neglect</u> of the <u>religious activities</u> demanded. Though painfully learned, yet I trust the lesson has been fully apprehended. From henceforth, Jesus must and shall have the uppermost seat in my heart.[69]

Though she did not note it at the time, Phoebe later revealed that she had delayed having the first child baptized. In retrospect at least this seemed to her an important symbol of a hesitancy on her part to "give everything to God." It was also a symbol of her preoccupation with trivial concerns rather than religious as she had delayed the baptism in part in order to sew special clothing for the baby. "I had spent hours of precious time in embroidering his garments," she recalled, and in busying herself with "little adornments requiring...a useless expenditure of <u>time</u> and expense ...."[70] She firmly believed God had judged her accordingly.

The second son, she felt, had been taken for a similar, though not precisely the same, reason. In this case it was preoccupation with the baby itself which was her fault. She had taken pains to attend to the before neglected "religious activities demanded" after the death of the first son, but when the second was born she believed that the obligation had been met. It was with "an unwarrantable complacency of feeling" that she concluded, "Now that God has made up my loss, I will <u>live</u> for this one dear object--I will have done with these

more extended expectations...."[71] The "lesson" she pre-
sumed she had learned in the first loss did not seem
relevant, for as she told her husband concerning the
second baby, "[God] has given him to replace the loss of
the other," and surely could not mean to take him too![72]
But she came to believe she had been wrong, as that
child also died in infancy leaving the Palmers child-
less. The admonitions from the Bible, "Thou shalt have
no other gods before me" and "I the Lord your God am a
jealous God" were at that point "experimentally apprehended" by Phoebe and she responded by throwing herself
with great guilt and remorse, ever more zealously into
religious activities and the pursuit of "entire devotion
to God."[73]

When another child was born to Phoebe and Walter in
1833, a daughter, Sarah, great care was taken not to
offend God yet another time. Phoebe's anxiety is evident
in her recollection of Sarah's birth: "I shall never
forget the chastened feelings with which I first looked
upon this beloved one. My heart seemed to be perfectly
subdued, and I indeed received her as a precious
loan."[74] The child lived, and Phoebe apparently maintained her level of pious activity outside the home and
her quest of Christian perfection.

In August of 1835 a second daughter was born, with
Phoebe and the baby barely surviving the birth process.
The near brush with death in connection with this child,
Eliza, inevitably set off all the old warnings so that
Phoebe once again lapsed into intense self-examination,
fearing anew that she had not done all she might for
God. The problem with assurance still unresolved, she
struggled with her strong sense of unworthiness before
God, concluding finally that if she were to die then she
would be admitted to heaven--but just barely. This

caused her profound grief.[75] Her resolve was to do better, but yet in less than a year Eliza Palmer was dead and a further "lesson" had to be discovered in the tragedy. The circumstances were painful; the child was burned to death in a nursery fire when the gauze curtains surrounding her cradle were ignited by a candle. Phoebe was distraught, having considered Eliza "an angel-like child, both in disposition and beauty of form."[76] In an extended passage in her journal she attempted to purge the wound:

Never have I passed through a trial so severe.... If it were not that the Heavenly Physician had applied the healing balm, I should shrink utterly from a review of the scene. But a life of Christian progress presents stepping-stones. Nature may shrink painfully from taking the leap from one stepping-stone to another, and the chasm below look craggy and fearful. But if helped forward by a divine hand, all will be well. I dare not doubt but I am being led forth by a right way, to a city of habitation.

After the angel spirit winged its way to Paradise, I retired alone, not willing that any one should behold my sorrow. While pacing the room, crying to God, amid the tumult of grief, my mind was arrested by a gentle whisper, saying, "Your Heavenly Father loves you. He would not permit such a great trial, without intending that some great good proportionate in magnitude and weight should result. He means to teach you some great lesson that might not otherwise be learned. He doth not willingly grieve or afflict the children of

men. If not <u>willingly</u>, then he has some specific design in this, the greatest of all the
trials you have been called to endure."

    From that moment the very distressing
keenness of the trial passed away.... Never
before have I felt such a deadness to the
world, and my affections so fixed on things
above. God takes our treasures to heaven, that
our hearts may be there also. My darling is in
heaven doing an angel service. And now I have
resolved, that the service, or in other words,
the time I would have devoted to her, shall be
spent in work for Jesus. And if diligent and
self-sacrificing in carrying out my resolve,
the death of this child may result in the
spiritual life of many.

    ...And now my whole being says, with a
strength of purpose beyond anything before
attained, "My heart is fixed, O, God, my heart
is fixed!"[77]

The Palmers had two more children who survived,
Phoebe and Walter Clarke, Jr., but the deaths of the
three would continue to haunt Phoebe the rest of her
life. She would write some twelve years after the death
of the third that "My precious little ones, whom God had
taken to himself, were brought to my recollection, as if
to admonish me.... I thought how fondly I had idolized
them. He who had said, 'I the Lord your God am a jealous
God,' saw the idolatry of my heart, and took them to
himself."[78] She was also troubled repeatedly by fears
that her husband would have to be "given up" as her
children had been.[79] Even the death of her mother at an
advanced age in 1856 was seen as a reinforcement of the
painfully learned earlier lessons. By then deeply in-

volved in camp meeting work, Phoebe believed herself
"more than ever detached from earth," through her
mother's death. Reminding herself yet another time that
"Surely, God takes our treasure to heaven that our
hearts may be there also," she resolved once again that
this loss "should be made the occasion of spiritual life
to many."[80] When her youngest child, Walter, lost two
children of his own in an eerie repetition of his
mother's experience, Phoebe quickly concluded that the
meaning was clear--God desired the "entire devotion" of
Walter and his wife.[81]

In addition to the deaths of the Palmer children
and the interior religious struggle Phoebe was undergoing, the third very important event of these years was
the decision by Phoebe and Walter to share a house with
Phoebe's sister, Sarah, and her husband. Though older
than Phoebe, Sarah had married later. She and Thomas A.
Lankford, a young architect, had married in 1831. By
this time the Palmers had been married several years and
had already suffered through the death of two infant
sons. Dr. Palmer's medical practice was flourishing and
he and Phoebe certainly had the means to maintain a
comfortable house at 54 Rivington Street which at the
time contained both Walter's office and living
quarters.[82] The house was no doubt unnecessarily large
for only two people, however, and the Lankfords were
invited to move in.[83] Though the details are not clear,
it appears that this arrangement was in effect from 1831
until the Lankfords moved from New York City in early
1840.

This house-sharing arrangement had two consequences
of note for Phoebe Palmer's life. One was the resolution
of her personal religious struggle under Sarah's guidance and the other was her involvement, again via

Sarah, in a religious gathering which eventually became
a forum for her to develop latent talents as a religious
thinker and revivalist. In the first instance it is
important to note that Phoebe and Sarah were both travelling very similar paths with respect to Methodist
spirituality. Both were wrestling with the twin dilemma
of assurance and Christian perfection. Sarah's problem
was less acute than Phoebe's, however, in that she had
at least undergone the requisite conversion experience
in dramatic fashion and could point to a definite time
as a child when at a camp meeting she had "burst into
tears" and gone "to the altar as a penitent," there
falling into a kind of swoon during which she felt her
sins forgiven.[84] Finding assurance of "heart purity" was
more difficult though, and while she claimed to have
begun seeking this "deeper work of grace" within days of
her conversion and even to have found momentary assurance that she possessed it, the assurance was fleeting.
The problem was, as it was for Phoebe, the emotions.
Sarah could not _feel_ the operations of divine grace as
she longed to, or as she thought she should. For years
her struggle continued, paralleling that of her sister.
She spent weeks in "prayer, fasting, and monastic pen-
ances" to little avail.[85] Her "breakthrough" finally
came in 1835 when, believing herself divinely led, she
read some pages in The Life of Hester Ann Rogers where
the English Methodist "saint" had written, "Reckon yourself dead, indeed, unto sin and thou art akin to God
from this hour. O, begin, begin, to reckon now: fear
not, believe, believe, and continue to believe...."[86]
This seemed to Sarah to be the answer to her problem.
Emotional evidence of her standing with God must be
eschewed; the troublesome Wesleyan belief in a palpable
"inward impression on the soul"--the "witness of the

Spirit" so elusive to Sarah--must be set aside, or at least subordinated to the act of belief, which must operate courageously and independent of any supporting "sensible evidence." Some sort of religious feeling might follow in the wake of believing, but it was not to be construed as grounds for assurance. Assurance, for Sarah, was to be in the act of believing itself. Whereas she had once complained, "I do believe, but I want to feel,"[87] she now concluded that she would believe even if she "had not a joyous emotion in forty years."[88] She recorded her resolve in these words: "I looked at the time and continued to say, 'Yea, Lord, from this hour, half-past two p.m., the 21st of May, 1835, I dare reckon myself dead, indeed unto sin.'"[89] Though she still wavered some after this, she came to identify this moment as the moment of her "entire sanctification" on the grounds that this was when she first dared to believe herself "totally dead to sin" and thus "perfected" by God without the impelling influence of strong emotion.

Sarah's "discovery" became the catalyst for the resolution of Phoebe's long standing internal conflict over assurance and Christian perfection even though Phoebe did not reach a settled peace until two years after Sarah. Having a definite "proneness to reason," as she called it, it appears that Phoebe needed to work through the logic of the view Sarah had embraced more fully before she was ready to espouse it herself. As her later theological writing reveals, she did this very thoroughly and her conclusions became the underpinning of her distinctive theology of "Christian holiness." An odd aspect of this is that Phoebe almost never credited Sarah for instruction or aid in her religious quest. As she recounted the journey in various reconstructions, it

was all a matter of "illumination" of Bible material by
the Holy Spirit.[90] Yet the record of events shows
clearly that Sarah reached "certainty" well before
Phoebe and that she was zealous to bring Phoebe along
with her into the "way of holiness" which she had discovered. Sarah "held [Phoebe] up constantly before her
Father's throne, earnestly beseeching Him to bring her
to 'the valley of decision,' and to set her apart for
Himself."[91]

By her own account at least, Phoebe was not passive
at this time, but was actively seeking what Sarah was
claiming to have found. Living in the same household,
their religious journeys could hardly have been kept
hidden from one another. In a passage interesting
because it reveals a dimension of Phoebe not elsewhere
seen, Sarah described an encounter between the two:

> I sought an interview with dear sister
> Phoebe before breakfast, telling her I
> intended spending the day in special fasting
> and prayer for her. I asked her to unite with
> me, saying, "I know you desire a more
> spiritual life." She playfully replied, "I
> must have my breakfast; but I'll pray." I was
> deeply pained by her apparent lightness. I
> went to my room, wept, and made this record:
> "This day shall be spent in fasting and prayer
> for my precious sister, asking that she may
> see the vanity of earthly joys and know more
> of spiritual life."
>
> A little before three p.m., that darling,
> almost twin sister, said to me, with streaming
> eyes, "Never did I see the vanity of earthly
> joys as to-day!" These were almost the very
> words I had recorded.[92]

In the wake of several such encounters, the loss of
a third child, and the accumulated weight of the ongoing, unresolved interior struggle, Phoebe finally
found a measure of peace along the lines laid down by
Sarah. She set aside the expectation of strong religious
feelings and the accompanying paradigm of religious
experience typical of nineteenth-century American
Methodism and claimed certainty and security, not in the
"witness of the Spirit," but in the act of believing.
She resolved no longer to expect "signs and wonders"
attending the work of divine grace within her. To have
done so for so long, she concluded, was "sinful." She
would instead rely on nothing except the Bible, which
she held to be the word of God to man, and "faith,"
which she defined as "taking God at his word relying
unwaveringly upon his truth" or taking "God at his word,
whatever [one's] emotions might be."[93] She saw that she
had been "much more solicitous about feeling than
faith"[94] and had been misled in this by putting too much
stock in the personal experience of others: "former
perplexities in experience had too frequently arisen
from a proneness to follow the traditions of men, instead
of the oracles of God."[95] She would in the future live
by "naked faith in the naked Word,"[96] regardless of her
feelings: "...the covenant was consummated between God
and my soul, that I would live a life of faith...though
I might be called to endure more complicated and long-
continued trials of my faith than ever before conceived
of...I would still believe, though I might die in the
effort, I would hold on in the death struggle."[97] Phoebe
believed herself now "entirely devoted to God" and
assured of her full acceptance by Him. The date was July
26, 1837.[98]

Though there came to Phoebe in this decision a certainty and "assurance" of her standing with God which she had not had before, difficulties clearly remained. She would reflect at some remove from the event:

It has often since been suggested that I gave myself up so fully to live a life of faith, that God has taken me at my word. And will you believe, the enemy sometimes tries to tempt me to be sorry for it.... You would hardly conceive how often he tries to make me think my faith a mere intellectual knowledge. I meet him by saying, it is founded on principles laid down by the eternal mind, and consequently immovable in faithfulness.... I trust him, and on the authority of his own word declare in strongest testimony, his faithfulness in fulfilling his promises. The fruits of holiness follow--I dare not doubt it.[99]

Though the ensuing effort sometimes left her mentally and physically exhausted, Phoebe held unwavering to her "discovery"--really Sarah's--and began to proclaim it as the key to vital spirituality, especially the attainment of the "deeper work of grace" of "entire sanctification."

Sarah Lankford's presence in the Palmer house not only was important in the resolution of Phoebe's long-standing religious struggle but it also paved the way for Phoebe to move out of an active but limited role in local Methodist church life to a much larger role in which she would gain national and even international prominence. Both sisters were energetic for various church causes, leading "young ladies' Bible classes" and participating in volunteer societies for the promotion

of missionary activity and charity work. Phoebe's dedication to these causes of course had much to do with the
"lesson" she had learned through the death of her
children, as has been seen. One of Sarah's several
involvements in this area was heading up two different
weekly "prayer meetings" involving women from the Allen
Street and Mulberry Street Methodist Episcopal Churches.
In 1835 Sarah proposed to combine these into one,
gathering at the Palmer-Lankford home instead of the
respective churches where they had been meeting. This
was done in August of that year. Meeting at 2:30 p.m.
each Tuesday afternoon, the session soon became known
simply as the "Tuesday Meeting."[100]

There is some question as to whether the main
purpose of the meeting from the outset was the special
promotion of holiness or "entire sanctification." This
clearly became its focus in time, but it appears that in
its early existence it was not distinctive from any
number of "female prayer meetings" being conducted.
Certainly Sarah had professed to being "entirely sanctified" just prior to August of 1835, but it was a full
two years before Phoebe claimed "the blessing"--and not
in connection with the meeting--and even longer before
Dr. Palmer made the same profession.[101] Whatever the
case, the meeting did move steadily toward single-minded
promotion of Christian perfection or "heart purity" as
the apex of Christian spirituality available to all
sincere seekers. By the time the meeting shed its women-
only character in 1839, it had become generally known as
the "Tuesday Meeting for the Promotion of Holiness."

At first Sarah Lankford was the acknowledged leader
of the meeting. Phoebe, though a participant, had no
special role, even though Sarah appears to have encouraged her to assume one. It is easy to imagine that

Phoebe's "trial" in 1836 (the death of infant Eliza) and her subsequent religious "breakthrough" in July of 1837 must have heightened her interest and involvement in the gathering, but by her own testimony she long shrank from taking the limelight in any connection, and this held for the Tuesday Meeting as well.[102] It was not until April of 1840 when the Lankfords moved to Caldwell-on-the-Hudson, some fifty miles from New York City, and it became impossible for Sarah to preside any longer, that Phoebe reluctantly became the leader. By this time the meeting had expanded to include men as well as women and had become an important vehicle for promoting "holiness" teaching as articulated by the two sisters.[103]

While it was the Tuesday Meeting which catapulted Phoebe Palmer into a role which would quickly expand far beyond the parlor at 54 Rivington Street, there were other activities occupying her time and energies in the years leading up to 1840. In April of 1837 Phoebe accepted an invitation to teach the "Young Ladies' Bible Class" at the Allen Street Church, which grew to between fifty and sixty members under her care. Though hesitant to take the responsibility at the outset due to poor health, she continued with the class for nine years until her health in fact forced her to resign.[104] By 1838 Phoebe was reporting that she frequently led Walter's Methodist "class meeting" because of his absence due to a burgeoning medical practice. His class would have been a male, or more likely a "mixed" class, and Phoebe's presiding over it a notable departure from custom.[105] In December of 1839 custom was violated all the more when Phoebe was appointed to head permanently a mixed class of her own, the appointment being "the first of the kind ever made in (New York City)."[106] It is not clear whether women led Methodist classes having both men and women members in other locales at this time, but whatever the case, Phoebe's success hastened the eventual wide adoption of the practice. Beginning the assignment, Phoebe set down in her journal the guidelines she would follow. These included furnishing each member with the Methodist Discipline and laboring to "enforce the necessity of being thorough Methodists," furnishing each with Wesley's tract "The Character of A Methodist," stressing the subject of holiness and asking each member to "pray at least three times a day for attainment of the witness," getting the members to bear one another's burdens, and impressing upon the class the importance of "praying for her who has charge over them."[107] By all accounts these principles were followed steadfastly.

As already noted 1840 was the year that Phoebe ascended to leadership of the Tuesday Meeting for the Promotion of Holiness, adding this responsibility to her other duties. Her star was definitely rising in the constellation of New York Methodism. Significantly, this was occurring in concert with renewed efforts within Methodism to strengthen what was widely seen as being an inadequate emphasis upon the "grand depositum" of the movement, Christian perfection. From 1832 periodic calls had been issued for Methodists to zealously "reclaim" their heritage, and measures had been taken to bring this about. One such measure was the Tuesday Meeting itself. Another was the creation of a monthly magazine for promoting "holiness" in the church by the New England minister Rev. Timothy Merritt. This occurred in 1839 after Merritt, then assistant editor of The Christian Advocate, became convinced that there needed to be a vehicle to make available contemporary accounts of persons claiming to have undergone the "deeper work of grace" of entire sanctification. To this end he established The Guide to Christian Perfection, the first issue of twenty-four pages appearing in July of 1839. The Guide developed a modest following under Merritt and several subsequent editors in the years prior to the Civil War.[108]

Such measures were underscored by a renewed call to "holiness" issued by the Methodist bishops in 1840, echoing concerns expressed to the General Conference by the leadership eight years before:

> Be not content with mere childhood in religion; but "...go on to perfection." The doctrine of entire sanctification constitutes a leading feature of original Methodism. But let us not suppose it enough to have this doctrine in our standards: let us labor to have the experience and the power of it in our hearts. Be assured, brethren, that if our influence and usefulness, as a religious community, depend upon one thing more than any other, it is upon our carrying out the great doctrine of sanctification in our life and conversation.[109]

The Tuesday Meeting, The Guide to Christian Perfection, and Phoebe Palmer's own multiplying activities all had as their goal precisely what the bishops were calling for, and this meant that they stood for the right things in the right place at the right time. They could hardly miss casting long shadows on Methodism--and beyond.

C. The Public Figure: The 1840s and After

1840 was a watershed year in Phoebe Palmer's life as it was then that she became "official" leader of the Tuesday Meeting for the Promotion of Holiness, a position which provided her with an ongoing forum for her developing ideas and leadership skills, and which gave her personal exposure to a wide spectrum of persons. It is necessary to back up just a bit to understand the full force of this assertion, for it may seem that a Methodist women's Bible society would be a poor place in which to achieve national prominence. Had the Tuesday Meeting remained simply a denominational Bible study group, Palmer would in all likelihood not have become the public figure which she eventually became. The Meeting, however, developed into something quite different from what it was originally intended to be and the key year in its transition was 1839. This was the year in which the first men attended the gathering, one of them being the notable philosopher, Thomas Cogswell Upham, Professor of Mental and Moral Philosophy at Bowdoin College, Brunswick, Maine. A Dartmouth and Andover graduate, Upham was a Congregationalist who had been a pastor in Rochester, New York briefly before going to Bowdoin. By 1839 Upham had established a considerable reputation on the strength of several philosophical works he had published including Elements of Intellectual Philosophy (1827), Elements of Mental Philosophy (1831), and A Philosophical and Practical Treatise on The Will (1834).[110] In December of 1839 he was spending considerable time in New York City overseeing the preparation of a new book.[111] Upham was accompanied by his wife who had already embraced the Methodist belief in "Christian perfection" through some contacts with Methodists who had apparently also directed her to the Tuesday Meeting during her New York visit.[112] Finding much help there, Mrs. Upham asked permission to bring her husband to a subsequent meeting, which she did, with the result that he became a believer

in and professor of "the deeper work of grace."[113]
Returning to Brunswick, the Uphams began a weekly holiness meeting there modeled on the Tuesday Meeting and
became outspoken advocates of entire sanctification.

Professor Upham's "second conversion," as Warfield
calls it, was a source of great satisfaction to Phoebe
Palmer who had been so instrumental in it. In 1841 she
noted in her journal: "Received a letter today, from
Professor Upham and lady. Our spirits were much re-
freshed by the cheering intelligence that he still continues firm in the witness of holiness.... They have
already opened a meeting at their house, similar to our
Tuesday Meeting.... Glory be to God in the highest, for
such witnesses."[114] The importance of the whole Upham
episode is of course that the professor broke the "sex
barrier"--from then on the Tuesday Meeting was a "mixed"
endeavor--and he and his wife broke the denominational
barrier, the meeting becoming increasingly inter-denomi-
national, attended by persons representing many
different ecclesiastical and theological traditions.
Phoebe Palmer thus became "mentor" to a widening and
ever more diversified circle.

Partly as a consequence of her inheriting the
Tuesday Meeting from Sarah, and also no doubt due to her
precedent-setting appointment as a "class" leader,
Phoebe began to receive invitations to travel outside
New York City to speak to groups of persons interested
in "going on to perfection." She was coming to be perceived as a zealous and articulate spokesman for a
concept official Methodism was clearly interested in
promoting. She was not yet thirty-three years old. In
the summer of 1840 she made her first "evangelism expedition" outside the city, visiting Rye, Williamsburg,
and Caldwell's Landing, the latter being the new home of

Sarah and Thomas Lankford. This initial expedition was not remarkable, but it was evidently attended by enough success that the invitations kept coming and increased in number.[115] Phoebe responded to these willingly, believing that "God has called me to stand before the people, and proclaim his truth," and yet at the same time with some hesitancy, knowing that the path before her was not well marked and could easily be a painful one to tread.[116] To encourage her and to legitimate her work to those who might be tempted to be critical or doubtful of her credentials, she sought "signs and wonders" in these early meetings but was disappointed when they did not materialize. In writing to a friend following a visit to Jersey City, New Jersey in 1841, she noted: "I cannot describe to you the weight of responsibility I at times, feel to be resting upon me, in view of the various calls, as they seem to be accumulating. By the manner in which I am sustained, I have no reason to think otherwise than that the invitations I receive ...should be regarded as the voice of God." However, she added, "Those extraordinary outpourings of the Spirit, which I am often led to anticipate, as a proof to others that I am called to this peculiar work, as was Moses and Gideon, seem to be delayed."[117]

Extraordinary or not, Phoebe's travels formed a widening sphere. From visiting towns a stone's throw from New York City in 1840, she travelled nearly to Philadelphia in 1841, visiting towns in central and southern New Jersey as well as Jersey City.[118] In 1842 she visited Bethlehem, Pennsylvania. The Bethlehem visit is interesting because it illustrates that Phoebe's sphere was widening, not only in terms of miles travelled, but also in terms of transcending her Methodist beginnings. She was invited to Bethlehem by Frederica

Böhler, a granddaughter of Peter Böhler, the Moravian divine who had so influenced John Wesley.[119]

Bethlehem was a center for the Moravian church in the United States and the purpose of Phoebe's visit was to stir the "slumbering" Moravians into a revival of piety like that which American Methodists were seeking, though there is no record that her efforts there had any unusual results.[120] Also in this same year Phoebe writes of being invited to a meeting sponsored by a Presbyterian minister which was attended by persons from several different denominations. Their serious interest in "heart purity" caused her to exult, "O, what a blessed day is ushering in upon us! Christians of different denominations meeting on one common ground, 'Holiness to the Lord.'" She also gratefully noted, with some surprise, their receptivity--clergy included--of her as a female in a non-traditional role as religious teacher.[121]

By 1844 Phoebe had travelled as far as Boston. In 1845 she visited the fledgling Wesleyan University of Middletown, Connecticut and addressed a meeting of the faculty. In 1847 it was on to Philadelphia and a Methodist camp meeting at Eastham, Massachusetts on Cape Cod. In 1849 Baltimore was added to her itinerary.[122]

The decade of the 1840s may be thought of as the period in which Phoebe Palmer laid the groundwork for her most active years in the 1850s and '60s. The '40s were certainly not insignificant, yet from the vista of the '50s and '60s these years appear like rather small beginnings. Still it was during the 1840s that Phoebe cultivated contacts made through the Tuesday Meeting, perfected her distinctive style of "holiness revivalism," and, probably most important of all, wrote and published three major books, The Way of Holiness (1843),

Entire Devotion to God (1845), and Faith and Its Effects
(1848). Also, the decade was punctuated by two serious
bouts with illness, which makes Palmer's accomplishments
in these years all the more notable.

Both periods of illness corresponded with periods
of literary output. It will be recalled that Phoebe had
written poetry ever since childhood. Occasionally she
was called upon to contribute material for special
church celebrations, and had done some anonymous or
pseudonymous writing for Timothy Merritt's Guide to
Christian Perfection and The Christian Advocate.[123]
Typical of her productions in this vein are the
following lines:

Christians, to arms! behold in sight
The treacherous, threatening sons of night!
To arms! or thou art put to flight,
     Attest thy glorious chivalry.
Armor thou hast. O! haste to use
Ere thou the skill to use it lose!
Powerless thou art if thou refuse
     To arm thee with this panoply.
Rise! clothed in strength, assert thy right!
Thou of the first born sons of light--
Christ is thy strength, and in his might
     Go forth, and his salvation see.[124]

Something quite different, however, began to flow
from Phoebe's pen in the 1840s. She began to articulate
the understanding of religious experience at which she
had arrived through her own interior struggle and which
she was already promulgating in the Tuesday Meeting and
in her travels. Her first efforts at this appeared in
serial form in several issues of The Christian Advocate
between October 13 and November 24, 1841 under the
title, "Holiness," and signed simply "P." Though these

articles bear little of the compelling personal style of most of her books, being much more didactic in tone, they are unmistakably the work of Phoebe Palmer, reflecting all the major themes and distinctive emphases of her system of thought.[125] Also, in their attention to basic principles these articles very clearly aim to promote the Methodist bishops' concern that the church not lose the "leading feature of original Methodism." In them Palmer raises and answers such practical questions as "what is gospel holiness, or sanctification?", "how may we enter into the enjoyment of holiness?", and "what will be the advantage of living in the enjoyment of holiness...?"

The articles were followed in less than two years by Phoebe's first book which, while reflecting many of the same concerns, placed them into a much different context, casting them in terms of a "spiritual autobiography." This very personal style modeled in The Way of Holiness (1843) would mark most all of Palmer's subsequent publications. Its effectiveness and popularity is attested to by the fact that the book went through three editions in its first year in print and was still being issued--by then in its fifty-second edition--some twelve years after Palmer's death.[126] Originally published anonymously (Phoebe still had mixed feelings about moving into the public arena), the second edition carried her own name, she explaining that upon seeing a gaudy billboard on a theater prominently announcing the names of the actors, she resolved that since "the servants of Satan...are not afraid or ashamed to let their names appear" certainly "the servants of the Heavenly King" should not object to being openly identified with their cause.[127] From then on she wrote under her own name, except for a series of articles which appeared in The Christian Advocate in 1857.

During the time The Way of Holiness was in preparation and The Christian Advocate articles were appearing,
Phoebe was suffering through a siege of ill health.
Through parts of 1841 and 1842 she underwent "much
severe pain of body," which at times rendered her "unfit
for mental effort."[128] Still she managed to write,
though she recalled nearly thirty years later that
"When the 'Way of Holiness' was written, I was in a very
low state of health, from which I had but little expectation of ever recovering. Much of it was written, while
in almost an agony of pain."[129] The nature of her illness is not clear, though it likely had something to do
with the evidently chronic problems which eventuated in
"Bright's Disease" in her later years.

Positive reception of The Way and continued invitations to travel and speak encouraged Phoebe to offer
more thoughts on "holiness" in print. This she did in a
second book, Entire Devotion to God: A Present to a
Christian Friend, published in 1845. Like The Way,
Entire Devotion was published under the shadow of poor
health. During 1845 and 1846 Phoebe suffered her second
major illness of the decade. As with the first illness,
the details of this one are sketchy, but she again at
least thought herself to be near death. Writing to a
close friend in July of 1845 she mentioned her ambiva-
lence about living or dying, excited at the prospects of
significant "usefulness" if she lived, but also content
in "expectation of shortly joining 'the disembodied
Saints.'"[131] She was so ill that it was necessary for
her to spend part of 1845 in recuperation at Long
Branch, New Jersey and to curtail severely her speaking
schedule during all of 1846.[132] It was during this same
time that she resigned from some of her local parish
involvements.[133]

Phoebe's health improved by 1847 and she resumed her travels and found time to write her third book of the decade, <u>Faith and Its Effects; or, Fragments from My Portfolio</u>, which was published in 1848. As the title indicates the book highlighted a crucial element of her "system" of thought, and in a sense "completed" her theological corpus. She was yet to write many other books, but they would for the most part elaborate and reiterate basic ideas set forth in the first three.

The year 1848 marked another departure for Phoebe, and for Walter, who was at this point largely an observer of the work being carried on by his wife. The Palmers transferred their long-standing membership in the Allen Street Methodist Episcopal Church, a prestigious church of considerable wealth and influence, to a small struggling "mission" congregation. The reasons given for the move in a letter to the pastor of Allen Street center on the needs of the new church, the "embarrassment of riches" at Allen Street, and a definite sense of calling felt by the Palmers to "bestow [their] labors on a part of the Lord's vineyard, where they are more needed...."[134] This move set a pattern by which the Palmers "pioneered" in a number of areas over the next twenty-five years, giving time and money freely to a variety of projects, usually evangelistic or charitable in nature. It also <u>may</u> indicate some dissatisfaction with Methodism as it was manifested at the Allen Street Church, although this is never explicitly mentioned by either of the Palmers. That this might be so is suggested by the fact that in the 1850s and '60s Phoebe became increasingly vocal about the need to uphold the "old landmarks' of Methodism and her fears that they were being abandoned. As some opposition to her teaching surfaced, she became convinced of deep problems

in the "house of faith," not only in terms of questionable beliefs but also as reflected in changing worship
styles, "fashonable dress," and the popularity of
"church fairs." These trends were more apparent in the
better established city churches than they were in the
"mission" outposts.

One other aspect of the first decade of the public
career which deserves mention is the fact that during
this time Phoebe continued to be wife and mother even
while expanding her sphere of activity outside the home.
By now her family numbered three children and though she
had domestic help, the demand on her time and energy
still must have been immense. Serious illness twice
during the 1840s is not surprising in this light. Also
it should be remembered that Phoebe's conception of home
life was of an intense, disciplined environment in which
both parents had heavy responsibilities, especially for
shaping the religious and moral nature of their children.[135] This had to be done in a consistent and systematic way. Phoebe struggled much with the tension between
these keenly felt family responsibilities and the "religious duties demanded," the tension made all the
greater by the hard learned "lessons" from a "jealous
God" in the earlier years of marriage. Somehow she
managed.[136]

All evidence suggests that the Palmer home was
indeed run as a tight, and very pious, ship. Family
"devotions" were held twice a day, morning and evening,
and included the entire household, domestics and house
guests. not exempted. Singing from the Methodist hymnal,
Bible reading (sometimes accompanied by exposition and
exhortation), and prayer constituted these sessions.
Meal times were preceded and followed by sung prayer.
Meal time itself focused on reciting memorized portions

of the Bible, discussing points of doctrine, or other "non-frivolous" activities.[137] Even social occasions were harnessed to religious ends. "All her happy relations with others were held in strict and utter subordination to Christ and His will.... She had no time for the mere interchange of formal, aimless social visitation. Her means and position were ample for such recreation and enjoyment, but her...recreations were all included under one head, 'One more day's work for Jesus.'"[138]

Phoebe was quite explicit about "family management," writing on the subject in several places. She believed it "far more desirable to rule by love than by fear," but also noted that "undue family restraint" is not a problem most families have to worry about. Far more prevalent is "the sin of Eli."[139] Christian parents should pray daily for their children, as she did for hers, and should direct all their training to the end of their "usefulness in the Church of Christ." They should be kept from "gay society" and "conformity to the world in dress."[140] Children should be raised in such a way that they are fit for "the service of the sanctuary," whether or not that ever becomes their actual calling.[141] With Phoebe's own children, Wheatley notes that they were all "intelligently converted to God before attaining the age of seven years."[142]

The year 1850 conveniently marks the beginning of the most active and most widely heralded years of Phoebe Palmer's public career. The stage having been well set in the 1840s, Phoebe now quickly moved to its center. This can be seen in her travel schedule which "exploded" from 1850 on. Longer and longer trips were added, new areas were visited yearly, and more places were visited than in the 1840s. In 1850, for example, Phoebe visited

Boston for the second time along with Springfield, Massachusetts; Carbondale, Pennsylvania; Providence, Rhode Island; the Oneida Conference "Ladies Seminary" at Oneida, New York; and several other points in western New York.[143] The Boston trip was made primarily at the request of Methodists, but also included two meetings at the home of a Mr. Watts, who was a lawyer and an Episcopalian. At these meetings Episcopalians, Presbyterians, and Unitarians were in attendance, Phoebe remarking that "They most appeared to be from among the first circles in the city."[144] In Providence she did some work among Baptists and found their response encouraging.[145]

A major development for Phoebe during the '50s was the addition of points in Canada to her itinerary. This greatly enlarged her field of influence and opened the door for a tour of Great Britain later in the decade. The first Canadian trip occurred in August of 1853 when she visited a camp meeting held on a farm owned by one Squire Mitchell Neville near Newburgh, Canada West (now Ontario). The meeting there was tremendously successful with five hundred people professing conversions and nearly that many "entire sanctification."[146] These results were anticipatory of Phoebe's subsequent visits, for her Canadian schedule, which she kept regularly from 1853 on, was often marked by unusual numbers of converts and strong support for her zealous promotion of Christian perfection as a "deeper work of grace."[147]

The years 1857 and 1858 mark a zenith in Palmer's career, and in American religious life generally. These years saw Phoebe--and Walter, who had begun taking a more active role in his wife's career--at the center of a religious revival involving many denominations and having as a major theme "Christian perfection" or "the higher Christian life." Wheatley described 1857 in the

Palmers' life as "Annus Mirabilis" and T. L. Smith has taken this up to characterize the generalized religious awakening of 1857-58 of which they were a part.[148] Though scholarly opinion is divided over the meaning and results of this revival, there is general agreement on its contours. It was largely urban, initiated and led by laypersons rather than professional clergy, and was characterized by noontime prayer meetings held in downtown churches and public buildings for workers on their lunch hour.[149]

Phoebe Palmer kept up a vigorous schedule throughout the winter and spring of 1857-58, the height of the revival, and reaped an abundant harvest everywhere she went. From Binghamton, New York she reported a "union" campaign supported by "all evangelical churches" in which hundreds were converted and "made perfect in love" including a granddaughter and great granddaughter of Jonathan Edwards.[150] In Owego, New York she led meetings at the Methodist church which spread out to include other groups. "All evangelical denominations have shared in the copious showers which have fallen on this portion of our Lord's heritage," she wrote. Presbyterians, Congregationalists, and Baptists all sought her time.[151] The story was much the same in such places as Providence, Rhode Island; Boston; Milford, Connecticut; Portland, Maine; and New York City.[152]

As in the previous decade, Palmer's heavy travel schedule, leadership of the Tuesday Meeting, and other involvements did not exhaust her resources; she still found time to write. In 1855 she published Incidental Illustrations of the Economy of Salvation, Its Doctrines and Duties, a collection of essays on various topics, "holiness" of course being a major preoccupation. In 1859 The Promise of the Father; or, A Neglected

Specialty of the Last Days, addressed to the "clergy and
laity of all Christian communities," set forth a case
for the right of women to "minister" in the Christian
churches, though not necessarily to occupy the preaching
office or to receive ordination. Also, in 1857 just
before the outbreak of the excitement of the "Layman's
Revival," Phoebe contributed a series of articles to The
Christian Advocate and Journal entitled "A Laity for the
Times" in which she argued vigorously for the "importance and expedience of requiring the individual membership of the Church to engage in personal efforts for the
salvation of the world."[153]

During these rarefied days of the fifties Phoebe's
head was kept from disappearing into the clouds by an
outbreak of controversy over her and her message. Though
the substance of the controversy belongs better in subsequent chapters, it ought to be noted here that the
strong positive reaction she engendered in so many who
attended her meetings and purchased her books was balanced by a very negative reaction in some others. While
Phoebe could claim prominent supporters for her work,
she drew some prominent critics as well. Chief among the
latter was Professor Hiram Mattison of Falley Seminary
in Fulton, New York. Mattison took exception to Palmer's
distinctive way of describing entire sanctification and
"the way" by which one obtained it, and to the very fact
that she as a layperson (and woman) had the temerity to
instruct others on the matter at all. He urged in print
that she "leave the subject [of Christian perfection],
with theology in general, where it properly belongs--in
the pulpits of the M.E. Church, and with the authorized
teachers of religion."[154]

Mattison had opposed Palmer's teaching in circum-
spect fashion in print in the early 1850s in the

Northern Christian Advocate, a regional Methodist paper published in Syracuse and modeled on the national Advocate seated in New York City.[155] Palmer had caught wind of this in her travels and through acquaintances and had gone so far as to write Bishop Edmund S. Janes requesting that he censure Mattison.[156] Apparently no official action was taken. As Phoebe's star rose ever higher, so Mattison's critique grew bolder and he finally went "national," though still rather circumspectly, in the August 2, 1855 issue of The Christian Advocate and Journal, never mentioning Palmer by name, but attacking certain well-known characteristic emphases of her "system" of thought.[157] Though not named in the article, Palmer felt the threat serious and obvious enough to respond, which she did in the November 15 issue.[158] Emboldened, and perhaps peeved, by her willingness to defend herself, Mattison launched a frontal attack, naming names, and citing chapter and verse in Palmer's various writings to substantiate his case that she had introduced questionable "new measures" into the church in connection with her propagation of "holiness."[159]

Phoebe was clearly shaken by the whole affair. Not adverse to controversy (Wheatley's protestations notwithstanding), she was apparently taken by surprise that her friends, notably editor Thomas E. Bond, at The Advocate would allow such an open attack as the November 29 article to go to print. Still, she was not without warning. Mattison had opposed her in his own territory for some time, and the article in the August Advocate represented an important expansion of his campaign against her. In a fascinating vignette Palmer described having a dream some weeks before the November Mattison article appeared in which she was attacked by wild animals, an especially large and fierce lion fighting her nearly to the death. "So intensely was my every particle of mental and physical energy called into exercise, in maintaining a successful grapple with this terrible lion, that I actually did not get over it for hours after I awoke," she recalled of the dream.[160] The meaning, at least in retrospect, seemed clear: "From this hour, I became settled in my convictions that some terrible conflict awaited me...."[161]

Though Phoebe did not respond to the open attack of the November article, others came to her defense. Letters in the December 6 issue of The Advocate supported her teachings.[162] Mattison kept up the fight two weeks later citing additional material from her writings to support his charges and drawing prominent Methodists into the controversy by name.[163] The battle continued on into January of 1856 with charges and countercharges.[164] Finally editor Bond put a stop to the matter declaring that no more articles of a "controversial nature" regarding Palmer's "theories" would be accepted by The Advocate and also noting in a parting shot that he personally considered her "essentially correct in her views of the Christian perfection which the Holy Scriptures hold out to believers; notwithstanding the...dispute about words, which may be suggested by the modes of expression which she sometimes uses, and which some have considered heterodox."[165] So, the controversy--at least in print--was at an end, though it was not to be the last opposition Phoebe would face despite the fact that her greatest popularity and success was just around the corner.

One final highlight of the 1850s was the extension of Phoebe's sphere of activity and influence from North America to Britain. Coming off the revival years of

1857 and 1858, the Palmers accepted an invitation to visit the British Isles, already enjoying considerable popularity there through the publication of Phoebe's books and the circulation of accounts of their work in the "British Provinces" of Canada. Evidently invitations had come their way from the earliest days of the Canadian visits, but they were unable to respond until 1859.[166] In June of that year they set sail, arriving in Liverpool on June 15.[167] In order to make the trip Walter gave up his successful medical practice, and never returned to it. He had, in fact, been moving in this direction for some time, routinely taking at least a month off to accompany Phoebe on some of her many travels.[168] With the onset of the tour, however, a nearly full partnership was struck with Walter playing an integral (though subordinate) part in all the evangelistic campaigns which they undertook.

The Palmers' success in Britain matched or exceeded anything they had known in North America. The visit stretched on for over four years with the Palmers having to turn down numerous very insistent requests that they return to the scenes of the previous "triumphs" to have one more go at the forces of apathy and "worldliness." Some opposition did surface before the tour was over, but on the whole their reception was astounding.[169] From the Isle of Wight to Scotland and Ireland they commonly drew crowds of 3,000 or more people, often having to turn overflow crowds away. Their invitations to seek Christian conversion or "entire sanctification" were answered by hundreds of persons at a time, and their meetings sometimes stretched on for nearly a month.[170] It was estimated that they accounted for ten thousand converts during their first year in Britain alone, a record Carwardine calls "enormously impressive."[171]

The Palmers returned to the United States in October of 1863 and Phoebe embarked on what was to be the final phase of her public career. Since both Walter and Phoebe had suffered some poor health under the stress of the British trip, they had decided to rest following their arrival home. This was not to be, however, for they "had not been at home two hours" before they were approached by a committee from the Allen Street Methodist Church urging their labors in an evangelistic campaign there. They accepted and spent several weeks at their former church, followed by one or two other engagements to finish out the year.[172]

1864 opened without the loss of a step it seems. The travel schedule of the 1850s was duplicated with trips to western New York, New England, Canada, and as far west as Mount Pleasant, Iowa. In Boston the Palmers had unusual success in "Union Meetings" at Tremont Temple originally scheduled for one day but which stretched on for ten days due to popular demand.[173] The toll was too much, however, and by the end of the year Phoebe was seriously ill, confessing that she had brought it on herself by "taxing herself too severely."[174] She resolved to do better in the future and for a year at least did, giving over most of 1865 to preparing Four Years in the Old World for publication and attending only one or two Canadian camp meetings during the summer.

In 1866 the pace quickened once again with several western locales being visited including Ann Arbor, Michigan; Chicago; Lima, Indiana; and Cleveland, Ohio; along with the usual Canadian and eastern states. In 1867 the main thrust of Phoebe's travel was westward with trips to St. Louis and Kansas City, Missouri; Leavenworth, Kansas; Lebanon, Illinois; Goshen, Indiana;

New Orleans; and Cincinnati, Ohio as well as eastern
visits to Philadelphia, Baltimore and Washington. It was
during this trip that the Palmers stopped at Oberlin,
Ohio and spent time in the home of the "patriarch" of
American revivalism, Charles G. Finney.[175] By 1870
Phoebe had literally traversed the continent, visiting
five towns in California that year in addition to numerous stops in the midwest and northeast.[176]

Response was still good in these years and yet
there is noticeable tendency for Phoebe to evaluate the
climate in the places visited negatively. More and more
often her impressions are that the subject of holiness
is unwelcome, or being suppressed, or that "worldliness"
generally prevails. The climate no doubt was changing,
but too Phoebe was in the years following the "British
interlude" seeing things through the eyes of a declining
woman in her sixties, rather than as a young woman in
her thirties with a great many new experiences and
opportunities coming her way.

Whatever the case, there is a kind of poignancy in
the records of the latter 1860s and early '70s which was
not there before. Visiting Upper Newton Falls, Massachusetts in 1866, she notes that the influence of Unitarianism and Universalism has led to a "general obtuseness
on the subject of everything that constitutes an orthodox Christianity...." Here her revival measures are
opposed as "too exciting."[177] From Illinois Wesleyan
University in 1869 she complains, "We have never to my
recollection, labored in a region of the country, where
what Wesley calls 'the Methodist testimony' has been so
slightly regarded."[178] The California churches in 1870
are "fallow ground" and typified by "so much profession
that scarcely approaches to morality."[179] And Albany,

New York in 1873 presents a situation "discouraging beyond anything I can tell."[180]

During this discouraging period in revivalistic work, Phoebe still had the very successful forum of the Tuesday Meeting (which continued even after her death) and acquired a new one as well in the form of The Guide to Christian Perfection, now named The Guide to Holiness. Phoebe had been a frequent contributor to The Guide from its beginnings in 1839 under Timothy Merritt and the Palmers had always been unflagging supporters of the paper and its message. Moderately successful under Merritt and some who followed him as editor, by the time of the Civil War The Guide had fallen on hard times, suffering "pecuniary loss" and "some serious embarrassments."[181] When the Palmers returned triumphantly from Britain in 1863 "it appeared necessary for the good of the cause" that someone of their reputation and means rescue the paper and give it new life, and this they did.[182] They purchased The Guide and another small struggling "holiness" paper, The Beauty of Holiness, originally founded at Delaware, Ohio but by then being published in New York City, combining them into the awkward The Guide to and Beauty of Holiness, a name which was soon dropped.[183] Having a subscription list of well under 10,000 when they acquired it, the Palmers eventually built it up to number nearly 40,000 subscribers by the end of the decade.[184] Phoebe presided over this resuscitation of The Guide as editor and was assisted for a time by her son-in-law, Rev. Elon Foster, and later by Walter, though the oversight was always mainly in her hands.[185] The Guide gave Phoebe an ongoing national forum from which to report her evangelistic travels and propagate her views of holiness.

By late 1871 the combined impact of over thirty years of zealous attention to the "religious duties demanded" and the chronic health problems that hobbled her periodically throughout her career had weakened Phoebe to the point that she found it necessary to cancel some scheduled meetings; she was now sixty-four years old. She spent some time at Masena Springs, New York hoping the rest would bring improvement in her health.[186] It did, at least temporarily, for 1872 and 1873 found her back on the road again. Still, she seemed to sense the return to activity was only temporary. She wrote in her journal, "I have...entered upon what has been, with thousands, the last decade of life. How many of our contemporaries have, during the past year, ended life's transient dream. The good Dr. Chalmers says, in contemplation of entering upon his sixtieth year, that he would regard this last seventh decade, when entered upon, as the Sabbath of life, and to be spent in preparation for his eternal rest beyond the grave."[187] In May of 1872 she and Walter visited Greenwood Cemetery which held "a multitude of dear ones, with whom we have taken sweet counsel" as well as the three deceased Palmer children. Noting the Palmer "monument," she recorded in her journal, "It is awaiting the time when this now active frame, shall cease its pulsations, and the spirit ascend to the God who gave it."[188]

By 1874 Phoebe was having to cancel scheduled meetings once again, but she still visited a number of camp meetings that summer.[189] In late summer and early fall her condition worsened. By September blindness had set in and she had become confined to bed.[190] She rallied briefly, prompting the optimistic line, "we are encouraged to indulge the hope that she may be again restored to health" in the November issue of The Guide.[191] The hope, however, was unfounded. Her condition turned suddenly grave and she died at 2:30 p.m. November 2, 1874, just weeks short of her sixty-seventh birthday.

She was mourned by many who knew her as author, revivalist, and indefatigable promoter of "holiness." Many of these in their desire to do justice to her memory overstepped even the bounds of "eulogistic license" to number her with the apostles or to proclaim her the most significant woman in the history of Christianity. The most telling tribute, however, is that of Walter, her partner and loyal supporter. He wrote in a letter to Mrs. Bishop Hamline, one of the couple's closest friends, the following:

I have told the Lord that mine was a peculiar trial, and that I needed to be indulged, for my loss was an uncommon one. I have endeavored to thank the Lord that He permitted me to have so much of heaven, for so many years on earth, to call my own.... You will pardon me, I know, if I say that her worth was not known, neither can language portray it. She was an angel on earth. She was the model mother, the loving wife, the perfect Christian lady. She was God's chosen one, and faithfully did she obey the instructions of His Word.... But, dear sister, forgive me, my dear Phoebe made up the most of me, and what there is left of me on this side of the river I want you to pray for as never before. I am not rebellious, but, O, the wound is so deep! [192]

Walter continued The Guide, the Tuesday Meeting, and a limited travel schedule for some time after, but without Phoebe none of them were quite the same.

CHAPTER III
A CLOSER LOOK: THE PREACHING CAREER

In all, Phoebe Palmer's public career spanned some thirty-four years, touching four decades of the nineteenth century. From 1840 when she emerged from a localized notoriety to take the first hesitant steps toward national and international prominence until her death in 1874, she worked single-mindedly to promote "the way of holiness." Her promotion of "the way" came to involve her in a variety of activities and enterprises, all of which outlived her. Her church and camp meeting involvement was carried on by her husband and her sister, Sarah, who became the second Mrs. Walter Palmer in 1876. As late as the 1890s Sarah was still leading a "holiness meeting" at the Methodist camp meeting at Ocean Grove, New Jersey.[1] The books which had been so popular continued to be published and find an audience.[2] The Guide to Holiness likewise continued to circulate, first under the editorship of Walter Palmer and then under Sarah Lankford Palmer, Rev. George Hughes and others. Despite competition from a host of holiness papers entering the field, The Guide survived until after the turn of the century.[3] The celebrated Tuesday Meeting for the Promotion of Holiness, where in a very real sense it had all begun, also went on without Phoebe, coming first under the leadership of Dr. Palmer (who had taken a major role in the meeting from the time he had given up his medical practice), and the joint leadership of Dr. and the new Mrs. Palmer (Phoebe's sister, Sarah), and finally, following Walter's death in 1883, guided by Sarah Lankford Palmer by whose initiative the meeting had been launched in the first place nearly a half century before! Sarah lived to see the diamond anniversary of the meeting celebrated in 1895, one year before her death.[4]

Phoebe Palmer's legacy goes beyond these enterprises, as we shall see, and yet they constitute the heart of her efforts to advance the "way of holiness." They were the instruments she chose to play to sound forth "holiness unto the Lord." In this chapter we shall look more closely at two of these "instruments" of holiness promotion, in order to define more precisely her role in nineteenth-century religious life and her lasting impact.

One fact which emerges from our survey of Phoebe Palmer's life is that she was clearly one of the most popular preachers of her day. Attendance at meetings and "protracted meetings" where she was the speaker rivalled that of any of the well-known revivalists of the time. Another barometer of her popularity and "success" as an evangelistic preacher is the number of "seekers" responding to her invitations to exercise faith to receive divine forgiveness for sin or the "deeper work" of "entire sanctification." This amounted to tens of thousands, as we have seen. Palmer herself would have been both comfortable and uncomfortable with this characterization of her work. Surely she would have admitted to getting results; she did in fact refer quite openly on numerous occasions--sometimes exhibiting something very near self-congratulation--to the turn-away crowds and overflowing "mourner's benches" which accompanied her travels. She would have hesitated, however, at the point of labeling what she did in these instances as "preaching." "Bearing witness" she would have called it, or "prophesying" or "exhorting," but not "preaching," at least preaching "technically so called."[5]

Here is an important issue which will emerge again in connection with Palmer's role as a spokesperson and model for "religious feminism." It grows from her reluctance to call her work "preaching" and the fact that she neither sought any official ecclesiastical office nor encouraged other women to do so, and yet at the same time authored a strongly worded and closely reasoned treatise defending the right of women to "minister" in Christian churches, including the right to speak publicly in order to edify, exhort, and comfort--i.e. to preach.[6] That is to say, Palmer both disclaimed that she "preached" (in a technical sense) and yet also redefined "preaching" in her book so that by her own definition she did indeed "preach." One catches the sense of the matter in this explanation:

> It is our aim, in addressing the people ...to simplify the way of faith.... Preach we do not; that is, not in a technical sense. We would do it, if called; but we have never felt it our duty to sermonize in any way by dividing and subdividing with metaphysical hairsplittings in theology.
>
> We have nothing more to do than Mary, when, by the command of the Head of the Church, she proclaimed a risen Jesus to her brethren.... We occupy the desk, platform, or pulpit, as best suited to the people in order that all may hear and see.[7]

She stood behind a pulpit and expounded on religious topics but she did not "preach," since for her preaching, as generally understood and practiced, in-

volved "metaphysical hair-splittings in theology." Elsewhere she related preaching to "oratorical display" and
"pulpits of pedestal eminence."[8] Since her activity did
not fit this description, she did not "preach" and she
refused to muddy the issue by claiming that she did or
that other women should. At the same time it would be
clear to anyone who read Promise of the Father that
Palmer did not consider the popular understanding of
preaching to be an adequate one. Preaching "in a technical sense" she found to be something quite different
than preaching in a biblical sense. The latter was
simply to explain the teachings or enforce the commands
of Christ and His apostles, edify, exhort and comfort,
open one's mouth for God, or speak as the Spirit of God
gives utterance.[9]

It is obvious that Palmer believed there needed to
be more of the biblical sort of preaching and less of
preaching "in a technical sense." In a letter to her
sister at the time of the 1857-58 "Prayer Meeting
Revival" she wrote, "We have had very little preaching,"
that is "preaching in the technical sense, according to
the ordinary idea of preaching in the present day."
Adding, "though I would not be understood to speak
lightly of the value of well beaten oil for the service
of the sanctuary," she declared, "yet never have I been
so confirmed in a belief...in regard to the sort of
preaching needed at the present day." Such preaching
ought to be the preaching of "apostolic times" when all
the members of the nascent Christian community, women
and children as well as men, scattered to explain the
teachings of Jesus, exhort, and "open their mouths for
God."[10] In this sense her own involvement with camp
meetings, protracted meetings in local churches, and the

Tuesday Meeting for the Promotion of Holiness indeed constituted a "preaching" career.

A. The Tuesday Meeting For the Promotion of Holiness

The logical place to begin to take a closer look at Palmer's preaching career is with the Tuesday Meeting for the Promotion of Holiness. This is so for several reasons. For one, Palmer's thrust into national and international acclaim occurred initially through her leadership of the Tuesday Meeting. It was here that she made and cultivated many friendships which later eventuated in invitations to travel outside New York City to address religious gatherings. It was also in connection with this meeting that she first developed and tested the distinctive system of thought which would be widely disseminated by her books and her evangelistic travels. Finally, it was the Tuesday Meeting which provided Palmer with her most consistent and longest lasting forum for furthering the teaching and experience of "holiness" among Christians, a fact which Phoebe herself recognized. Writing in her sixty-fourth year to her intimate friend, the widow of the Methodist bishop Leonidas Hamline, she noted, "I sometimes say to Dr. P., that if we had never lived for anything else but the Tuesday afternoon meeting, we shall have enough to praise the Lord for forever."[11]

The phenomenon of the Tuesday Meeting is fascinating. The modern student is most struck by the very simplicity of a thing which came to have such large impact throughout North America. The factors involved in the founding of the meeting have already been noted, and they are very simple: two conventional Methodist women's "prayer meetings" were combined into one and began to meet in a home shared by the Palmers and Lankfords. Over

time the combined meeting began to focus more and more
exclusively on "holiness," reflecting the religious
experience and understanding of Phoebe Palmer and Sarah
Lankford, and men began to attend. In 1840 Phoebe replaced Sarah as leader of the group and held that role
for better than thirty years.

The conduct of the meeting was equally simple.
Convening in the Palmer home at 2:30 p.m. each Tuesday
for one hour and a half, a minimally structured "social
religious company" sang hymns, prayed, heard a brief
exposition of a selection from the Bible (by all accounts this was kept to a minimum), and shared personal
accounts of religious experience. Firsthand descriptions of the meeting make plain that the sharing or
"testimony" aspect was by far the most important and
took up the greatest amount of time. There was no sermon
or lecture and the one in charge, generally Phoebe
Palmer though others served in her absences due to
travel, functioned more as a discussion leader than as a
"special speaker." Many times the meeting moved toward
an evangelistic climax with persons present being given
opportunity to seek forgiveness of sin or the experience
of entire sanctification. On these occasions it assumed
something of the form of the "inquiry meeting" or "anxious meeting" used by the revivalists of the day. Persons anxious about their spiritual state could raise
questions and be instructed and prayed for by any
present.

"In these meetings the utmost freedom prevails,"
wrote an observer, and this seems to have been one great
attraction of the Tuesday Meeting.[12] Though a set pattern was followed from week to week, there was a great
deal of latitude within this pattern. Once the "prelimi-
naries" were completed (hymn, corporate prayer, brief

exhortation), any person present might give an account of his or her religious pilgrimage, read or quote from memory passages from the Bible, lead the group in a spontaneous hymn or chorus, relate some personal need or problem and perhaps request prayer from others present, or offer some insight or word of exhortation. The goal was a relaxed interchange of views quite distinct from "church," something like a pious parallel to the social gatherings of the "children of the world" where "in intelligent, social converse, heart meets heart in unrestrained fellowship."[13] Of course the freedom and interchange of views was not altogether unrestrained, for the meeting was "for the promotion of holiness" and it was to this end that everything was to be done. Views explicitly opposed to the teaching on entire sanctification which prevailed in the Palmer circle would not have been tolerated, though there is indication that specific points of doctrine were on rare occasions the focus of controversy.[14] On the whole it was well understood that the meetings exhalted "holiness" and that all were welcome so long as they fit one of three categories-- witness to holiness, sincere seeker after holiness, or interested observer at least open to the teaching being aired in the assembly. Even though representatives of a host of theological traditions and religious bodies were typically present, doctrinal distinctives were subordinated to the common stress on holiness. And, as noted, the evangelistic motive was an important part of the gatherings.

The evangelism thrust is well illustrated by the experience of one of the best known Tuesday Meeting "converts," Thomas Cogswell Upham. The first man to break the sex barrier of the previously all-female meeting, Upham attended at his wife's invitation in

1839. Formerly a Congregationalist pastor in Rochester,
Upham was at the time Professor of Mental and Moral
Philosophy at Bowdoin College, Brunswick, Maine and a
noted philosopher.[15] His wife had early in 1839 attended
a Methodist protracted meeting and there heard for the
first time the doctrine of Christian Perfection explained. Interested enough to seek a follow-up interview
with a woman who had spoken in the meeting, Mrs. Upham
began a personal study of the matter which concluded in
her publicly declaring in May of 1839 that she had been
entirely sanctified. Professor Upham did not embrace his
wife's views at this time, but he did note later that it
was "early in the summer of 1839" that he came "by a
series of special providences" to "examine the subject
of personal holiness...."[16] In this state he travelled
with his wife to New York in December to handle matters
relating to the publication of a new book. Mrs. Upham had
presumably been directed to the Tuesday Meeting by her
Brunswick Methodist friends, for she soon fell in with
the Lankford-Palmer circle there. Finding a "spirit of
freedom, which invited inquiry and discussion, together
with the clear witness of this grace (i.e. entire sanctification)," she asked that her inquiring husband might
attend. The ladies agreed and the next week he was
present along with several other men invited by Phoebe
Palmer so that Upham would not feel out of place.

Upham later recounted that his introduction to the
Tuesday Meeting had been "providential" and that he had
been "exceedingly happy" in attending a "number of meetings which had exclusive reference to the doctrine of
holiness and to personal holy experience."[17] It was in
fact through these, along with related conversations
with Phoebe Palmer and Sarah Lankford, that he was
enabled to lay claim to the "deeper work of grace"

already espoused by his wife. This occurred on December 27, 1839 following an evening of conversation with the two sisters. Phoebe noted that he posed many questions to her and that as she answered them to his satisfaction his "desire for the present attainment of the blessing of entire sanctification" became "more ardent."[18] Feeling a great burden for Upham, she spent time alone later that night "wrestling with the angel of the covenant, in his behalf."[19] The nature of her concern is interesting: "I saw that the Redeemer's Kingdom needed an advocate in the denomination of Christians to which he belonged (i.e. Congregationalist) in defense of this doctrine. Standing, as he did, with an important college, it was greatly desirable, that he should be a witness of its attainment."[20] Here was a noteworthy non-Methodist who was on the brink of accepting, and if accepting no doubt promoting, "perfectionist" teaching. He would be a great "catch" for the cause, and Palmer pursued him with strenuous prayer, pledging once again to God the "entire devotion" of her life to divine service, this time in exchange for Upham's entire sanctification. The next day, Friday, December 27, Upham visited Palmer and witnessed to having experienced a "very powerful manifestation of the Spirit [of God]," not quite an explicit avowal of entire sanctification, but enough so that Palmer considered it a definite answer to her prayer and Upham himself considered it a signal day.[21]

Professor and Mrs. Upham returned home to Maine about the middle of January, 1840 and immediately commenced a meeting modeled on the Tuesday Meeting, apparently the first of dozens of such duplicates to appear over the next several decades. It was in connection with this meeting that Upham was finally able to explicitly profess "the great blessing of holiness" some two or three weeks after leaving New York. Writing to Phoebe in March, Upham noted, "I feel my great obligation to your interesting little circle, and trust that your Saviour will abundantly support and reward you."[22] Mrs. Upham appended to the same letter an exultant note of her own: "O! Could you see and hear my dear husband talk, in our little meeting, how happy you would be, because you have begotten him in the gospel. You have seen him trembling and afraid; now, could you see him, you might perhaps feel that he was strong in the Lord, even as you."[23]

Some six months later Upham was still expressing his debt to the Tuesday Meeting ("To me, personally, it was in religion, the 'beginning of days'") and to Phoebe Palmer, his "respected and beloved sister," who had helped lead him into "the way of holiness."[24] Upham was Palmer's first important "convert," of which there would be many more, and in these very earliest days of her "preaching career" she was much buoyed by the success. Noting in her diary for March 31, 1841, "Received a letter to-day, from Professor Upham and lady," she reports that "he still continues firm in the witness of holiness" and that they have begun a meeting "similar to our Tuesday meeting."[25] Commenting on this, she reveals the significance she attached to it: "His establishment in the possession of this blessing has tended much to the confirmation of my own faith. I can never look back upon the solemn covenant engagements entered into at that time, in reference to this specific object, without adding fresh fuel to the fire of devotion."[26]

Upham did become, as Palmer anticipated, a major advocate of holiness teaching and produced a number of writings in support of the cause, most of them penned during the same period in which Palmer was gaining her own fame as a writer on holiness themes. Among these were Principles of the Interior or Hidden Life (1843), The Life of Faith (1845), The Life of Madame Catherine Adorna (1845), Life and Religious Opinion and Experience of Madame de la Mothe Guyon (1847), A Treatise on Divine Union(1851), and Absolute Religion (1873). As can be seen by these titles, Upham's view developed in a decidedly mystical direction, drawing heavily on the "Quietist" tradition in Christianity for paradigms of "holiness" of "entire sanctification." That this eventually led to a rupture in the relationship between Upham and his "spiritual mother," we shall see.

The content of the Tuesday Meeting, as has been noted, consisted largely of accounts by various individuals of their religious experiences, or words of instruction or exhortation to the group concerning the "way of holiness." Very often the vocabulary and conceptualization were reflective of Phoebe Palmer's distinctive views, though this was not always the case. Sometimes rather vague, general references to "holiness" or "the presence of the Holy Ghost," or "the power of an indwelling Christ" constituted the substance of the remarks, while occasionally speakers would wander off from "the way" altogether. The following are excerpts either from actual transcriptions of testimonials or paraphrased summaries which give a bit of the flavor and range of the typical Tuesday meeting session. These are drawn from various periods of the life of the meeting.

Rev. Henry Belden (Congregational minister): "I have loved to give my testimony to the power of the cleansing blood of Jesus for many years. He has saved me from all sin.... I came out of that sad error that we are justified by faith, but after that we are to pro-

gress by works. We are justified and sanctified by faith. What we have faith in Jesus to
do for us, He doeth it."[27]

"Sister" Drake: "I am but a child. The
Lord helps me. As I go on in the Christian
life it becomes more and more simple.... I
never loved God as I have for two or three
years past. I seem to be like a little child
who knows its mother is about. It seems to me
that God has come to me. He is my power, my
strength, my rest.... Trust Him, and He will
fulfill every promise."[28]

"Sister L---": "Was kept and saved by the
blessed Jesus, and she was made superior to
all the annoyances of life. She was saved, not
from trial, but from sin. There was a time
when her will was in opposition to God's will,
but everything now seemed to waft her God-
ward.... Her heart was full of love to God and
to the world."[29]

Rev. William Taylor (Methodist minister):
"The difference between the consecration of
instructed believers and that of the sinner is
this. The sinner does not consecrate at all.
He has nothing to consecrate. He is a felon
under condemnation. His is a surrender, not a
consecration, and made mainly from fear. The
converted soul...has given back to him blessings lost through sin. He now has something to
consecrate. He...sees that he is able to...
offer himself a living sacrifice, holy, and
acceptable to God through Christ."[30]

"Sister" Lois Smith: "At the time she was
convinced that it was her privilege to be

cleansed from sin, she had been going over the
various points of consecration, but did not
apprehend the way till she heard a sermon text
'Go on to perfection.' Afterwards...she rose
and said...'They say the altar is Christ,' and
the Bible says the altar is holy and sanctifies the gift. I know that the gift is poor
and mean, but the altar is holy and I know the
gift is sanctified.' She resolved to retain
this position till convinced of her error.
While waiting for the testimony the words
came, 'Now are ye dead to sin and alive to
God,' and she had since been reckoning herself
dead, and had the blessed testimony of the
Spirit [of God]."[31]

Dr. Charles Cullis (Episcopalian physician): "If anything is true, it is God's Word.
It is precious to me, I would rather feed on
it than on anything in the world.... The promises (of the Bible) are to be accepted by
faith. 'All things ye desire when ye pray,
believe that ye receive them, and ye shall
have them.' The promise does not hinge on
feeling, but believing.... I should as soon
question my existence as to doubt God's word.
Take God at His word. Does not the blood (of
Jesus) cleanse from all sin? It cleanses, it
cleanses! It cleanses the moment we believe."[32]

"Sister" Clark: "Thought it a great
blessing to have sanctified common sense. To
be fully set apart for God does not mean that
we are to take leave of our common sense, but
to have our judgement and reason sanctified.

We are to live in the world as lights...and
doing everything with a single eye to the
glory of God.... When we do all to the glory
of God, it enables the commonest duty. She
once heard Mrs. Palmer say 'she put on her hat
to please the Lord.' Housework had always been
a drudgery to her because she lacked physical
strength; but one day, as she was cleaning
paint, the thought came that she was doing it
for His glory, because a dirty house is not to
His glory, and immediately her soul merged out
into freedom; and since that time she had
enjoyed doing everything, as mother, wife,
housekeeper, and the routine of life, for the
glory of God."[33]

Rev. Freshman (Canadian Methodist minister identified as a "Jewish Witness"): "I have
often read of these meetings, and I am glad to
be here. The Lord has done great things for
me. I was brought up in a religion opposed to
'Him of whom Moses in the law and the prophets
did write.' It could give me no peace in life,
or consolation in death. But, blessed be God,
He opened my eyes, and led me to see that I
was a sinner. God has adopted me into His
family and applied the blood of Jesus to my
soul. He has honored me in putting me into the
ministry, as also my dear father, formerly a
Rabbi, who labored faithfully for fifteen
years in connection with the Methodist Church
in Canada.... I have been trying to follow in
his footsteps. I have come into the enjoyments
of perfect love, since which God has graciously blessed my labors."[34]

Analysis of these typical Tuesday Meeting "testimonials" renders nothing startling or surprising. In
fact the most startling or surprising thing about them,
considering that the Tuesday Meeting had such consequence for the holiness movement in American religion,
is that these statements are so ordinary. They are
altogether typical of nineteenth-century "Evangelicalism." Except for some specific reflections of Palmerian
theology (e.g. the importance of "consecration"; "the
altar sanctifies the gift"; "the promise does not hinge
on feeling, but believing"), the emphases are largely
those of "Common Sense Evangelicalism" or "Romantic
Evangelicalism," both important strains in the dominant
religious outlook of the nineteenth century.

"Common Sense Evangelicalism" drew heavily upon the
Scottish Common Sense School of philosophy articulated
by such thinkers as Francis Hutcheson, Thomas Reid, and
Dugald Stewart. These thinkers, in reacting to the em-
pirical psychology and epistemology of John Locke, particularly its more troublesome aspects developed by
George Berkeley and David Hume, developed a system of
thought which placed heavy emphasis on the validity of
"common sense" analysis of the workings of human consciousness. By this means they claimed to be able to
demonstrate the ultimate reality of such things as immortality, rewards and punishment after death, the existence of a fixed moral law, and the nature of the moral
law. They held that human beings experience the objective world without the mediation of ideas, and that
humans are in themselves genuine causes and not merely
"reactor mechanisms" which are simply acted upon by
outside stimuli. Religiously such a system helped to
shape a variety of Christian movements which stressed
the reasonableness and benevolence of God, held that God

worked through certain fixed, discernible "means," saw the person as active rather than passive in his or her salvation, and understood grace to be available to all rather than dispensed selectively only to the elect. In short, "Common Sense Evangelicalism" in theological terms represented a clear "Arminianizing" of American Christianity, moving it away from the dominant Calvinistic tradition of the seventeenth and eighteenth centuries and toward more "Methodist" categories of thought. [35]

"Romantic Evangelicalism" infused into the "common sense" thrust of Evangelical religion emphases upon the feelings or emotions, Jesus as the center of the Christian system (often exalting His "personality" and His immediate availability to the believer), and upon a sentimental extolling of women, children and parenthood as ideal symbols, and even embodiments, of grace. Romantic Evangelicalism was also highly individualistic.[36]

The "common sense" and "romantic" strains are evident in the above Tuesday Meeting testimonies. All either imply or make explicit the fact that the way of salvation is clear and reasonable and that God is utterly benevolent. Several stress the moral responsibility of both converted and unconverted. A number are sentimental, describing the divine-human relationship in parent-child terms (Drake and Freshman) or exalting the domestic role (Clark). Some are "Christocentric," stressing friendship with or imitation of Jesus (Beldon, "Sister L---," Freshman). Six of the testimonies are, as expected, explicitly "perfectionistic," making reference to being saved from all sin or enjoying "perfect love." Of these, four (Belden, Taylor, Smith, Cullis) have recognizably "Palmerian" emphases. In all, these are unremarkable religious statements, quite typical of

American Protestantism in the nineteenth century. Even
their perfectionist concern is not a denominational or
sectarian oddity.[37]

While the conduct and content of the Tuesday Meeting were not extraordinary, certain other facets of it
were. For one, it was strongly egalitarian and provided
opportunity for much participation by laypersons.
Though many ministers attended, recorded testimonies and
accounts of the meetings indicate that they did not
dominate or control the proceedings. And their contribution was just what it was for all others--a description
of their own religious experience, a verse quoted from
the Bible, or a word of exhortation. This is quite
amazing considering the fact that several dozen ministers from various denominations were commonly in attendance.[38] One interesting incident in this connection
concerns an unidentified minister, "known by reputation
to tens of thousands of the religious and literary
world" who visited the Tuesday Meeting for the first
time. Expressing his desire not to be "brought out"
(but, one suspects, expecting to be), he sat in some
obscure corner of the Palmer's parlor. When he finally
concluded that he really was not going to be given
special recognition or called upon to address the assembly, but by then desiring to do so, he found himself ill
situated to gain the floor. Only after repeated attempts
was he able to make himself seen and heard, only one
among the many.[39] This was quite typical of a situation
in which the "ministry does not wait for the laity,
neither does the laity wait for the ministry.... These
comingle as one...."[40] Even Phoebe Palmer herself,
though keeping a firm hand on the helm, did so by means
other than monopolizing the floor. Dr. Roche noted that

when speaking "she consumes no more time than would be allowed to another."[41]

Among the laypersons who were routinely given access to the Tuesday Meeting on an equal footing with the professional clergy were many women. This was an egalitarian gathering in terms of gender as well as in terms of professional and non-professional roles in the church. The meeting was singular enough in its being led by a woman, and this singularity was underscored by the attendance of full participation of many other women.[42] If recorded testimonies are to be taken as an accurate indicator of female participation, fully as many women as men would be heard from at a typical gathering. Proclaiming the credo "whether male or female, all are one in Christ Jesus," the Tuesday Meeting seems to have quite successfully acted this out in its own structure.

This egalitarian thrust to the Tuesday Meeting was undergirded by Phoebe Palmer's theology. Throughout her public career she taught the full propriety--indeed, necessity--of lay action in the church and in religious causes. Her concern was not so much for lay government of religious institutions as for the obligation of the laity for carrying out the mission of the church through proclamation and evangelism, teaching, and works of compassion. This emphasis was not itself new, being a characteristic of American Christianity owing to the voluntarist system of denominationalism, revivalism, and the pietist imprint, but Palmer helped to give it new rationale through her evolving "pentecostal" theology.[43]

Taking as her starting place the biblical book of Acts, particularly the chapter two account of the day of Pentecost, she held that in the "dispensation of the Spirit" (i.e. the state of the Christian community since Pentecost) all Christians are given gifts which they are expected to use for extending and building up the church. The use of these gifts will result in the creation of a "holy working class of Christians in all the various denominations...."[44] Such is the implication of Acts 2, thought Palmer, where all who were "filled with the Holy Ghost" began "to speak as the Spirit gave utterance," entering into "united ministrations" which resulted in the conversion to Christianity of three thousand persons in one day.[45] In that event "the ministry of the Word" was no longer "confined to the apostles," but was rather laid upon a divinely prepared "laity" for the times."[46]

Marching in step with men in this spiritual army were many women. Their prominent inclusion in fact was considered by Palmer to be a special characteristic of the "last days" (i.e. the period of history since Pentecost). Daughters as well as sons of God could expect to "prophesy" and have the Spirit of God "poured forth" upon them.[47] Palmer declared that "calling out female laborers" would mark a "revival of Christianity after the apostolic fashion."[48]

In a series of articles in the Christian Advocate and Journal in the winter of 1857 Phoebe punctuated her "theology of the laity," proclaiming that "The cause of Zion now demands that every soldier enlisted under the banner of Christ...should come up to the work."[49] To this end she exhorted pastors, "endeavor to cause your people to feel their individuality in regard to the demand of the Head of the Church for personal effort."[50]

Such were the convictions behind the operation of the Tuesday Meeting which accounted for its emphasis on personal testimony rather than preaching or lecturing by one designated person and its recognition of the importance of the contribution of laypersons as well as

professional clergy, women as well as men. The forum of
the Tuesday Meeting was to be a microcosm of a Christian
Church carried along by the fervent joint activity of an
egalitarian corps of Holy Spirit endowed workers.

Implicit in this egalitarianism of the Tuesday
Meeting is an element which was clearly reflected in the
group's makeup as well as being made quite explicit in
Phoebe Palmer's public statements. This is interdenomi-
nationalism. Though having Methodist roots, the gathering quickly became interdenominational, gaining its
initial notoriety, in fact, from the involvement of
Congregationalist Professor and Mrs. T. C. Upham, and
the conversion to perfectionist views of Professor
Upham. Over the years many Congregationalists along with
others from various ecclesiastical and theological traditions would support the Tuesday Meeting and the wider
ministry of Phoebe Palmer which grew out of it. Already
by 1842, non-Methodists familiar with Palmer through the
Tuesday Meeting were inviting her to address "holiness
meetings" of their own. At one of these Rev. William
Hill, a Presbyterian minister at Newburg, New Jersey,
sought and professed to experience entire sanctification. Within weeks, he and two other fellow ministers
who had followed him in his profession of Christian
Perfection were tried for heresy and expelled from the
Presbyterian ministry. One of these, Henry Belden, subsequently became a Congregationalist pastor and remained
an outspoken supporter of perfectionist teaching and
Phoebe Palmer.[51]

Notwithstanding the rough handling of Belden and
Hill, three Presbyterian ministers were reported as
being present at the Tuesday Meeting in 1844.[52] By 1845
"persons of different denominations" are present including one who "unable to sustain the shock of power"

(apparently the presence of divine power in the meeting), "sunk down overwhelmed" and a Baptist minister who "confessed his belief that holiness was indeed a doctrine of the Bible" and who "lamented his want of it."[53] By the mid 1860s Baptist, Congregationalist, Dutch Reformed, German Reformed, Presbyterian, and Episcopalian, along with Methodist ministers are being reported in attendance, to say nothing of the laypersons present.[54] George Hughes' fiftieth anniversary commemoration of the Tuesday Meeting includes testimonies from representatives of all of these groups plus the Society of Friends.[55] Phoebe Palmer herself wrote late in her life of attending a meeting of "Orthodox Friends" and finding there those who had attended the Tuesday Meeting.[56]

As with lay participation, Palmer explicitly justified this interdenominational or ecumenical character of the Tuesday Meeting and of her revivalistic activities generally. She held that Christian Perfection was a "leading doctrine of the Bible" rather than a doctrine "peculiar to any sect" and so should be proclaimed by and to all Christians.[57] She agreed, along with nineteenth-century American "restorationists" like Thomas and Alexander Campbell and Barton W. Stone, that the "oneness of Christians, in heart and in effort," is "just what Christ, the Founder of Christianity, set forth as a fundamental principle if we would have the world believe in the divinity of his claims as a Saviour."[58] She thought that the embrace of the doctrine of holiness by all denominations would "shake the world, and bring in the reign of Christ," i.e. inaugurate the millennial rule of Christ on earth.[59] In a development of the same "Pentecostal Theology" which underlay her advocacy of lay and women's rights, Palmer held that the promise of Pentecost was not only that all Christians, male <u>and</u> female, would be called upon and empowered to "preach" and evangelize, but that Christians would co-operate "as one" in the effort. In a letter which reveals her views at this point, as well as her estimate of the Tuesday Meeting as a significant model, Phoebe wrote to her close friend, Mrs. Bishop Hamline, concerning some ecumenical holiness meetings in Canada,

> Have you observed how greatly the Lord is blessing the ministers and people of other denominations in connection with the 'Conventions on Holiness' held in churches of various denominations? We attended one of the conventions held in an old established Episcopal Church, a few weeks ago. It was a season of Holy Ghost power. Male and female disciples participating with unreserved freedom. Congregational, Episcopal, Baptist, Presbyterian, and Methodist ministers, as one, witnessing of the great salvation.

> The Tuesday Meeting seems to be the general rallying point with these dear brethren of various denominations. The Lord is blessing and diffusing the savor of the meeting in a remarkable manner.[60]

The interdenominational dimension of the Tuesday Meeting is at once remarkable and ordinary. It is ordinary in that the nineteenth century saw many attempts at Christian unity either in terms of actual organic union such as that envisioned by the Disciples of Christ/ Christian movement, or in terms of practical cooperation such as occurred in connection with the early frontier camp meetings or the host of voluntary societies formed for evangelization and the reform of American society. The Tuesday Meeting and Phoebe Palmer's concern for

Christian unity under the banner of "holiness to the
Lord" are not anomalous in this light.

The remarkable thing, however, is that the Tuesday
Meeting pursued its ecumenical course even after interdenominational cooperation had begun to break down in
Protestantism generally, becoming more, rather than
less, interdenominational with time. Its greatest
strength came in a time when denominational self-con-
sciousness was beginning to reassert itself in many
communions as witnessed by the breakdown of the Congre-
gationist-Presbyterian Plan of Union, several celebrated
heresy trials within the Presbyterian fold, and the
travails over various issues--notably slavery--which led
to schisms in several of the major denominations and the
formation of northern and southern Baptist and Presbyterian bodies, northern and southern Methodist bodies,
and the Wesleyan Methodist and Free Methodist
churches.[61]

Furthermore, the Tuesday Meeting, and Palmer's work
as a whole, promoted Christian unity on a precariously
slim basis, that being a doctrine which was popularly
thought of as a denominational distinctive of Wesley's
heirs. That Christian Perfection could become the point
of convergence for so many different religious traditions is little short of astounding! The fact that it
did clearly shows the revivalistic and pietistic leaven-
ing of nineteenth-century American religious life, a
process to which Methodism itself contributed no little
part.[62]

In order to assess fully the Tuesday Meeting the
question of its inspiration or sources after which it
might have been patterned needs yet to be raised. It
seems here that the Methodist tradition itself was the
main source and inspiration with its highly developed

system of small group meetings. Within Methodism the society, the class, the select band, and the "Love Feast" all operated on a basis very similar to that of the Tuesday Meeting.

The society was the very foundation of early Methodism under John Wesley in England. The concept, which was first seen in the famous "Holy Club" conducted by Wesley, his brother Charles, George Whitefield and others at Oxford in the late 1720s and early 1730s, appears in connection with John Wesley's stint as a missionary in Georgia for the Anglican Society for the Propagation of the Gospel in Foreign Parts in 1736-37. It reappears in England in 1738 when Wesley, together with the Moravian Peter Böhler, formed a religious "society" in London, and it became the chief vehicle by which Wesley spread his concern for seeking "true holiness" within the Church of England. He seems to have borrowed the society idea from the "society movement" within Anglicanism, with which his parents were much in sympathy, which had its roots deep in early continental Pietism, and from the Moravians with whom he associated much during his crucial period of theological formation in the 1730s. The society movement would have been an earlier influence, reinforced by the Moravian idea of "ecclesiolae in ecclesia" ("little churches in the Church") during later contact with that movement.[63]

The society was not a full-orbed church, but rather a "meeting for spiritual fellowship in a setting of devout informality."[64] It was a gathering of the "saved" and those seeking to be "saved" for mutual support, edification, and exhortation. Wesley did not conceive of the society as a substitute for services of public worship, but as a supplemental means of spiritual growth. Begun according to this vision, the Wesleyan societies of course over time grew into a "sect" which eventually withdrew from the Church of England.

In America Methodist societies were formed by the first Methodist lay preachers in the 1760s. Of those attending Methodist preaching, perhaps thirty or fewer would be constituted into a society of "hard core" Methodists, submitting to discipline as prescribed by the General Rules, and committing themselves to mutual spiritual care and pursuit of "holiness." The society was thus the basis of membership in Methodism, with perhaps several hundred non-members making up the Methodist preacher's wider "congregation."[65]

Over time, both in England and in America, two subgroups of the society developed, these being the class and the select band. The class was usually limited to about fifteen in size, with the band even smaller, usually numbering not more than five or six. These smaller groups, meeting in various homes under lay leadership, "bound the society with the ties of a spiritual family" by means of prayer, testimony, and counsel in an intimate setting.[66] The smallest unit, the band, though promoted in America by Thomas Coke and Francis Asbury as ideal agencies for the cultivation of Christian Perfection, maintained a precarious existence and finally gave way altogether to the larger class, though the bands were a bit more long lived in England.[67] However, interesting in light of the development of special holiness meetings in the New York City area in the 1830s is the fact that as late as 1819 certain New York City Methodists were still forming small "holiness" bands and holding prayer meetings. These were "composed only of such as have experienced the blessing of perfect love, or those truly awakened to feel the necessity of it and who are steadily seeking for clean hearts."[68]

One other unique Methodist institution, similar in design to the societies, classes, and bands, was the "love feast." Building on Moravian precedent, Wesley introduced the love feast to his "Methodists" as a quasi-sacramental occasion marked by the serving of plain bread and water (rather than the usual communion bread and wine) and extempore prayer and testimony. Only those in full membership in a Methodist Society were permitted to attend. Wesley held that warrant for such a gathering was to be found in the "Agape" or fellowship meal of the primitive Christian Church.[69] The love feast in American Methodism was frequently held in connection with Quarterly or Annual Conferences and always as a part of camp meetings, and could arise more or less spontaneously on other occasions as well. So popular was the practice that it often threatened to supplant Communion or the Lord's Supper as a central sacramental occasion among Methodists.[70]

With this structure to guide them, is it any wonder that Phoebe Palmer and Sarah Lankford should have turned to an informal, lay oriented, small group meeting to promote the renewal of holiness within Methodism? As daughters of the Methodist Episcopal Church, both had been members of classes. Phoebe led a class for a time, and they had attended many love feasts.[71] The idea of a special "select group" nurturing its members through prayer, testimony, and counsel was natural. There was even precedent for such a group to be focused narrowly on the pursuit of Christian Perfection.

Of course the Tuesday Meeting soon outgrew the "small group" aspect of the traditional Methodist gatherings, sometimes numbering three hundred in attendance, though it did maintain the other elements of society, band, and love feast.[72] In doing so it gave birth to a numerous progeny, some 238 meetings for the promotion of holiness in operation throughout the United States, Canada, Britain, New Zealand, and India by the time George Hughes wrote his golden anniversary testimonial in 1886.[73] As the soul of the "holiness movement," the Tuesday Meeting in New York and in its offspring elsewhere had a long and useful existence. Even in the twentieth century holiness churches were still holding "Tuesday holiness meetings" as a part of their regular program.[74] Many connected with the movement would likely have agreed with George Hughes' laudatory assessment of the Tuesday Meeting as the "place above all others" where he had "received the greatest light on holy Scripture" and "enjoyed the purest saintly fellowship." It was, he wrote, "without a parallel. No meeting like this has a place in church history. The number saved through its instrumentality is beyond computation." Heaven, he thought, would be "immeasurably richer for the holding of it," and it would be a "subject of happy converse among the glorified throughout eternal ages."[75]

B. Pre-Civil War American and Canadian Church and Campmeeting Ministry

The Tuesday Meeting for the Promotion of Holiness, as central as it was to Phoebe Palmer's career in the public eye, and as extolled as it was by those influenced by it, was probably not in the long run her most important vehicle for promoting "entire devotion to God." Her revivalist travels and her writings were more important. Both grew initially out of the Tuesday Meeting, but both eventually far surpassed it as effective means of reaching large numbers of people with a persuasive presentation of her religious views.

The travels began inauspiciously but mushroomed into important extended "campaigns" which matched those of the better known revival practitioners of the day. Though she is not given place in the standard histories of American revivalism, as has been noted, she has been seriously slighted by the omission.[76] Her travels took her literally from coast to coast in the United States, into Canadian territory and to Great Britain, and drew thousands to crowded halls, churches and outdoor camp meeting sites.

In this kind of religious activity Palmer was far from alone, for the nineteenth century was the great century of revivalism in American Christianity. Periods of religious fervor reaching across denominational lines and touching most regions of the country characterized the times. Religiously, the century was "born in revival" with the embers of the first "Great Awakening" of the eighteenth century not yet fully cooled, especially in the American South, and new sparks beginning to kindle fire in the Northeast and the western frontier. These new sparks led to the so-called "Second Great Awakening" which McLoughlin dates from 1800 to 1830, though such precise dating is somewhat arbitrary as McLoughlin himself recognizes.[77] The century ended with the death of Dwight L. Moody in 1899, perhaps the most widely acclaimed revivalist of the whole century and the one who made revivalism "a big business."[78] Moody's campaigns were, variously viewed, either part of a third "Great Awakening" or significant preparation for it.[79] Whatever the case, between the second Great Awakening and Moody, revivalism "permeated most of the American denominations, and contributed much to the common style of Protestant life." It was "the most powerful engine in

the process of American church growth, frontier accul-
turation, and benevolent reform."[80]

A major aspect of revivalism was the revivalist who
on a full-time or part-time basis crisscrossed the country preaching and seeking converts to Christianity. The
"protracted meeting," a series of religious gatherings
held daily (or even more frequently) and lasting a week
or longer, became the main tool of the revivalist in his
or her work. In the nineteenth century protracted meetings featuring more or less professional revivalists
figured prominently in national "awakenings" and also
effectively served local congregations seeking to be
"revived" from perceived religious apathy.

To this extent Phoebe Palmer's emergence as a revivalist is not singular. Revivalism was the order of the
day; by the 1840s its machinery was firmly in place and
Palmer's denomination, the Methodist Episcopal Church,
was a most enthusiastic user. However, the major revivalists, both Methodist and non-Methodist, were men.
Here Palmer's climb to fame is singular. She became the
first of a very small group of women who emerged from
the swirl of nineteenth-century revivalism as full-
fledged revivalist "preachers." Many women found greatly
expanded roles within the context of revivalism due to
its focus on individual religious experience rather than
traditional ecclesiastical structures, its stress on lay
activism as a sign of genuine conversion, and its intense mobilization of support agencies to strengthen and
perpetuate revival related activities and goals. This
has been documented by a number of students. Still,
these new larger roles were rather clearly circumscribed
and only a handful of women tested the boundaries to the
point of challenging the men for the right of being
professional itinerants.[81] That such challenge should

occur was virtually inevitable, however, given the wide ranging revival activities which women assumed and the theology which undergirded their activism. "Perfectionist" theology was especially potent in this regard.[82] The real wonder is that more did not follow the path to its logical conclusion. As it was, besides Phoebe Palmer only Margaret ("Maggie") Newton Van Cott, the first woman to receive a local preacher's license in the Methodist Episcopal Church (1869), and Amanda Berry Smith, a black "holiness" revivalist during the last third of the nineteenth century, achieved anything more than local or regional notoriety, though a few other women had become "preachers" or "evangelists" by the turn of the century.[83]

Palmer's assumption of the role of revivalist was not unanticipated, yet it did not happen without considerable hesitation and soul-searching on her part. As has been previously seen, she had become a noted part of New York City Methodism by 1840, largely on the strength of some published poems and articles, her role as leader of a Methodist "class" having both male and female members--the first woman to head such a class in the area-- and her inheritance of major responsibility for the Tuesday Meeting from her sister, Sarah. From this base she began to be invited to travel outside the city to share her ideas on the "way of holiness." The record does not indicate what form these earliest travels took, whether Palmer "preached" in the manner she later would or was presented in some other sort of form.[84] Probably informal and Tuesday-Meeting-like settings grew into more formal and larger occasions over time. Whatever the case, the earliest outings were unremarkable, Phoebe noting that while she had desired "extraordinary outpourings of the Spirit" as proof to others (and no doubt also to herself) of divine approval of her fledgling career, these had not occurred.[85]

Even though the early outings were not all Phoebe expected them to be, they did give her a wider exposure and led to still more invitations. By the second "season" of travel (1841) numerous conversions were beginning to occur in connection with her visits and persons were claiming to have experienced the "deeper work" of entire sanctification. She wrote to her husband of a meeting in which "over fifty stood up as a token that they entered into covenant to give themselves to be wholly the Lord's."[86] She also noted that she found it difficult to write regularly because so often during the day "The room is almost filled with company, who desire to see me."[87] Such response should have buoyed her, signalling the divine endorsement she sought--and it did to some degree--but there was still tension and hesitation. Even after several years of growing public acceptance and "success," she reported, "My nature still shrinks from this," but she also affirmed that she desired to know and do "the will of God, however crossing to the flesh it might be" and that when she did this, "grace always sustains."[88] She also remembered how at first "the enemy" had "tempted her with thoughts of being away from home without her earthly protector, and other suggestions of like bearing."[89] Evidently at some point along the way the tension slackened and the "extraordinary outpourings of the Spirit" she hoped for began to occur in such measure that her always logical mind could not deny their meaning. By the close of her career she could claim with evident conviction, "So fully has God made my commission known to my own soul, and so truly has He set His seal upon it...in the conversion of thousands of precious souls, and the sancti-

fication of a multitude of believers, that even Satan
does not seem to question that my call is divine. It has
been many years since I remember to have had a temptation to doubt."[90]

From 1841 on Palmer's desire to do "the will of
God" led her away from home more frequently and took her
longer distances. Her itinerary lengthened. For roughly
the first twenty years she traveled without husband or
children. That her children should be left at home with
their father and domestic help should not be surprising
given the painful "lessons" Phoebe had learned through
the loss of three children about the priority of God and
"religious duties" over all other things, especially
prized children. At one point she noted the difficulty
to which this set of priorities sometimes led, but also
observed that "by endeavoring to make all things subservient to the duties of religion, showing manifestly
before my family that I seek first the Kingdom of God
and its righteousness, God honors the intention and adds
needful sustainments."[91] She also sends a message to
Walter for "those precious little ones": "tell them Ma
sends one hundred kisses each."[92]

That this practice was uncommon hardly needs mentioning, yet its radical nature has been obscured by the
fact that in later years Phoebe and Walter together
formed a revivalistic "team." In the earlier years,
however, Phoebe was pioneering alone in a man's world.[93]
Walter Palmer was clearly a key part in Phoebe's decision to launch out into these uncharted waters and to
sustain the voyage once begun. It was Walter who presided over the home during Phoebe's extended absences.
It was Walter who went into the publishing business in
part to enhance his wife's reach as an author. It was
Walter who appears never to have bridled at a role which

cast him as something very close to "Mister Phoebe
Palmer." And it was also Walter who financed some of
Phoebe's travels, a little known fact about her revivalistic career being that she often served without honor-
arium.[94] In an early "revival report" to Walter, Phoebe
ventures that he will not oppose her extending her trip
and that in fact she is certain his "heart will exult"
at the news that she has experienced encouraging results.[95] There is no evidence that she was mistaken.
Quite the contrary. In an undated, but obviously somewhat later letter she wrote to Walter from Boston: "The
longer I live, the more I see how needful we are to each
other. If I have been in any degree useful, it has been
greatly owing to the fact, that the Lord has given me a
husband who seems ever to have appreciated me beyond my
worth, and whose encouragements have been very, and I
think, absolutely needful to me, in the prosecution of
the work to which the Lord has called me."[96]

As Phoebe, with the encouragement of Walter, expanded her itinerary, certain patterns began to emerge
which would characterize her career as a revivalist. One
of these was the continued use of the "small group"
(these groups sometimes became quite large) meeting, an
essential component of the Methodist tradition in which
Palmer was steeped, and a widespread feature of the
"social religion" of nineteenth-century Protestantism
generally.[97] Though Palmer more and more became the
"headliner" of expansive, often interdenominational
protracted meetings, the Tuesday-Meeting-like small
group gathering continued to be a profitable avenue for
setting forth the "way of holiness."

One reason for this was no doubt the fact that
Palmer was identified throughout her career as the leader of the "famous Tuesday Meeting for the Promotion of

Holiness," so that it seemed natural and proper to present her in her most noted medium, the "social religious gathering." As a result of the whole socio-religious transformation wrought by revivalism, of which they were a major expression, such gatherings were more widely open to women than other religious structures, a fact which made them continually useful adjuncts to the more male-dominated techniques with which Palmer began to experiment. Through them she could always get a hearing. When she visited Wesleyan University, Middletown, Connecticut in 1845, rather than "preaching" to faculty and students, an act that might have aroused opposition in that setting, she met them in typical Methodist "class meetings" where she presented holiness as the duty of the present moment.[98] Similarly, when visiting Boston in the spring of 1850, while holding meetings in two Methodist churches, she conducted meetings somewhat like the Tuesday Meetings, focusing exclusively on "holiness." She also held two informal "social religious gatherings" in the home of an Episcopalian lawyer, attended largely by Episcopalians, Presbyterians, and Unitarians, all of whom would typically have had considerable difficulty with a woman in the pulpit. Here, however, they sat for an hour and a half as Palmer explained what she believed to be "the principles of Bible consecration, giving throughout, experimental illustrations," and they responded with tears and assurances of their hearty agreement.[99] Later that same year, as part of her stay in Springfield, Massachusetts, she helped to "resuscitate" a meeting for the promotion of holiness.[100] Even in England, between 1859 and 1863, the social religious gathering was a frequently used evangelistic tool which opened perhaps otherwise closed doors to Palmer.[101]

These kinds of meetings dovetailed nicely with another sort of religious gathering in which Phoebe found much success, the camp meeting. Born on the frontier as a potent tool for religious conversion and community building, camp meetings found special favor with Methodists who soon domesticated the original frontier phenomenon, establishing permanent campgrounds near urban concentrations of church members. It was to these summer encampments that Palmer began to go.[102] Here she would conduct meetings somewhat like the Tuesday Meetings, focusing exclusively on Christian holiness and its attainment. These would be part of the larger program which included several preaching services, "prayer meetings" and "love feasts." These "holiness meetings" Palmer would conduct as a combination inquirer's meeting and evangelistic preaching service. Persons interested in attaining Christian Perfection would be given opportunity to confess their need and inquire after the "way of holiness," after or before which Phoebe Palmer would strongly exhort them as to the requisite steps for entering "the way." The meeting usually closed with an "altar invitation," giving seekers after holiness an opportunity to put feet to their concern by entirely devoting themselves to God while kneeling at the altar or mourner's bench, and thereby experiencing the "deeper work of grace" of entire sanctification. Referring to such meetings in a letter to her sister, Sarah, Phoebe notes, "As usual with us, the afternoon meetings are largely devoted to the theme of present, personal holiness.... It is only to give opportunity to seekers of the great salvation, and the altar is crowded."[103] Of another occasion she reports, "Our afternoon meetings have been very largely attended," adding that ministers and laypeople alike "have prostrated themselves in humility before God" seeking holiness, and "have not sought in vain."[104]

In the course of developing these camp meeting gatherings as tools for promoting entire devotion to God, Palmer pioneered three "new measures" which were of great consequence not only for her career but also the "holiness movement" which grew largely from her work and began to take institutional shape in the years following the Civil War. These "new measures" were mainly adaptations of more or less common revivalist techniques to the specific purpose of leading persons into (and confirming them in) a "second work" of God's grace following the initial conversion experience.

The first of these was the "holiness altar invitation" extended specifically and exclusively to those already converted Christians who were seeking the deeper, second experience of "entire sanctification." What is possibly the first one of these on record occurred during a camp meeting at Belleville, New Jersey in 1844, Palmer's fifth "season" of travel. Here at Palmer's suggestion the minister in charge of a preaching meeting invited specifically those who were "seekers of present holiness" to pray at the "mourner's bench."[105] This became an increasingly popular practice which Phoebe cultivated in her camp meeting rounds. Interestingly, on this same tour Palmer had complained of the lack of preaching on holiness at the Trenton camp meeting, observing that "the people were hungering for food, which they did not get" and declaring it "a mistake to suppose that first principles are all that are required at camp meeting"; Christian Perfection must also be urged upon the already converted.[106] Here Palmer was moving from the somewhat limited sphere of the afternoon holiness meeting to the wider sphere of the general preaching meetings of the camp schedule, contending that "holiness" ought to be the preoccupation of both. More and more the camp meetings at which she appeared took on a holiness coloring. It was not a large step from here to the National Campmeeting Association for the Promotion of Holiness and its program of avowedly holiness camp meetings that did so much to bind the holiness message to the machinery of American revivalism, and to determine the direction of the holiness movement after 1867.[107] These connections will be further explored in chapters V and VI.

The second "new measure" pioneered by Palmer was the "believing meeting." This was a step beyond the "inquiry meeting," though it retained elements of it. It was an attempt to systematically bring persons to the point of believing God for present holiness, a keynote in Palmer's doctirne. The seeking, the praying, the instruction would now be done; persons would be exhorted and given opportunity to act. Such climactic crisis had long been a part of Palmer's methodology of promoting holiness. She already used "altar invitations" as part of her afternoon camp meeting holiness gatherings, and urged general "holiness altar invitations" in camp meeting preaching services. The new wrinkle was structuring this ritual into a special meeting. This gave the procedure a focus and urgency, as well as psychological and social support it did not have in the other settings. Palmer first tried the technique in 1858, at the very height of her popularity, in connection with a revival at Charlottetown, Prince Edward Island.[108] In her own words, this innovation began as follows:

> I think it was last Tuesday afternoon (perhaps the friends at the Tuesday meeting were praying for us). Said I, to the crowded assembly convened, "We sometimes have prayer

meetings, and these are most important; now let us have a <u>believing</u> meeting. If one must exceed the other in importance, surely it must be the latter, inasmuch as without <u>faith</u> it is <u>impossible</u> to please God."

Many had, during the heart searching exercises of the preceding days, come to a point where they had a right to look for the present fulfillment of the promise of the Father. The sacrifice had been brought to the altar, but it is <u>faith</u> that brings the power and claims the <u>tongue of fire</u>.... Oh, what extraordinary demonstrations of the power of faith followed.... It is not enough to wait and pray for the descent of the tongue of fire. There is something to do... Through the power of the Spirit, the offering is brought to the altar, and just at that point the <u>command</u> meets us, "<u>believe</u>," and unless this command be obeyed...the consuming fire does not descend.... Would that I could portray the scene we witnessed at this "Believing meeting." All the ministers on the District, with the exception of one, were present, and not one, I think, but received the baptism of fire.[109]

With the usefulness of the technique thus validated, more and more of Palmer's meetings tended to become "believing meetings." The exhortations, "It is not knowledge you need, but ACTION," and "It is only for <u>faith</u> to demand the needed grace NOW," were pressed ever more vigorously.[110] This theme was always a strong element in Palmer's religious teaching, but it was not until the advent of the "believing meetings" that this method found its perfect institutional embodiment.

The third "new measure" pioneered by Palmer was the "altar testimony." Probably this was not an altogether new practice originated by her, but the putting of an old one to new use. Certainly the "testimony meeting" had popularity among revivalists generally, and the major feature of the Methodist "love feast" was personal accounts of religious experiences. The Tuesday Meeting also incorporated personal testimony. In addition, the conversion experience, which in revivalist fashion occurred in the context of a protracted meeting or camp meeting, could lead to spontaneous testimony at the "mourner's bench" or "anxious seat" that one had received divine grace in answer to prayer of repentance for sin.[111]

The difference in what emerged from Palmer's camp meeting and protracted meeting work was that such "altar testimony" became institutionalized and mandatory. One was expected to testify to saving or sanctifying grace immediately upon receiving it in the prescribed fashion. One did not wait for a special meeting and it was not optional as to whether such testimony was made. Many are the times when Phoebe declares the necessity of public testimony, especially to entire sanctification, beginning with the moment of reception of "the blessing," but continuing ever after if one would retain the blessing.

Hughes relates how Walter, when he was accompanying Phoebe, would elicit "altar testimony": "Passing around the altar, extending his hand to one and another of the newly adopted ones, he would say, 'My brother (or, my sister), what has the Lord done for you?'"[112] Thus the seeker would be led to immediately verbalize what he or she understood their new religious standing to be and in this supportive setting be confirmed in it.

Phoebe was less gentle in this exercise than Walter, but then it was her conviction which was behind the practice, and it was an intense conviction. She taught, along with her emphasis upon "naked faith" as the key to receiving the "deeper work" of entire sanctification, that a chief and necessary expression or demonstration of "naked faith" was to testify publicly to having received "the blessing" once one had made the required "entire devotion" of oneself to God. This was to be done in the absence of any validating "signs" or evidence whatsoever (e.g. great emotion, subjective sense of acceptance by God, etc.). To testify without any thing upon which to stand except the promises of the Word of God as recorded in the Bible was for Phoebe the ultimate demonstration of "naked faith." Taking the words of St. Paul, "For with the heart man believeth unto righteousness; and with the mouth confession is made unto salvation" (Romans 10:10) as her starting place, and understanding "confession" to refer to public testimony, Palmer argued that such was absolutely essential for "salvation," and entire sanctification was the crowning element of salvation according to her Methodistic views.

To a minister struggling with assurance of his being made holy, Palmer admonishes: "your error has been in not confessing with your lips (God's) faithfulness in fulfilling his promises. Your heart has believed, but your lips have not fully, freely, and habitually made confession."[113] To another she poses the question, "Is (God's) word evidence sufficient to rest your faith upon?" If it is, she counsels, "you will not hesitate in making confession with your mouth. If you are not willing to do this, it proves that your faith is yet defective...."[114] And then, lest there be any confusion she adds: "do not forget that believing with the heart, and confessing with the mouth stand closely connected, and 'What God hath joined together, let not man put asun-

der.' To the degree you rely on the faithfulness of God,
O hasten to make confession with the mouth of this your
confidence...."[115] This emphasis became a major--and
controversial--part of her teaching, and, through the
innovation of "altar testimony," of her revivalist technique as well.[116] Both carried over to the various
"holiness" organizations which began to appear in the
closing years of the nineteenth and early years of the
twentieth century.

Though small "social religious gatherings" and camp
meetings proved to be open doors to Phoebe Palmer and
effective means for the propagation of her passionate
concern for "entire devotion to God," they were not her
only forum. She also held "protracted meetings," or what
amounted to the "camp meeting come to town." The practice was a well established one in Methodism by Palmer's
day, although it was relatively new in non-Methodist
circles, being introduced there largely though the work
of revivalist Charles G. Finney.[117] The protracted meeting did all the things which the camp meeting intended
to do, only the physical setting was a little different.

It was in connection with these "urbanized camp
meetings" (and one day public meetings, since not all of
her work was carried on over an extended period of time)
that Palmer most fully approached "preaching." As noted
earlier, according to her own definition of "biblical
preaching" she did in fact preach, though she would not
admit to its being "preaching, technically so called."
In the small group meeting and the camp meeting Palmer
was still a kind of "testifier," a lay person sharing
her own experience and religious insights in a setting
which might best be described as "structured informality." In the church or hall meeting, however, Palmer was
the preacher of the hour, doing all the things a Finney
would do; occupying the pulpit, taking a text, present-

ing an exhortation calculated to persuade hearers to repent and turn to God or seek to more fully enter the "way of holiness" (always replete with stories and illustrations), issuing an "invitation" to the anxious to pray and be prayed for, and praying with an instructing those who responded to the invitation.[118] According to the evidence, this was perhaps Palmer's most effective medium of all, as well as being the one in which the participation of a woman was the most exceptional.

In the camp meeting ministry a report like "two hundred were blest" in the course of an encampment was typical. The protracted meetings, however, which peaked for Palmer in the religious excitement of 1857-58 in the U.S. and Canada included meetings of three or more weeks' duration and reports of upwards of 800 "pardoned" or "entirely sanctified" under Phoebe's "preaching."[119] In these cases her presence in a town was often announced by "show-bills," a flourish she found hard to accept, but which she finally rationalized with typical revivalist logic, concluding that "If being thus announced, would bring out one more person, and that one person would be spiritually aided, it should be made the occasion of grateful ascriptions of praise..."[120] The British tour, which followed hard on the heels of the North American "Laymen's Revival" produced even more spectacular results. At Newcastle-on-Tyne Phoebe and Walter were persuaded to remain for thirty-five days and the names of 1300 "converts" were recorded. Services were conducted four times a day![121] At Sunderland in three weeks' time the names of 2,011 were recorded, with as many as 3,000 in attendance at one service.[122] Here Phoebe was reaching scores with her message and enjoying acceptance and tokens of success equal to that of any revivalist of the time.

The question which naturally suggests itself in this connection is, what sort of "preacher" was Phoebe Palmer? What was it about her that drew the crowds and persuaded persons of the truth of her message? Unfortunately--and inexplicably, considering her popularity--contemporary accounts are few. The most complete is Roche's description which appeared in The Ladies' Repository, a Methodist magazine published in Cincinnati in part to instruct its readers in virtue through presenting biographies of exemplary women. The picture drawn is thus no doubt an idealized one, though it is probably generally accurate in its portrayal of Palmer's distinctive qualities as a speaker, for much the same picture emerges in all the extant accounts. The article bears quoting at some length.

In addressing an audience her position is erect. In spirit, subject, and manner she indicates no confusion. Her intellect and action reveal discipline and self-control. She has enough gesture for either vivacity or effect, and it is easy and appropriate. She never appears to be in a hurry, though not tedious in any of her exercises.... Her articulation is distinct and deliberate, and her voice, that is clear, has sufficient compass for the largest churches in which she officiates. She is calm and free from vociferation, and is rarely vehement. Her style is clear, concise, and colloquial. In the structure of her sentences there is nothing elaborate or involved.... In her communications there is more of logic than rhetoric. She does not, however, attempt any severe or protracted reasoning, but lays down her premises and reaches her conclusions in a way that is sim-

ple, direct, and vigorous. Her forms of speech
are often axiomatic.... Her discourses are
replete with Scriptural illustration and her
design is transparent.

Her spirit is intensely earnest, and in
the strongest utterances, in the periods of
her profoundest emotion, when compassion for
the sinner and concern for the professor move
her soul, her entire nature sways under the
pressure. Her words, action, countenance dis-
close the struggle that is within....

It is not the custom of Mrs. Palmer to
name a text, but when the meeting is under her
direction she desires her husband to open the
services with reading the Scriptures, from
which, after a few easy and pertinent remarks
by the Doctor, she derives her theme. She may
occupy twenty minutes or even an hour. Circumstances influence the matter and length of her
discourse. Her prayers, exhortations, experiences, and addresses all have the impress of
her own individuality. Her character as a
religious teacher is fixed, and her services
are uniform.[123]

One recognizes here the consummate urban revivalist, very nearly approximating a female Finney, it would
seem. There is the "countenance disclosing the struggle
that is within," but there is no "vociferation" like the
frontier camp meeting exhorter. There is just enough of
the theatrical to keep it interesting. The style is
clear and colloquial, logical and liberally sprinkled
with biblical allusions and illustrations. The speaker
is deliberate, direct, and "intensely earnest." She also
communicates her own individuality. This pretty much
sums up the best popular revivalist and evangelical

preaching of the nineteench century. It appears that
Palmer was simply a gifted--and, by 1866, well-polished--
public speaker who offered a clear and simple message in
the common vernacular of "respectable revivalism."

This picture is confirmed by the other accounts of
Palmer's ministry. One who was instrumental in extending
her work to Canada remembered her "intense earnestness"
and the impact she made on "both head and heart." He
also recalled that she was "cool and deliberate," her
"voice clear, utterance distinct, words carefully considered and well chosen." She was, he thought, "a perfect
model of modesty and confidence."[124] An observer of the
British tour reported to the British Standard, an English
Congregational paper, that Palmer's addresses "mingled
simplicity, earnestness, and power" and noted that the
services were "more characterized by solemnity than
excitement," nothing "boisterous or unbecoming the house
of God" taking place.[125] Another British writer also
commented on the "remarkable solemnity" of the proceedings, a particularly sensitive point to the British who
had been scandalized at the antics of a few rougher
specimens of American revivalism earlier in the century.[126] A writer for the Watchman described Phoebe's
preaching at Carlisle, in the north of England, as
"clear, pointed, and scriptural," and as "addressed more
to the understanding than to the feelings of her audience." He also noted her tendency to punctuate the
message with "striking incidents."[127] Yet another
British correspondent, present at services on the Isle
of Wight, described a sermon characterized by "urgency
and explicitness" and centering on "the nature and importance of present holiness, and the necessity of a
minute and most careful attention, on the part of believers" to the matter of their entire devotion to

God.[128] American Methodist Bishop Edmund Janes thought Phoebe to have a "clear understanding, good reasoning powers" and "a calm, easy, yet impressive and effective utterance."[129]

The "secret" of her revivalistic success then, according to these descriptions, seems to be that she had mastered the medium and used it effectively. No eccentric histrionics apparently set her apart from other competent revivalist practitioners of the time. Her uniqueness was in her sex and the particulars of her message, the latter factor still to be explored in greater detail in the following chapters.

As has been seen, in the 1840s Phoebe Palmer itinerated in enlarging circles from New York City while conducting the Tuesday Meeting there and writing, publishing three major books during the decade. As important as these years were to articulating her religious views, fashioning her style of "holiness revivalism," and gaining recognition as a religious teacher and leader of note, they were in the long run but preparation for the 1850s and early '60s, which mark the pinnacle of her public career.

An important part of the dizzying climb of the 1850s was the extension of travel into Canada by Phoebe. Her popularity preceded her first appearance there in 1853 by means of her books, Canadian visitors to the Tuesday Meeting, and a series of excerpts from her writings published in The Christian Guardian, a Canadian Methodist Magazine. In August of 1853 Palmer made her first visit to Canada laboring at a camp meeting held on a farm in Canada West (now Ontario), and saw gratifying results with a reported 500 converted and nearly that number professing "entire sanctification." In Wheatley's opinion, this meeting "gave new life, and a fresh impetus to camp meetings in Canada."[130] It also led to invitations to speak in area churches following the camp. That the largest portion of the six thousand new members reported by the Wesleyan Methodist Conference of Canada in 1853 came from this region visited by Palmer cannot be attributed solely to her, but neither can it be discounted as indicating in some measure her impact there.[131]

From this time on Palmer returned to Canada regularly for summer camp meetings and urban protracted meetings. It was in this connection, in fact, that Walter began to travel with Phoebe in the summers, leading to their close association during the religiously charged years of 1857-58 and permanent "partnership" from 1859 on.

Closing out the 1857 "Canadian tour," the Palmers arrived at Hamilton, Ontario in early October on their way to Albany and home. Planning to stay only overnight, they attended a regular Thursday evening prayer meeting of the three Methodist churches in Hamilton, where they were persuaded to speak. Only about seventy people were present. Phoebe urged them to be diligent in their efforts to win the unconverted (her series "A Laity for the Times" had appeared in the Christian Advocate less than a year before, urging the same on all Christians). As a device to translate their concern into specific action (compare the "believing meetings" and the "altar testimony"), she proposed a meeting be held the next evening to which those in attendance would bring neighbors and friends. A number committed themselves to invite as many as possible and to bring at least one. The crowd appearing the next night overran the appointed room so that larger facilities had to be found. As usual, dozens responded to the invitation to pray for pardon from sin or "present holiness." These in turn were challenged to seek the conversion or sanctification of others, special meetings for that purpose being appointed for afternoon <u>and</u> evening the next day.

The result was that the Palmers remained at Hamilton for nearly three weeks of such meetings and spent another twelve days at London before actually heading home. During these weeks hundreds presented themselves for conversion or entire devotion to God and a tremendous wave of lay activity drenched the region.[132] Phoebe wrote home of "bands of newly baptised disciples" composed of men, women, and children, going everywhere "preaching the Word," and of some organizing themselves as "bands of soul-savers" with a written constitution committing them to "use every possible means, in their individual and collective capacity, to pluck sinners as brands from the burning."[133] Back in New York, she estimated that not less than two thousand persons had been converted during the October meetings with hundreds more receiving the "baptism of the Holy Ghost," adding "I would speak with carefulness before God....I believe this to be a low computation."[134]

The revival excitement outlasted the Palmers, continuing on for some time after their departure. One of the three Hamilton Methodist churches originally involved had to almost immediately enlarge its facilities to accommodate increased attendance and a fourth Methodist church was built during 1858 to handle the larger membership which the revival helped to spawn. Membership increased between 1857 and 1858 by nearly 55% and church attendance by over one thousand in the Hamilton churches.[135] Also notices of revival were carried in the New York <u>Christian Advocate</u> in November, perhaps contributing to the spread of similar lay-centered religious fervor there and in other areas of the United States during the winter of 1857-1858.[136]

The Palmers returned to unusual religious concern at home. What would come to be called the "Prayer Meeting Revival" or "Laymen's Revival" was just coming to life. Weekly noontime prayer meetings had commenced in early October in a local church, just about the time the revival in Hamilton was catching fire, and had become daily by the time the Palmers returned to New York. By midwinter these had spread throughout the city, sponsored by churches of various denominations and interdenominational agencies like the Y.M.C.A.[137] Some met in theaters and music halls. Other cities experienced similar interest with prayer meetings being organized in places like Park Street and Old South Church, Boston, the Metropolitan Theater in Chicago, and the American Mechanics Auditorium in Philadelphia.[138]

A number of factors seem to have coalesced to create the religious concern expressed by the meetings. On the narrowly religious level there had been efforts throughout 1856 in New York to visit homes and organize Sunday Schools in "destitute areas," as well as other areas of the city, involving some two thousand lay volunteers from various churches. The first noon prayer meetings, in fact, were for these volunteers. Other cities had copied the New York plan.[139] Also, New School Presbyterians were holding "revival conventions" in various cities in the fall of 1857 urging fasting and prayer for "national revival" and preaching to that end. Important city-wide "protracted meetings" in places like Boston, Rochester, Philadelphia and Cincinnati featuring revivalists Finney, the Methodist James Caughey, and the Baptist Jacob Knapp occurred in 1856 and 1857.[140] Also there was the work of the Palmers and their newly emergent emphasis on lay responsibility for evangelism as reflected in Phoebe's "A Laity for the Times" articles, her preaching in Canada during 1857, and her soon to be published book, The Promise of the Father.

In addition other factors were at work creating a socio-political climate ripe for revival phenomena. There was the financial collapse and panic of September 1857 and the following winter which threw many persons, especially in northeastern urban areas, out of work, a factor even Phoebe Palmer recognized.[141] Employers and financiers perhaps feeling guilty about contributing to the collapse through deception or speculation and out of work employees seeking consolation turned to evangelical religion.[142] There was also heightened tension in American society generally, and the churches especially, over slavery, the violence in "Bleeding Kansas" escalating in 1856-1857, the Dred Scott decision being handed down in 1857, and two churches, the New School Presbyterians and the Methodist Episcopal Church (North) quarreling throughout 1856-1857 over the issue along with interdenominational agencies like the American Bible Society and the American Home Missionary Society. Here revival was seen as a means of smoothing the differences and healing the breaches. Even President James Buchanan supported the revival, attending meetings near his home at Bedford Springs, Pennsylvania.[143] Closely related to this in promoting revival would be the optimistic millennialism and reformism of the 1820s, '30s and '40s which sought the perfection of American society and the ushering in of the reign of Christ on earth. This was a movement that, while jolted by the sectional conflicts of the '40s and '50s, was not yet dead. One also cannot discount Protestant concern over Catholic growth by way of increased Irish and German immigration in mid-century, or more general anxiety over the "great evils" of the burgeoning urban centers. These may also have contributed to enthusiasm for the evangelical religion of the revival as a means of coping with an altered social reality.[144]

Whatever the precise mix of factors, religion seemed to take precedence over all other concerns for a time. The noon prayer meetings were packed. Churches held protracted meetings which resulted in scores of converts. Various denominations joined together for city-wide "Union Meetings." In all of this the Palmers shared as highly visible promoters, running here and there in response to the invitations which poured in upon them. Now among the best known revivalists in the country, their presence was thought to practically guarantee large numbers of converts and a revitalized religious life for the group that would have them.

The expectation seems usually to have been fulfilled. At Owego, New York, the Palmers held four and five meetings a day in churches of different denominations. Naming Baptists, Presbyterians, Congregationalists, and Episcopalians along with Methodists, Phoebe claimed they all were sharing "in the copious showers which have fallen on this portion of our Lord's heritage." She also suggested this might herald the dawn of the millennium.[145] "Religion seems to be the order of the day here," she reported.[146] At St. John, Nova Scotia meetings ran on for twenty-three days with six hundred converts, including some Roman Catholic converts to Protestantism.[147] At Charlottetown, Prince Edward Island, it was eight hundred names recorded, about four hundred being seekers of entire sanctification.[148] Everywhere the story was the same. God's Spirit was sweeping across North America in unprecedented measure--

so it seemed for those who were at the center of the revivalistic fervor.

C. The "British Isles Interlude," 1859-1863

But the excitement was not confined to the western shore of the Atlantic Ocean. Britain also was rustling to the "winds of the Spirit." As the American revival began to cool in 1859, it cast a few live embers eastward which fanned into flame throughout the British Isles, bringing revival to much of Ireland, Scotland, Wales, and England. As in the United States these were generally lay-centered affairs, resulted in thousands claiming conversion, buoyed the churches, and were widely reported in the secular press.[149]

As in America, the British revivals were not quite as spontaneous as they appeared to contemporaries. British churches, like American, had been directing attention to the need for religious quickening ever since the publication in 1853 of the report on the religious census which underscored the churches' weakness in the chief industrial cities and among the working classes generally. The various Methodist bodies especially had been holding "special religious services" (essentially protracted meetings), but so too had Congregationalists and Baptists, favoring meetings in theaters and halls designed to attract working people, minus most of the trappings of usual "revival services."[151]

The economic factor was at work in Britain too as it was in the U.S. The winter of 1857-58 was a bleak period of lagging trade, falling wages and unemployment. Large increases in poor relief were reported.

Into this situation came news of the North American events. The religious and secular press reprinted

"revival intelligence" from such sources as the New York
Tribune which were giving heavy coverage to revival
related happenings. Some American "eyewitnesses" visited
Britain to tell the story. This publicity reached flood-
tide in 1859, the year the greatest excitement appeared
in Britain. In many places quite blatant copies of
American techniques were instituted, including noon
prayer meetings with large lay participation, "union"
protracted meetings, and even American-style camp meetings. In Wales, Humphrey Rowland Jones, a Welshman who
had preached in the U.S. for four years, returned to
Wales solely to "promote a similar movement to what was
going on in America."[152] The "Welsh Revival" ensued.

In all of this there were many stimuli, as in North
America, but a major one seems to be simply the presence
of the "sympathetic community" linking North American
and British Protestants which had been built up through
the nineteenth century primarily by a succession of
American revivalists itinerating throughout the British
Isles. Asahel Nettleton, Edward Norris Kirk, James
Caughey, Charles Finney, and others traversed Britain in
the years prior to the American Civil War.[153] Meeting
with various degrees of success, all had helped to stamp
an American revivalistic impress on British Christianity. With the outbreak of revival enthusiasm in North
America in 1857-58 and the inevitable British interest
in it, the "transatlantic pipeline" began to flow once
again. In July of 1857 Caughey arrived at Liverpool and
embarked on a two year tour. He would be back again in
1860. Finney followed in December of 1858. In 1859
Britain welcomed the young Edward Payson Hammond and
Phoebe and Walter Palmer.

Phoebe Palmer was at the apogee of her North American Career by 1859, and in the context of the times it

was a logical and almost inevitable step for her to undertake a "victory tour," as it were, of the British Isles. She had turned in impressive results consistently in the "British Provinces" of Canada and had only the "old world" left to conquer. Besides, revival fire in North America was beginning to cool while in Britain it was just finding fuel, presenting the promise of receptive audiences for a while longer at least. Audiences in Britain were indeed receptive, and what began as a visit of undetermined length in June of 1859 turned into a nearly four-and-one-half-year, almost continual revival campaign which constitutes a major chapter in Palmer's life and career.

The Palmers had given thought to a British trip as early as 1845, though considering Phoebe's still hardly "veteran" status as a revivalist at that point, it appears the trip would have been more vacation and "fact-finding trip" among British Wesleyans than revival campaign. They had planned to travel with American Methodist bishop Leonidas Hamline and his wife.[154] The trip did not materialize. In 1856--by then Phoebe's books were readily available in England and her work in Canada was well-known--a trip was considered again, this time it would seem at the behest of British clergy and laypersons who saw her as a potent catalyst of religious awakening. Again the trip had to be deferred.[155] Finally, in the summer of 1859 further hindrances were removed and the tour was begun. It appeared to the Palmers that "there was such a concurrence of circumstances as to make it evident that the finger of the Lord" pointed toward England.[156]

The Palmers left New York on June 4 and arrived in Liverpool June 15. Their crossing was memorable in that it threw the Palmers in with a group of people with whom

they did not seem to be familiar or altogether comfortable. The first chapter of <u>Four Years in The Old World</u>
is preoccupied with descriptions of various ministers
on board who, clearly not of the pious Methodist or
revivalistic stamp which Phoebe considered essential,
whiled away their time "playing at various games" (e.g.
chess, dice, etc.). Their "jocose laughs" and general
lack of ministerial dignity she found offensive and
troubling. That one of these was a "well-known professor" in Union Theological Seminary, New York, Palmer
considered "frightening."[157] Still she found consolation
in striking up acquaintances with her "own kind" including a music teacher who had found the "blessing of
holiness" through reading her <u>The Way of Holiness</u>,
thinking about the Tuesday Meeting at home, and organizing early morning prayer gatherings. She thought she
might have made a spectacle of herself in the latter
instance, but considered the effort a fitting rebuke to
the wine drinking and "merry carousal" which characterized the ships facilities during most of the day.[158]
Interestingly, the Palmers also, upon seeing obviously
pious persons from "steerage" present at Sunday service,
decided to "go among the steerage passengers and make
friends," which they did. Here they found kindred souls
among whom they held religious services several times
during the crossing. Phoebe thought these, though "men
of low estate" by "worldly" standards, to be "of
Heaven's nobility."[159]

Second class was not to be their lot in England,
however, for their first days were spent on the estates
of wealthy admirers, and they would benefit continuously
throughout their time there from the generosity of
affluent benefactors.[160] Arriving at Liverpool on June
15, they were met by a Wesleyan minister from the area

who had seen a notice of their voyage in The Guide to Holiness and who shepherded them through to passage to London, seeing that they boarded the first night with a lady who had "been blessed" through reading Phoebe's Entire Devotion to God. Phoebe's first impressions of England are telling, for they evidence the attitude that would color her evaluation of much of what she encountered there. The people are kind and courteous, but "Every thing appears so ancient and sombre, as though grown hoary with age." It "looks like the Old World!"[161]

In London the Palmers visited the usual tourist spots and some places of special interest to Methodists, e.g. John Wesley's City Road Chapel and his grave. They also attended a number of religious services, including one gathering fashioned after the Tuesday Meeting. At St. Paul's Cathedral Phoebe had her first look at Anglicanism and she was unimpressed. She thought the service to have "little spirituality" and to be suspiciously "papal." She also thought Anglican clergymen who were "experimentally pious" to be "surely the exception rather than the rule." This was an opinion of the English Church she would voice on many occasions throughout her stay in the "old world."[162]

The Palmers did not hold formal services until they had been in England nearly a month. When they did, the results were not immediately heartening. The receptive audience they had expected did not materialize right away. Preaching first near Manchester, Phoebe comes as close to being discouraged as she ever does prior to the sometimes difficult post Civil War years back in the U.S. There are few seekers who answer the invitations to repent or seek holiness. "Now it is certain we have seen greater things than these under our labors in America," she writes with palpable understatement, but lest she seem petulant quickly adds, "but the Lord has been teaching me such lessons in regard to the infinite worth of one single soul, that I would not dare think or speak as though it were a light thing, though...but one solitary soul had been snatched from the grasp of the adversary."[163] The tune would change soon enough. Before long, overwhelmed with success upon success, Phoebe would be judging each campaign greater than "anything we remember to have witnessed either in America or Europe."[164]

In early September they proceeded to Newcastle-on-Tyne, a shipbuilding and coal center in the northeast of England, and here it was that their efforts finally began to bear the sort of fruit to which they had grown accustomed in the U.S. and Canada. Their host was Rev. Robert Young, pastor of Brunswick Chapel, district chairman (i.e. "presiding elder" or "district superintendent" in American methodist parlance), a lifelong revival promoter and friend by correspondence of the Palmers.[165] Young no doubt prepared the ground thoroughly, and his effort together with the news from North America must have created an atmosphere of expectancy which was more promising than anything the Palmers had yet encountered in the British Isles.[166] Their success was immediate. Within only a few days of arriving Phoebe's early misgivings about Britain were gone and she was certain she had never witnessed "a more glorious work" than that unfolding at Newcastle.[167] It was, reverting to language she had used of the 1857-58 North American excitement, a "pentecost of modern days."[168]

The numbers are impressive. The Palmers stayed for thirty-five days, holding various sorts of services four times a day. The crowds in Brunswick Chapel, the largest non-Anglican place of worship in northern England, sometimes numbered two thousand. The total number of those professing conversion or entire sanctification, carefully recorded by "secretaries," was set at thirteen hundred for the campaign. Reporters for various religious papers visited the services, filing their dispatches in London or other places, comparing what they saw to the "times of Whitefield and Wesley." One of these issued a pamphlet entitled "A Night At Brunswick Chapel" which passed through several editions. At the close of the protracted meeting, the leaders of the chapel presented an official resolution to the Palmers, commending them for their work and inviting them to return.[169]

Thus buoyed, the Palmers moved on to Sunderland, a shipping port and rail center near to Newcastle and part of the same Wesleyan district. News of Newcastle of course preceded them, and some from Sunderland had probably even been present at Brunswick Chapel. Anticipation was high and once again impressive results were seen, Phoebe early on concluding that "The work here bids fair to exceed anything we remember to have witnessed either in America or Europe."[170] She was right, at least so far as statistics were concerned. In twenty-nine days of meetings (the Palmers had intended to stay only two weeks) 2,011 names were recorded, with as many as three thousand present in some of the services. Phoebe was especially impressed with numerous coal miners and sea captains whom she exhorted and counseled.[171]

Here the Palmers encountered a problem they would meet with again in Britain, an architectural style in the churches which made it difficult to invite penitents and seekers to the "altar," "mourner's bench," or "communion rail." In contrast to U.S. churches or camp meeting facilities, most British church buildings had only a "communion rail," and this was often too small of

an area to accommodate the numbers who responded to
Phoebe's "sermons." At Sunderland, Walter quickly in-
novated, announcing, "In view of the fact that we cannot
invite you forward for want of room, we desire to know
where you are in order that we may make our supplica-
tions on your behalf. The Saviour of sinners is willing
to save you, wherever you may be; and let all who desire
to seek the Lord raise the right hand." The several
hundred responding were then requested to keep their
hands raised "until heaven's recording angel" could
write their names in "the book of God's remembrance."[172]

As useful as this technique appeared to be--and it
was used from time to time thereafter--it did not accord
well with Phoebe's "theology of responsibility" which
called for action of a bolder sort than simply raising
one's hand for prayer if one would be "saved" or "made
holy." For her a trip to the "altar" was an essential
first step, at least in the context of a protracted
meeting or camp meeting. Given this, she held out for a
different sort of solution to the problem of church
architecture. This led to one of the really interesting
incidents on the British tour. In Glasgow, Scotland in
early 1860 the Palmers found themselves in a church
especially short of "altar" space even by British standards. In the first service Walter resorted to raising
hands, but Phoebe was troubled and "earnestly sought
unto the Captain of the hosts of Israel" for a better
solution. That solution, when it came, was to physically
modify the front of the church so it would better accord
with revivalistic custom. In approaching the leadership
with the request, Phoebe typically left them no ground
upon which to stand. Would Lord Nelson, Wellington, or
Napoleon "have hesitated, if the success of a battle
might depend on any sort of change of fixture imagin-

able...irrespective of cost, risk, or trouble?", she asked. "Did not portions of your own army, in the Crimean War, sit up all night to cast up bulwarks, dig trenches, etc., all to secure an earthly victory?" Would God's army do any less to win spiritual victory? Not this time anyway, for "Most nobly did the brethren conclude at once to risk the matter." By 4:00 a.m. the next morning there were carpenters at work in the church, and before long a "neatly carpeted platform enclosed by a railing" was in place. The result, of course, was that hundreds of seekers were able to take the required path to salvation.[173]

Scotland also provided Phoebe another opportunity to voice reservations about established churches and the religious life of the people. As an American revivalist, Palmer saw the Scottish church as moribund, and as a Wesleyan, she saw it as hopelessly fettered by rigid Calvinism. Many Scottish church members were "strangers to the doctrine of conversion," she believed, and dozed "under the opiate of a [false] religious profession."[174] She even had harsh words for Scottish Wesleyans, whom she thought lacking in "aggressiveness" and in need of someone like "our American bishop, Asbury" to lead them.[175]

By the end of the first year in Britain, the Palmers' fame was considerable. A couple of incidents illustrate the "celebrity" status they had attained. The one occurred in Leamington, near Warwick, in late 1860. There photographs of the Palmers made in Edinburgh were sold by the local Wesleyan society to cover the expenses of the special meetings. Phoebe did not object, though she found it humorous.[176] The other occurred sometime later at Epworth, John Wesley's birthplace. An item from the Wesleyan Times says it all: "Dr. and Mrs. Palmer spent the last week in the small town of Epworth.... The friends at Epworth had two objects in view, in inviting Dr. and Mrs. Palmer; viz., to raise funds to defray the expenses of a larger organ, and the salvation of sinners. Both are in great measure accomplished. To God be all the praise!"[177]

Being "celebrities" and much in demand did not insulate the Palmers from their share of opposition and controversy while in Britain, however. As in the U.S. some troubled surfaced, but the issues were somewhat different. Whereas in the U.S. it was Phoebe's doctrinal views which came in for the most criticism, in Britain it was her right to preach, the Palmers' "American-style" revivalism, and their advocacy of teetotalism.

The first issue surfaced only briefly and early on in the tour. During the highly successful and highly publicized revivals in the north in 1859 there were Wesleyans who refused to support the work because they held that Phoebe's "preaching" was "diametrically opposed to an inspired apostle's precept," making reference to St. Paul's charge that "women keep silence in the churches" (1 Corinthians 14:34-35). Robert Young, the Wesleyan district chairman, came to Phoebe's defense in print, as did Catherine Booth, the co-founder of the Salvation Army, who was present at some of the Palmers' early revivals and was much influenced by Phoebe Palmer's example to take up a preaching career of her own.[178] Of course, Phoebe was well equipped to defend herself, having published Promise of the Father before departing for England. Her critics were simply reflecting a long-standing Wesleyan wariness of "female exhorters" that went back to an 1803 resolution of the Wesleyan Conference which restricted women from addressing sexually mixed assemblies. This was apparently widely ignored, however, good evidence for this being the steady stream of calls which came Phoebe's way throughout the four years in Britain.[179] It was still an issue that could call up some feeling, but it seems not to have dogged Palmer much beyond the campaigns in the northeast.

The second issue too was rather fleeting, though it did more damage in the long run than the first. It centered on the Palmers' style of revivalism. No practices in particular came in for criticism. The concern was rather for the free-wheeling, independent nature of their campaigning generally. The same issue had arisen periodically within British Methodism throughout the nineteenth century, even resulting in organizational fractures in the Methodist movement, so the Palmers were not the first to provoke it. From the colorful Lorenzo Dow at the turn of the century on, British Wesleyans had wrestled with the whole matter of the "irregularity" of itinerant revivalists.[180] A tour by the American James Caughey between 1841 and 1847 had brought the matter to a head. The Wesleyan Conference in 1846 had adopted one resolution asking American Methodist bishops to "recall" Caughey because of his lack of ecclesiastical supervision, responsibility, or control, and another forbidding Caughey's employment in Wesleyan pulpits.[181] The Caughey incident was not all that far in the past when the Palmers appeared on the scene in 1859, and Caughey had just recently been back in England, ending a two-year tour just as the Palmers were beginning theirs.

The Palmers were no doubt aware of the problem; the concern is evident in Phoebe's remark from Sunderland that "Here, as elsewhere we have labored, we have enjoyed much satisfaction in our efforts in connection with the beloved ministry.... Our design has never been to work aside from the ministry and membership of any church, but only under God, as <u>laborers</u> <u>together</u> <u>with</u> <u>them</u>." On another occasion she emphasizd, "Our invitations are <u>official</u>, as we do not accept any other."[182] All indications are that the Palmers were indeed scrupulous at this point. However, their lay status and American origins were sufficient to call up old fears and as early as the summer of 1860 some in Wesleyan Conference leadership were making more or less official pronouncements condemning "extra revival efforts."[183] The Wesleyan Conference of 1862 went further, resolving that superintendents should not allow persons "not amenable to our regular discipline" into their chapels. In the debate the Caughey case and the problem with Dow early in the century were both specifically mentioned, suggesting definite "troublesome American" overtones were present in the decision, though the Palmers themselves were not mentioned by name.[184]

Whatever the case, the Palmers were surely apprised of the decision, though curiously make no mention of it to the folks at home. What is mentioned is a serious illness which Phoebe contracted very shortly after the Conference action in July of 1862. It was serious enough that it took the Palmers out of revival work altogether for several months and led Phoebe to record, "Several days I was flickering between the two worlds...day after...day.... I knew not which wave would bear me to the eternal shore."[185] Whether the concurrence of the illness and the Conference restriction on "irregular" evangelists was anything more than coincidence is of course impossible to say, but it was December before the Palmers were fully active again, and from then until their return trip to the United States in October of 1863 they labored largely in chapels of the United

Methodist Free Churches and the Methodist New Connexion, both more democratic and lay oriented segments of the British Methodist movement than the Wesleyan Connexion which had spurned them, and more accepting of American-style revivalism.[186]

The third challenge to the Palmers was, on balance, the most difficult of all. It seems to have discouraged them to the point that their enthusiasm for the work in England waned considerably in the days following. It is surprising that they didn't run into the problem sooner than they did and that they weren't prepared for it when it came, considering that their friend Caughey had run up against the same difficulty in England in Wesleyan circles in the 1840s. The "difficulty" was the Americans' advocacy of teetotalism. In America, by the 1830s Methodism had become quite strongly "teetotal," while in England no similar development had occurred. The result was two quite different understandings of the nature of the Christian use of alcohol.[187] Caughey had broached the issue immediately in his preaching in 1841, calling for total abstinence by devout Methodists, but had been rebuffed by official action of the 1841 Conference which ordered Wesleyan chapels closed to teetotal meetings. He had still managed to find sympathetic English Wesleyans, but the opposition was quite vocal.[188] Given this, one would think that the Palmers would have been sensitive to the issue, and yet on the other hand it is consistent with Phoebe's insensitivity to other aspects of British religious life that they were not. It is also consistent with her uncompromising stand against sin of any sort in the life of the Christian believer that she should have been outspoken over what she conceived to be an especially vile "sin." At any rate, the Palmers preached teetotalism from the outset of their British ministry,

but, while raising the "repelling countenance" of some
"in high places," did not for a while face any widespread
opposition.[189]

   The crisis came after more than a year of successful revival campaigning. In Poole, in southern England,
the Palmers received a note from an anonymous church
member informing them that the "most noted maltster in
town" happened to be circuit steward and Sabbath-school
superintendent of the Wesleyan chapel. Shocked, the
Palmers investigated and found the story to be true. Not
wanting to be "reprovers general," as Phoebe put it, and
take on the problem alone, and yet believing such a
situation to be a hindrance to the possibility of any
religious renewal taking place, the Palmers asked to be
relieved of their obligation at the end of one week. "We
felt deeply," Phoebe wrote. "To our minds it seemed a
sin far more insulting to the god of heaven than that
which prevented him from leading forth his hosts to
victory in the days of Achan."[190] The superintendent
"with tears" begged them not to go. Phoebe struggled
with the matter for several days, becoming "really ill"
in the process, imagining that this might be "the death-
knell of our revival services in England."[191] She finally concluded that they could not continue "unless the
accursed thing was removed," and the Palmers ceased
their work though they did not immediately leave Poole.
The brewer was "waited upon"--by whom it is not clear--
and apparently given an ultimatum. According to Phoebe,
"prizing the gains of sin more than his membership or
his love for souls," he withdrew from the church.[192] The
way now open for revival, the Palmers resumed their work
and on that very evening "twenty souls were born into
the kingdom, besides several who received the sanctifying seal."[193]

The incident provided Phoebe the opportunity to
expound once again upon the state of the English
churches as she saw it. She was grieved to see an "almost universal bowing down to the great god Bacchus" in
an otherwise "enlightened" country. Lest she be misunderstood, she wrote, "were the habit of partaking of
intoxicating beverages confined to the acknowledged servants of sin, or the lower order of the people," things
would not be so bad, "but the habit prevails equally
among church members and ministers as with avowed world-
lings."[194] From her perspective a greater indictment
could hardly be made.

The abstinence issue did not go away, though
Phoebe's worst fears were not realized. Still, one cannot discount the effect of it in noting the somewhat
diminished results the Palmers achieved through the rest
of their tour. And the issue did reappear from time to
time, with sometimes devastating effect. For example, in
Banbury in late 1860 the Palmers again encountered a
point of view different from theirs. As at Poole an
important Wesleyan lay leader was involved in brewing
and selling alcohol, and Phoebe also struggled with
seekers who did not see "strong drink" as a "sin" needing to be renounced in order to pursue the "way of
holiness." She again became depressed, "so ill that it
seemed dubious" whether she should "be able to engage
any more, in this place in the blessed toil of bringing
souls to Jesus."[195] She did continue but the response of
the people dried up with few seekers answering "altar
invitations." Phoebe let go with one last blow aimed
directly at those who would not embrace teetotalism,
preaching specifically on the topic, and thus the revival ended with minimal results and bruised feelings all
around.[196] Significantly, not long after at Maidenhead,

the Palmers for the first time saw most of the congregation leave when they issued invitations for persons to
stay after their first meeting to commit themselves to
revival. At the close of the campaign Phoebe noted that
it had "not been a work of such overwhelming interest as
at some other places...."[197] Sometime later the problem
reared again at Windsor when it was discovered the
chapel basement was being rented out for liquor storage.
This time, however, the offending brew was removed
and the protracted meeting continued with "great
victory."[198]

D. The Final Years, 1863-1874

While the Palmers were in England dealing with
success and opposition, they were also being entreated
by their friends and supporters back in the U.S. to
return and give leadership to the battle for holiness
there. Much of the time they were away the Civil War was
unfolding and there was a strong sense among religious
people that the promise of the great revival days of
1857-58 had been squandered. Religion had not saved the
Union. The nation was now at war and all were preoccupied with the war effort. Religion was no longer the
"order of the day." This was reflected in decreased news
of and interest in revivals as well as declining church
membership statistics.

Phoebe was made aware of this religious malaise by
her American correspondents who from time to time sent
along materials to support their case that the Palmers
were needed at home. One of these was a copy of the
western Christian Advocate, one of several American
Methodist papers by that name, which carried an editorial decrying the sickly state of American religion. It
troubled Phoebe greatly. Writing home, she mentioned the

article and the state of things in "poor dear America,"
noting that, "For hours after I perused it, the subject
stood up absorbingly before me, and exerted such a
controlling influence, that though I had retired to
sleep, I could [not sleep]." She went on to lament the
loss of fervent religious concern in wartime "when death
is so rapidly gathering his victims, for eternity," and
added, "I do not wonder that you express yourselves as
you do in regard to our coming home." Still, she was not
certain that their work in Britain was done; "we dare
not come, until we are sure it is by the command of the
Lord of the vineyard."[199] The letter home was dated
January 7, 1863. In exactly nine months the Palmers were
on their way back across the Atlantic to the United
States.

Back home, the Palmers' friends who wanted their
return so badly wasted no time enlisting them back in
the cause, almost literally meeting them at their door-
step and prevailing upon them to begin a protracted
meeting at the Allen Street Methodist Church in New York
City. Having both suffered some poor health in the later
stages of their trip, Walter and Phoebe were intending
to rest, but their resolve gave way in the face of
intense pleading. Even after Allen Street, they held
other meetings right on through the end of the year.[200]

Another project awaiting them upon their arrival
was the proposition that they purchase the venerable
Guide to Christian Perfection and resuscitate it as the
chief literary organ of perfectionist teaching. Having
fallen on hard times, it needed a financial shot in the
arm and some fresh editorial enthusiasm. Walter supplied
the former and Phoebe the latter, as The Guide was
purchased before the year was out, and soon had increased its circulation nearly sixfold.[201]

From late 1863 until the summer of 1874, Phoebe set about busily reclaiming--or perhaps better, enhancing--her title as one of the premier revivalists of the day and the best known advocate of Christian holiness. She faltered a bit in 1864, becoming seriously ill under the combined weight of the never-recovered-from British tour, the resurgent demands for her preaching in the U.S. and the newly assumed responsibility for The Guide to Holiness, as it was now called. After resting through much of 1865 during which time she prepared Four Years in the Old World for publication, Phoebe was back to something like full strength by 1866.

Response to Phoebe and her message in these years was still good, and in some places quite remarkable, but as noted in the previous chapter, there is a noticeable tendency for her to evaluate the climate in the places visited negatively.[202] With the proliferation of rail lines, stimulated in part by the Civil War, Phoebe's U.S. travels were taking her farther from home than ever, but bringing her less of a sense of satisfaction and "victory" than before the "British interlude."

There seem to be three major reasons for the change. For one, the Free Methodist schism had occurred in 1860 while the Palmers were in England. In this major event in the history of American Methodism, a substantial body of preachers and lay people had seceded from the Methodist Episcopal Church and had formed a new body which they called the Free Methodist Church. The factors involved in the split are complex, but among them was a concern that Methodism was slighting its historic witness to Christian Perfection or "holiness."[203] This was a theme Phoebe Palmer had voiced in her labors between 1840 and 1859 and was a strong motivating element in her crusade to secure "entire

devotion to God." In fact, the principal founder of
Free Methodism, Benjamin Titus Roberts, had professed
the "deeper blessing" of holiness under Palmer's ministry at a camp meeting in 1850.[204] Though there was never
any formal connection between them, the paths of Roberts
and Palmer were parallel to the extent that they both
promoted holiness with uncommon zeal. And it was not
difficult for those within Methodism who saw any "holiness crusade" as potentially divisive to conclude that
their fears were confirmed by the rise of the Free
Methodist movement. To these it seemed that preaching
holiness as a "specialty" would surely lead to schism.

Leaving the U.S. while the Free Methodist controversy was in progress but not yet resolved, Palmer
returned to a situation where American Methodism had
just experienced its third fracture in sixteen years.[205]
It was traumatized, and because of the most recent
experience (Free Methodism and its "Palmerian" stress on
holiness) understandably wary of outspoken holiness
advocacy. In this context Palmer's work could not help
but be hindered. Her services were sought with less
enthusiasm than before the British tour. The correctness
of this interpretation tends to be borne out by some of
Palmer's most unreservedly negative assessments in the
1860s and after. She scorches the Central Illinois Methodist Conference in saying, "We have never to my recollection, labored in a region of the country, where
[holiness] has been so lightly regarded."[206] Ninety-nine
out of a hundred ministers, she judges, are "resolved to
keep down everything in the Conference favoring holiness
as a specialty...."[207] The reason is not hard to find;
Illinois, along with the Genesee Conference of New York,
was a hotbed of Free Methodism. It had been worked by
one John Wesley Redfield, a free-lance revivalist, who

had brought a generally contentious band of Methodists which grew up around him together with B. T. Roberts' forces in the east.[208] Palmer herself was aware of the source of the problem, noting that "the Free Methodists had done much harm [in Illinois] by factious and schismatic proceedings, and had brought the profession of entire sanctification into wide disrepute."[209]

Much the same went for other areas as well. In upstate New York Phoebe found very rough going in these latter years. Buffalo and Utica were especially recalcitrant--and major centers of Free Methodism. In Buffalo "the bones have been exceeding dry" and in Utica "Methodism seemed dying out," the Presiding Elder taking pains to "crush out all definite testimony on the subject of holiness," Phoebe reported.[210] The reason for the opposition? The Presiding Elder regards special holiness promotion as "synonymous with free Methodism."[211] This was an incubus Palmer had not had to face before and its presence made the years after 1863 an increasingly difficult struggle at times. Phoebe still had her following, and her editorship of The Guide to Holiness in these years gave her a wider exposure than ever before, but she was also finding more polarization over holiness teaching than she ever had before.

There was a second reason for declining enthusiasm for Palmer's brand of holiness revivalism in these years and it is related to the first. While very few Methodists were prepared to go so far as Roberts and his cohorts to fight for holiness, there was a growing sense in the post-Civil War years that there needed to be some more effective means for promoting perfectionist doctrine and experience than those that had been used. This sentiment found expression in the organization of "holiness camp meetings" and the formation of a National

Campmeeting Association for the Promotion of Holiness
(NCAPH) in 1867.[212] Palmer had no direct involvement in
this, though as noted earlier she had called for greater
emphasis on holiness at Methodist camp meetings. Also,
as in the case of B. T. Roberts, one of the founders of
the NCAPH and its first president, John S. Inskip, just
happened to have professed entire sanctification in
connection with her ministry.[213] And it was widely believed by those promoting holiness through the camp
meetings and the other agencies the NCAPH would later
spawn, that though Phoebe never officially became a
member of the association (she and Walter did work in
some "national holiness campmeetings" during the final
years of her career, and The Guide regularly carried
NCAPH news), they were her true spiritual sons and
daughters. Said one who was an officer in the Association at her death, "The present National Campmeeting
movement for the promotion of holiness owes its inception largely to the inspiration and labors of our sister
[Palmer]."[214] Said another referring to "camp meetings,
protracted meetings, and conventions for the promotion
of holiness," then flourishing, "we regard her as the
mother of all this movement."[215]

This understanding was not lost on those who opposed the holiness camp meetings because they saw in
them potential for the same sort of polarization and
divisiveness that had appeared in the Free Methodist
schism just short years before. The two were parallel
movements in their passionate promotion of Christian
Perfection, and the NCAPH shared with Free Methodism at
least an implicit critique of the Methodist Episcopal
Church as needing to be revived toward greater spirituality. And the common link in both was Phoebe Palmer
with her twenty plus years of holiness revivalism. By

the time of her death criticism of the NCAPH had become quite outspoken even in high places. Typical was an article which appeared in the prestigious Christian Advocate (New York) attacking a tract fund being promoted by the Association. It charged that,

under the profession of Holiness--a doctrine justly precious to our people--a few men whose ministerial influence and position have been acquired under our itinerant system... have first, organized themselves into an association to choose their own time and place of service, and, next, have set themselves to the task of establishing a publishing system institution not recognized in our economy, but claiming the support of our pastors and people.

It further characterized the NCAPH as "an irresponsible agency" the outcome of whose work would be "another and mischievous secession."[216]

In fact, such concerns of NCAPH critics would come to be realized as the organization grew in size and complexity, acquiring a life of its own. It eventually gave rise to "holiness" papers and a whole body of "holiness" literature, full-time "holiness" evangelists often having very tenuous ties with Methodist ministerial discipline (or that of any other church body), and regional and local holiness associations or "holiness bands," in addition to a network of holiness camp meetings. The ultimate result would be official censure of extra-church holiness activities, discipline of holiness evangelists, and schism as many of the most zealous holiness advocates responded by organizing their own churches. All of this brewing storm hung over Phoebe Palmer in the waning years of her career as a revivalist

The third factor in Palmer's more negative assessment of the last years is theological. Simply put, Methodism in these years was moving down a quite different theological path than that taken by Palmer and her associates. The "old paths" were being abandoned. Again, this is a large issue, but its essence is that Methodism, and the American churches generally, were undergoing a massive revolution in thought brought about by a host of forces, not the least among which were Darwinism and "Higher Criticism" of the bible. This revolution would cause questioning and reassessment of the whole theological enterprise and in many cases radical reinterpretation of traditional points of doctrine. In Methodism the traditional understanding of Christian perfection would be dissected again and again.[217] Though the full flowering of the revolution would not occur until after Palmer's time, its first shots were being sounded already in the post-1863 era, helping to make the last years of a truly illustrious revivalistic career bittersweet.

CHAPTER IV
A CLOSER LOOK: PHOEBE PALMER
AS RELIGIOUS THINKER

American religious history furnishes ample evidence
that the successful revivalist is not necessarily a
careful thinker. Raising the goal of bringing persons to
conversion or elevated states of piety above all other
considerations has usually resulted in revivalists de-
pending upon a "holy pragmatism" or "spiritual in-
stincts" rather than systematic thought. The experience-
centered pietism at the core of revivalism has also
encouraged this. D.L. Moody's often quoted retort to the
lady who expressed disagreement with his theology, "My
theology! I didn't know I had any," could well serve
scores of revival preachers who, busy "saving souls,"
put off thinking much about the faith they commended or
the methods they employed.[1]

Phoebe Palmer both fits and does not fit into this
pattern. On the one hand she knew she had a theology and
was very explicit about what it was and the steps by
which she had arrived at it. As concerned about saving
"souls" as any revivalist, she nevertheless also believed that ideas have consequences and that authentic
religious experience is indispensably tied to sound
theology. By word of mouth and in print she constantly
articulated those ideas which she had concluded were
"sound" and which she held to be central to Christian
spirituality. Her theology was no "afterthought," as
may be seen in the fact that Palmer commenced her output
of articles and books at almost the same time she was

embarking upon her public preaching career and was often
known to audiences first through these. Many times her
writings were what opened the way for her to visit a
place in person. Her revival technique as it developed
in the years after 1840 was guided by an already exis-
ting framework of thought, rather than the other way
around.[2]

On the other hand, even though Palmer was very
self-conscious about the theology which served as a
guide for her public preaching career, like all revivalists her main concern was individual religious experience. This means that hers is a very practical theology
which eschews strictly theoretical considerations in
favor of those things which have a direct "payoff" in
terms of bringing about the desired religious experience. One might even say that Palmer's thought constitutes in its essence a "theology of means" pertaining to
"holiness," so preoccupied is she with actually getting
persons to the place where they are made "holy" and live
lives of "perfect love." In this she is much like her
contemporary, Charles G. Finney, whose Lectures on Systematic Theology revolve around soteriology and moral
obligation, relegating a cursory look at "Divine Sovereignty" to the very end.[3] Also, it will be seen that
while Palmer's system of thought supported her preaching
career in a way perhaps singular among nineteenth-century revivalists, it did arise to a great extent out of
a kind of "holy pragmatism" which can be observed at
work in her own religious pilgrimage.

A.   Holiness The Burning Passion
While Palmer's system of religious thought was one
of her most important and original contributions to
nineteenth-century American religion, it has been too

often overlooked. Either her "activism" on many fronts
(e.g. evangelism, social amelioration, "foreign"
missions, expanded roles for women in the churches) has
been allowed to dominate her story, or else the assumption has been made that her thought is little more than
a faithful version of Wesleyan teaching transmitted to
her through American Methodism.[4] In fact, her activism
grows out of her theology, and her thought is a major
departure from the standard expositions of Wesleyan
Methodism, a fact recognized more fully by some of
Palmer's contemporaries than by some recent students of
her times.

The body of religious thought Palmer expounded for
better than thirty years was first, last and always
riveted to "holiness" as its central theme. By no means
was her thought a "systematic theology" in the sense of
a comprehensive ordering of Christian thinking about
God, the cosmos, the nature and end of humankind, etc.
Systematically arrived at, and systematically
communicated, to be sure, its focus was narrow rather
than comprehensive. It was a "theology of holiness"
which sought mainly to develop the implications of two
basic convictions: 1) "it is absolutely necessary that
you should be holy if you would see God"; 2) "holiness
is a blessing which it is now your privilege and also
your duty to enjoy."[5]

These convictions about holiness grew out of
Phoebe's own interior religious struggle and the manner
in which it had been resolved. As seen, hers was a
protracted struggle which went on for eleven years
before she was able to achieve a degree of certainty
that she had entered into a state of holiness by a
definite, datable (July 26, 1837) consecration of
herself to God and exercise of faith that her gift was

accepted and that she was henceforth freed from
intentional sinning and perfected in love toward God and
humanity. Her Methodist upbringing taught her that such
a state was the ultimate goal of Christian spirituality,
while her own experience and the guides she found most
helpful provided her with a model of "the way" to
achieve the goal. From that time which marked her entry
into a life of "holiness," Phoebe unflaggingly and ever
more aggressively urged all who would to join her. For
those willing to follow, she set forth in clear steps
the path they should take.

Her first systematic exposition of holiness found
its way into the Christian Advocate and Journal in the
fall of 1841. By then the recognized leader of New
York's Tuesday Meeting for the Promotion of Holiness and
a fledging revivalist with two brief "campaigns" away
from home to her credit, she decided in response to
urging from her growing coterie to address a broad
Methodist audience with the message she had been pressing in more limited circles. Signing her articles only
as "P" (even The Way of Holiness would appear in 1843
anonymously at first), she sounded notes that would
become familiar to thousands in the following decades.

As with all her writings, these articles are
strongly evangelistic as well as didactic. Not only is
she instructing her readers about the nature of holiness
as a conceptual and experiential reality, but she is
also the revivalist seeking to bring her audience to a
point of decision and action. Immediately taking the
discussion out of the realm of the merely theoretical,
she begins the very first installment by asking her
readers to consider, "What does God say to me on this
subject [of holiness]? What does he now require of me in
relation to it? And how should these requirements affect

my present conduct?"[6] The shape of the answer is suggested by the verse from the Bible to which she points,
"Follow peace with all men, and holiness, without which
no man shall see the Lord" (Hebrews 12:14), which leads
her to conclude that it is "absolutely necessary that
you should be holy if you would see God."[7] Lest one
agree with the conclusion but desire to consider the
matter at leisure, Phoebe is ready with the revivalist's
stock retort: "Scores will be in the eternal world
before the return of this day next week"; thus the
matter must be decided now.[8]

Her reference to the Bible signals that it rather
than "the traditions of men" is the "text-book" for the
seeker after holiness. The "experience or practice of
this or that professor [of holiness], however high in
experience or station" is not to be accepted as normative. Only the "Word of God" is an infallible guide.[9]

Having thus established the urgency and importance
of the topic and the source of her authority, Palmer
proceeds with definition. What she writes here would not
change substantially during the years of her public
career. "Gospel holiness" is

That state of the soul which is attained by
the believer when, through faith in the infinite merit of the Saviour body and soul, with
every redeemed faculty, are ceaselessly presented, a living sacrifice to God; the purpose
of the soul being steadily bent to know nothing among men, save Christ and him crucified,
and the eye of faith fixed on the Lamb of God,
that taketh away the sins of the world.

Holiness is an entire salvation from sin;
a redemption from all iniquity. The soul
through faith having laid upon that altar that

sanctifieth the gift experiences <u>continually</u>
the all-cleansing efficacy of the blood of
Jesus; and through this it knows the blessed-
ness of being presented faultless before the
throne and...gaining new accessions of wisdom,
power, and love, with every other grace,
daily.[10]

Though partial to the terms "holiness" and "sanctification" (especially the first as evidenced by her
writings) as those most often used in the Bible and thus
"most significantly expressive of the state intended,"
she allows that other terms such as "entire consecration," "perfect love," and "wholly the Lord's" are
synonymous.[11] Taking "sanctification," she traces its
essential meaning of "set apart" through the Bible,
stressing that the people of God are everywhere required
to "come out and be separate" (2 Corinthians 6:17).
"Holiness" is the state of the Christian believer who
has "come out" by consecrating or devoting all of his or
her "body and soul, with every power" to God and whose
inner being has been purified by the "renewing of the
Holy Ghost." Such a one is "sanctified."[12]

In an interesting aside to this main theme, Palmer
calls attention to the fact that some Methodist ministers neglect, misunderstand, or openly oppose this idea
of holiness even though it is the "established view" of
Methodism and a clear teaching of the Bible. Their
problem, she thinks, is that they have not experienced
this "second blessing" themselves. The irony of these
unsanctified Methodists is compounded by the fact that
some prominent clergymen from another denomination have
recently embraced the idea of holiness as a "distinct
blessing" after months of Bible study and soul searching
and are now active allies in the cause. Though she does

not mention names, she almost certainly had in mind the
"Presbygationalists" Asa Mahan and Charles Finney who by
1841 had made Oberlin College in Ohio a center of perfectionist teaching. During several crucial winter
months in 1836-37 the two had explored together the idea
of holiness or perfection, arriving at some very Meth-
odist-like conclusions. Both soon published books declaring their views and became aggressive promoters of
holiness teaching.[13] Mahan especially was a frequent
contributor to The Guide to Christian Perfection from
its founding in 1839 through the years Phoebe Palmer
edited it in the 1860s and early '70s as The Guide to
Holiness.

In the third installment in the Advocate the heart
of Palmer's burden, her unique "theology of means," is
spelled out with clarity. The appeal for holiness and
the definition of holiness were nothing new to mid-
nineteenth-century Methodists. In answering the question, "How may we enter into the enjoyment of holiness?", however, Palmer breaks new ground. In some
respects her views are not novel, as for example her
urging that the "intention be fully fixed to live a holy
life" and that one be open to "deep searchings of the
Spirit [of God]."[14] In several other respects, however,
she establishes principles which would distinctively
mark her teaching for the next thirty-three years,
bringing both acclaim and controversy.

One of these is the contention that one must be
"willing to be sanctified on the terms specified in the
word [i.e. Bible]," a rather obvious point, given her
regard for the Bible as her "text-book," and at the
surface level not out of keeping with traditional expositions of holiness. Yet in filling this with very
specific meaning, Palmer creates something new. Quoting

scripture, "Come out from among them, and be ye separate, saith the Lord, and touch not the unclean thing" (2 Corinthians 6:17; cf. Isaiah 52:11), she declares that the seeker cannot expect to be made holy unless certain things are renounced. This process of renunciation precedes the actual attainment of holiness. Only when it had been completed is one on what Palmer elsewhere calls "believing ground," ready to exercise faith that God accepts the "sacrifice" offered and bestows "perfect love."

Illustrating the point, all her examples have to do either with persons fearful of avowing sanctification openly or hesitant to give up "idolatrous" or "unrighteous" attachment to persons or things. That is, "coming out from among them" and being "separate" seems for Palmer to involve mainly the psychological process of identifying with a potentially (in some cases actually) unpopular ideology and the social group which espouses it. There is the minister, now a proponent of holiness, who sought it for nine years (cf. Phoebe's eleven-year struggle), experiencing "much anxiety and perplexity on the subject." His problem was preferring the honor of "the world" to the honor "that cometh from God only." Only when he resolved to give up "that honor that cometh from the world" and declared himself "willing to literally have my name cast out as evil" was he able to attain the "second blessing." Similar is the one (Palmer herself?) who feared publicly "professing the blessing" should she attain it, yet, faced with the requirement to "give up all," finally conceded and immediately was sanctified. Others have wrestled with "attachments... forbidden by the word," i.e. friendships or romantic involvements with "unbelievers," or, as in Palmer's own experience, preoccupation with one's child or spouse.

When these were given up, such ones became at once "happy possessors of the perfect love of God."[15] So, argues Palmer, the "terms specified in the word" for sanctification to occur begin with renunciation, the particulars of which may vary somewhat for each seeker but which will likely follow the lines of the examples she offers.

Here Palmer is face to face with an old theological conundrum, namely the relation between human choice and effort and the grace of God in salvation. Whereas the Calvinist tradition in Protestantism emphasized the divine side of the equation, underscoring ideas of divine sovereignty, predestination and unconditional election, the Arminian tradition, which is home to Methodism and to Palmer, emphasized the human side, i.e. the ability and necessity of human beings to respond to God's gracious offer of salvation.[16] Palmer is very explicit about her view, though one may ask whether her logic is consistent. She is an Arminian (she doesn't use the term) who sees the process of salvation as synergistic, involving the cooperation of God and humankind. There is that which God does and that which we do. She writes, "we must most emphatically be co-workers with God," for while there are those biblical references to God sanctifying persons, there are also those such as "Sanctify yourselves, therefore, and be ye holy" (Leviticus 20:7).[17] For the seeker after holiness, this means that he or she must comply with the "terms" set down for them, after which God will fulfill his end of the bargain, as it were.

In this "exchange" is where it becomes difficult for Palmer and she in this early article introduces an element of ambiguity that would dog her teaching always. First, she argues that though sanctification is received

through faith ("it is by <u>believing</u> that we are brought
into this blessed state of soul"), true faith simply
cannot be exercised until "the sacrifice of body, soul,
and spirit" is made. Once such sacrifice has been made,
however, true faith is possible, and at this point it
becomes the seeker's <u>duty</u> to believe. If faith is not
immediately exercised, God is grieved and dishonored.[18]
There is thus a heavy burden here on the seeker to
initiate and sustain the climb to holiness, first "coming out and being separate" and then "believing." This
is the obligation of the human "co-worker."

Yet in explicating the "duty to believe" which
arises when an "entire consecration" has been made,
Palmer suddenly introduces a new element: such belief is
made easy by the recognition that one's entire consecration has been accomplished "through the assistance of
[God's] grace." The logic here is that since God enabled
you to come this far--you did not do it on your own--it
is clear that he means to complete the process, i.e.
accept your "sacrifice" and impart freedom from sin and
"perfect love." Thus, Palmer tries to offer grounds for
believing which should make faith a simple next step
after entire consecration. Since the whole process is of
God, the seeker should understand his or her longing
after the blessing and renunciation of the "world" as
grounds of assurance that God is at work within and will
bring the process to fruition. Thus Palmer seems to want
to have it both ways: the seeker must meet divine conditions <u>in order for</u> God to respond with "his part of the
engagement," and yet at the same time confidence and
assurance is to be taken from the fact that the whole
process is begun and carried along by God's grace. That
this was a trouble spot in her system is indicated by
the fact that Palmer later shifted the grounds for

believing and also addressed the whole matter of faith
as she understood it at length in her book, Faith and
Its Effects (1848). In both cases she stressed more the
"contractual" nature of sanctification and less the
overarching role of grace.[19]

A related set of ideas, distinctive to Palmer's
system, which she presents in this connection includes
the relationship between faith and feeling and the role
of the "altar." The faith and feeling issue is one to
which she returns many times, mainly it would seem
because she perceived many persons wandered from "the
way of holiness" because of mistaken ideas of the matter. She herself had been one of these, long entertain-
ing what she later came to believe were false notions
which kept her from being holy. The problem, as she saw
it, was believing one needed some powerful emotion to
carry one to the point of exercising faith for sanctification, and that if one did not strongly feel what one
took to be divine influence on one's inner being, one
could not believe for sanctification. Palmer argues that
this is getting the matter backwards; in fact, faith is
required for there to be feeling, feeling being a
"fruit" of faith. However, even here she hesitates to
affirm that feeling is a necessary or inevitable product
of faith, holding that God may very well withhold feelings of "ecstasy" or assurance even to one who has
exercised faith in order to "test" or "try" the genuine-
ness and strength of that faith. The less feeling, the
greater the challenge to subsist alone on faith. The
greatest religious heroes, in fact, have been those
whose faith has been the least supported by any sensible
confirmation (e.g. Abraham in the Old Testament). In
such cases, "A holy unyielding violence" of will and
resolution is required, and this is the essence of true
faith.[20]

Helpful in all this, Palmer thinks, is the image of
the "altar," her treatment of which became perhaps her
most distinctive trademark.[21] Once again quoting her
"text-book," she refers to a fragment of a verse from
the Gospel according to Matthew, "the altar sanctifieth
the gift" (Matthew 23:19).[22] Noting that the source of
these words is an Old Testament reference to the practice of animal sacrifice among the ancient Hebrews
(Exodus 29:37), she turns to Dr. Clarke to explain that
reference. Adam Clarke (1762?-1832) was an esteemed
British Methodist theologian and Bible scholar whose
six-volume commentary on the Bible became widely popular
upon its publication in America in 1824. Clarke had
written: "This may be understood as implying, that whatsoever was laid on the altar became the Lord's property,
and must be wholly devoted to sacred purposes."[23] This
is easy enough to understand in the context of Hebrew
belief, but that is not Palmer's main concern. She holds
that the altar of sacrifice is but a "type," i.e. a
prefiguring and foreshadowing of something yet to come,
the "antitype," namely Jesus. Her idea here is grounded
on three sources: the venerable tradition of biblical
typology in the Christian Church, the teaching of the
New Testament book of Hebrews that though the altar of
sacrifice does not figure literally in the new "covenant" between God and humanity initiated by Christ,
Christians have a substitute "altar," and "Dr. Clarke's"
interpretation of Hebrews as meaning "The Christian
altar is the Christian sacrifice, which is Christ Jesus,
with all the benefits of his passion and death."[24]

Again, none of this is novel in and of itself, but
the way in which Palmer combines the elements and fits
them into her "theology of means" is very singular. As
she explains it, when something (i.e. the seeker's

entire devotion of self) is placed upon the altar (i.e.
Christ), it becomes holy by virtue of the sanctity of
the altar. Of this there can be no doubt for the Bible
plainly states that "the altar sanctifieth the gift,"
and Dr. Clarke has written that the gift on the altar
"must be wholly devoted to sacred purposes." Hence, when
the sacrifice is sincerely offered, the desired result
(one's being made holy, freed from sin, etc.) will
ensue, and will ensue the very moment that the offering
"touches the altar." "Rest now and forever here," she
counsels, "and you are NOW, and shall eternally be, the
SAVED of the Lord."[25] Palmer intends this "altar principle" as a source of assurance to the seeker after holiness who is following her method of attainment, and it
clearly served this purpose for her and for many who
embraced her teachings. It also implied a kind of automatic endowment of all the qualities inherent in the
idea of "holiness" or "perfection," however, and in this
sense became a source of considerable criticism for her
detractors. Though she does not develop the idea at
great length in these articles, she does later on in
many places, making it in effect the linchpin in her
system.[26]

In two final installments in the Advocate Palmer
addresses the question, "What will be the advantages of
living in the enjoyment of the witness of holiness to
ourselves and others?" Her answer develops four important ideas.[27] The first idea is that those who have
entered "the more excellent way" will enjoy the "witness" (i.e. have grounds for confidence) that the "sacrifice" of "all the powers of [their] bodies and minds"
is acceptable to God and is made holy. The concept of
the "altar" which "sanctifieth the gift" is of course
important here, but having already touched on that,

Palmer now refers more generally to this confidence as
resting on a "holy chain of inferences," a "just process
of reasoning" involving scattered verses from the Bible
("warranted by the word"). The significance of this, she
thinks, is not simply that religious seekers may know
themself to be perfected, thereby having some sort of
sense of satisfaction in having achieved such a lofty
pinnacle of spirituality, but that they may consequently
a̱c̱t̲ with a clear conscience, confident that their per-
formance of "religious duties" springs from pure motivation (a "purity of intention"), giving them power and
freedom to "labor in faith." Palmer thinks that many
persons struggle at this point and because of doubts
suggested by "the accuser of the brethren" are robbed of
the faith to do heroic things in promoting Christianity.
The biblical "heroes of faith" were able to accomplish
what they did precisely because they had such an assurance of their standing with God as she believes is
available to all who are "entirely devoted to God."[28]

The "heroic things" Palmer has in mind are quickly
spelled out in her development of the results of being
holy. The fully sanctified Christian is enabled to be a
witness to "the higher state of grace" into which he or
she has entered--i.e. those confident of their own sanctification become vigorous promoters of "entire sanctification" to others. "Those who themselves live in the
enjoyment of the direct witness [of holiness] c̲a̲n̲n̲o̲t̲
f̲o̲r̲b̲e̲a̲r̲ ̲u̲r̲g̲i̲n̲g̲ ̲i̲t̲ ̲u̲p̲o̲n̲ ̲o̲t̲h̲e̲r̲s̲." The reason why more are
not fearlessly declaring a "salvation from a̲l̲l̲ sin" to
others is that there is too little understanding of the
assurance which arises from the "holy chain of inferences" which are "warranted by the word." The timidity
she sees about her prevails because "one is waiting for
the other" and each makes the "standard of the other's

experience a criterion for his own" instead of "making
the requirements of the word the only standard." This
results in a "comfortable state of mind" in the Church
in which comparatively few are aggressively confronted
with the fact that it is "absolutely necessary for the
safety of the soul to be living in the enjoyment of
holiness." This can be reversed, she thinks.

There are also other "heroic" things done by persons secure in their sanctification which carry special
benefits to the world at large, according to Palmer.
These all arise from the fact that sanctified Christians
hold nothing as their own, understanding that all that
they have is "entirely devoted to God." Specifically,
time, abilities, and money are to be devoted to "holy
purposes." Though such purposes are not identified here,
elsewhere Palmer makes quite plain that among these
would be selfless involvement in all the work of the
Church as well as special works of charity and social
amelioration (e.g. visiting and evangelizing prisoners,
giving money to the poor, maintaining orphanages,
etc.).[29]

Finally, Phoebe turns to those who constitute for
her a "holiness hall of fame," an assortment of persons
who may serve to both inspire and judge the seeker of
Christian Perfection. Among these are John and Charles
Wesley, John Fletcher, Mary Bosanquet (Mrs. Fletcher),
William Carvosso, Hester Ann Rogers, Francis Asbury, and
William McKendree. Though, according to Palmer, no one's
experience is to be normative for another, she comes
close to commending these as "models" of spirituality to
be imitated. That all are eighteenth- and nineteenth-
century Methodists is an important indicator of the
boundaries of her awareness of or interest in Christian
spirituality. Many of these names are met with repeatedly in Palmer's writings.[30]

A favorite, by whom Palmer was influenced in many ways, as argued elsewhere in this study, is Hester Ann Rogers, an eighteenth-century English Methodist (1756-1794) whose spiritual autobiography was first published in America in 1814 and widely read. Since Palmer seems to have cut her "religious teeth" on Rogers' Memoirs, and identified closely with her, it is not surprising to find her lifting this pious woman up from among the others named as the most worthy example of holiness. She recounts her courageous decision to break with "gay, fashionable society" in order to "come out" and be "separate" from "the world," the ridicule she endured, her long single-minded struggle after holiness (cf. Palmer's own pilgrimage), and her final achievement of the goal. Most important of all, "hundreds...were brought into the [Methodist] society through her instrumentality" and many "brought into the enjoyment of perfect love through her example, prayers, and writings."[31] Her life is thus a paradigm of holiness--the seeking, the finding, and the energetic advocacy in the wake of finding. Her life, says Palmer, shouts "go and do likewise."

Now on reflection, it is clear that the essential ideas in Phoebe Palmer's system of religious thought are all present in this early essay. Though she would write dozens of articles, "preach" hundreds of times, and publish lengthy books over the next thirty-three years, she would largely reiterate or amplify the ideas developed in The Christian Advocate articles. Even in the one case where there seems to be a major shift of emphasis, the seed has already been planted here.[32] Thus, her system was in place by 1841, articulated clearly and forcefully. There was still a crucial element yet to come, however. Hardly had the Advocate articles appeared before Phoebe was at work on another holiness tract, but this one of a different sort. In it, though her ideas remain remarkably stable, the medium of their presentation changes. From the heavy didactic tone of the Advocate articles Palmer moves on to a much more personal, informal, "popular" style and it is this that marks her most highly acclaimed works.

The new style tract was The Way of Holiness, first published anonymously in 1843, but destined to go through over fifty editions with Palmer's name firmly attached.[33] Just how she came to put her thoughts into this new mold is not clear though it is likely that the works of others which influenced her most played a part, these being the spiritual autobiographies of eighteenth-century British Methodist women like Hester Ann Rogers, Mary Bosanquet, and Lady Maxwell, as well as other "lives" of Methodist "saints" like William Carvosso and William Bramwell. Although Palmer's The Way is very similar to these works, there is a curious Victorian diffidence at work in her statement, one which prevents her from ever using the pronoun "I." This results in a very personal revelation of her own interior religious pilgrimage being written in the third person throughout. It is uniformly "the sister" and "she" whose entry into "the way of holiness" is recounted.[34]

Another factor encouraging the new style may well have been the siege of illness Palmer underwent during the book's preparation. She did not expect to recover from the unnamed malady and labored in "an agony of pain" which sometimes brought her work to a standstill.[35] Thus it would seem that Palmer may have conceived of The Way as a "last will and testament" to be left to fellow seekers after holiness. This might help to account for the intimately personal style. As it

turned out, however, she lived, the book became enormously popular, and the style was perpetuated as an
obviously apt vehicle for her ideas.

One might also view The Way as reflecting the growing influence of Romanticism on American religious life
in the nineteenth century. Certainly the vaunting of the
individual self, which constituted a major theme of
Romanticism, can be seen in Palmer's preoccupation with
her own experience, and yet, on the other hand, it
should be noted that it is not so much the "subjective
self" of feeling and intuition which she prizes as the
"thinking self." And her tendency to construe her own
journey in universal terms reflects the rationalist as
much as it does the romantic.[36]

Whatever the case, given the book's autobiograph-
ical nature, it is a key resource for determining at
least some of the steps by which Palmer arrived at the
ideas in her influential system. As she very carefully
recounts the twists and turns of her pursuit of spiritual perfection, one can see the key ideas crystallizing
and falling into place.

An overarching factor in The Way is Palmer's drive
to find and teach a shorter route to spiritual perfection than the standard one espoused by nineteenth-century Methodists. Posing the question, "is there not a
shorter way?" the opening chapter resoundingly answers,
"Yes...THERE IS A SHORTER WAY! O! I am sure this long
waiting and struggling with the powers of darkness is
not necessary. There is a shorter way."[37]

The certainty Palmer professes here, it becomes
clear, arises from several insights which came to her
during the course of her decade-long struggle to find
holiness and assurance of her standing before God. The
first was that the Bible is a surer guide to spiritual-

ity than the experiences of other persons. Through much trial and error Palmer came to believe that relying upon another's experience was likely to take one on a circuitous path, while the Bible marks out plainly a direct, and hence a shorter, path to perfection. One following the Bible way would reach the goal quickly and confidently while those following the advice of others were likely to detour unnecessarily from the main road, and perhaps even to miss their intended destination altogether. Frustrated in her pilgrimage, Palmer at some point resolved to be a "Bible Christian," taking the Bible alone as the "rule of life." From that point forward she discovered that "former perplexities" fled, leaving a "much clearer light beaming upon her path." This fresh illumination enabled her to see the utter "simplicity of the way" of holiness, each specific step being "distinctly marked" by an emphatic "Thus saith the Lord."[38] Now instead of the ambiguous or contradictory guidance offered by fellow travellers on the journey, she was certain she had explicit and infallible direction from the one who had engineered the road system upon which she travelled. This would surely hasten the trip.

The trip would be shortened too by the discovery that the traveller need not wait for some impelling influence to carry him or her along to the destination. Palmer rails against a kind of "passiveness" which had kept her from enjoying the blessing she had sought from God. It had been suggested to her that she must wait to feel sufficiently deep convictions of her need of being perfected before she could expect the perfecting to be accomplished. Never certain her state of conviction quite measured up--"weeping because she could not weep" --she eventually discovered a different view of the matter in her new "textbook," the Bible.[39] There she found the simple command, "Be ye holy."[40] Stark in its simplicity, Palmer understood this as a requirement admitting of no delay. To her the logic of the matter was simple: if God had declared his will that his people should be holy (or "perfect" as Matthew 5:48 has it), then they should "<u>now</u> be holy."[41] What could be plainer than one's duty to comply immediately with the will of God? The burden is upon the seeker after holiness, and he or she is instructed to <u>do</u> something, not to wait for something to happen. If one were to speak of "conviction" being necessary to the process, that might be permissible, but one should understand that conviction is not a state of emotion. "<u>Knowledge is conviction</u>," declares Palmer, expressing her insight into a "simple truth before unthought of."[42] One need only <u>know</u> the requirement of God for personal holiness in order to enter into "the way."

This of course shortened the journey by eliminating the necessity of self-examination and careful attention to one's subjective states in the pursuit of holiness. It also placed responsibility squarely upon the shoulders of the individual to initiate the journey at once, for there was no reason or excuse to hesitate once the requirement to be holy was known.[43] Palmer found this discovery to be exhilarating (but also at the same time a little depressing) since she had for a long time been assured that God required holiness but had "never deemed this knowledge a sufficient plea to take to God" to receive a "present bestowment of the gift."[44] Now she knew her knowledge was sufficient conviction and so "with renewed energy, began to make use of [it]."[45]

This led Phoebe first to a roadblock, but ultimately to a further insight which also contributed to shortening the journey to holiness. The roadblock was her tendency to look at holiness as something virtually beyond her reach. Even though it might be a plain command of God, she wondered how she, an "unprofitable servant," might become "perfect." For eleven years the goal eluded her. The insight which finally set aside the roadblock was that holiness turns on "entire consecration" or the devotion of all one's powers to God and his service. This is in fact the very essence of holiness. Palmer had stated the idea in the Advocate articles: "Gospel holiness is that state of the soul which is attained by the believer when...body and soul, with every redeemed faculty, are...presented a living sacrifice to "God."[46] Previous to her discovery she had thought of holiness as something more esoteric ("some great and undefinable exercise," she had called it).[47] Yet upon reaching a place where she believed she had devoted "the entire services of her heart and life to God" in the pursuit of holiness, she was astonished to find the Holy Spirit impressing upon her that she had by this actually entered the long sought state! "What! wholly the Lord's?," she had sensed the Spirit suggesting. "Is this not the holiness that God requires? What have you more to render?"[48]

Here again, as with the teaching on the nature of conviction, the emphasis is on the action of the seeker. Holiness does not "happen" to one. It comes through a resolute willing that all one is and has shall be at "God's disposal." In order to be holy, "man must act," Palmer emphatically declares.[49] Thus, when the requisite action has been done, the desired spiritual state has been achieved. With this discovery, Palmer's journey toward holiness was shortened to the point of being almost over, but not quite.

Still remaining to be dealt with were the place of grace, faith, and assurance. Though clearly stressing the responsibility of the human seeker after the holiness demanded by God, Palmer stopped short of ascribing the attainment of the goal exclusively to human effort. Though holiness was a state "attained by the believer" and consisted essentially of the entire devotion of one's "heart and life to God," there was something left to God.

Phoebe was not insensitive to the danger of placing herself very near the outer border of the Protestant tradition through emphasizing human activity as the key to salvation. In the narration of her experience she pauses to reflect on the matter: did the "determination to consecrate all to God," to "be wholly the Lord's" actually bring about "entrance into the new and living way" of Christian Perfection, she asks?[50] Though she has seemed to suggest just this, here she retreats a bit, reminding herself that a finite and sinful being could surely not accomplish this alone. Only the "blood of Christ" could do it, she affirms, citing Titus 3:5: "Not by works of righteousness which we have done, but according to his mercy he saveth us."[51] Thus, she holds that the "sacrifice" of self is an acceptable "offering" only because of what God has already done through Jesus. That is, one could not expect a holy God to accept the imperfect and sinful offer of a human self as a fit gift, were it not that God had graciously seen to it that Christ "bore the sins of the whole world in his own body," and through his death brought about reconciliation between God and sinful humanity. Hence, one comes to God for forgiveness of sin and to be sanctified or made holy through Jesus, as it were. It is "His sacrificial death and sufferings" which are the "sinner's plea."[52] That is, God accepts the condemned human sinner because of what Christ did, so long as the sinner offers himself or herself through the mediation of Christ and according to his "merits" rather than according to any merit of their own. In this way, Palmer believes, God, "in his infinite love," has "provided a way by which lost, guilty men may be redeemed, justified, cleansed, and saved."[53] However, with this affirmed, she adds quickly, "Yet she conceived that it was by these pious resolves [to consecrate everything to God] she was enabled thus to be a <u>worker</u> <u>together</u> with God."[54]

In this connection Palmer next recounts the genesis of her "altar theology," an idea already introduced in the <u>Advocate</u> articles, and no doubt a mainstay of her preaching and teaching ministry by this time. It ties together her excursion into the classical Protestant teachings of salvation through faith in Christ and a further distinctive insight of hers concerning the "shorter way" to holiness. Having just affirmed that God graciously provides the way which can be travelled by those seeking "full salvation," she once again finds herself at a roadblock when she returns to her description of how the human traveller may successfully traverse the way. The difficulty is wrapped up with the nature of faith and assurance. As Palmer understands the process, the "second work of grace" which brings holiness, or full salvation, or Christian Perfection comes by faith in Christ, just as does the "first work of grace," that being justification and forgiveness of sin. But this second step also comes by the "pious resolve" of the "co-worker" with God. The fact that these two dimensions work together leaves one without a completely satisfactory ground of assurance that the goal has been reached, when it has, since one half of the "transaction," as it were, depends upon something other than the action of the human "co-worker" in making an entire consecration of himself or herself (implied in consecration is also a renunciation of the things of "the world," according to the Advocate articles). One may know when a point of full consecration or "entire devotion" has been reached, but how may one be assured that the "sacrifice" has in fact been rendered acceptable to God through Christ?

Palmer resolved the problem to her own satisfaction through another insight which she believed she was given by the Holy Spirit through her searching of the Bible. She fastened upon a verse from the Gospel according to Matthew (23:19) speaking of the Jewish sacrificial altar and the sacrifices offered upon it. Jesus, mocking the casuistry surrounding the use of oaths, notes that according to the prevailing teaching swearing by the altar is acceptable, but swearing by the sacrifice offered on the altar is taboo. "Fools and blind," the gospel has him saying, "for whether is greater, the gift, or the altar that sanctifieth the gift?" The implication is that it is the consecrated altar which hallows that which is placed upon it, rendering the distinctions about oaths both misguided and ludicrous.[55]

Palmer was not concerned with the matter of oaths, however. For her the key point of the words ascribed to Jesus was that they asserted that the sacrifice is sanctified--i.e. made holy--by virtue of the altar upon which it is offered. Understanding the entire consecration which she held to be necessary for spiritual perfection as akin to the Jewish practice of offering animal sacrifices to God, she found this reference relevant to her situation. It told her that in fact the human act of entire consecration was the nub of achieving holiness. While she formally recognized the Protestant doctrine of salvation through divine grace rather than human "works," and, steeped in that doctrine, knew that ultimately any state of spirituality was a "gift," her reading of the Matthew passage took the uncertainty of having to "wait upon God" out of the matter and threw the responsibility for achieving the goal of holiness back upon the seeker. To reach the level of "entire consecration" was to be guaranteed that this offering was acceptable to God through Christ and that "an entire salvation from sin" was granted, with "new accessions of wisdom, power, and love, with every other grace" to follow. "By 'laying all upon this altar [i.e. Christ]'," she declared, she "laid herself under the most sacred obligation to believe that the sacrifice became 'holy and acceptable,' and virtually the Lord's property, even by virtue of the sanctity of the altar upon which it was laid, and continued 'holy and acceptable,' so long as kept inviolably upon this hallowed altar."[56] "I cannot believe that there is any lingering on the part of God in fulfilling his promises to the seeking soul," she wrote. "When we come to him in the way of his requirements, we are met with his blessing." The "work is accomplished the moment we lay our all upon the altar."[57]

Here then was assurance for Palmer which even preceded the act of faith necessary to complete the journey to holiness. Assured now that the act of entire consecration on her part brought her into a state of holiness, but still sensitive to the need to ground spiritual attainment upon grace and faith alone, she holds that it is only by faith that the "transaction" is completed.

The faith issue was one with which Phoebe struggled long and hard. It will be recalled that following the lead of her sister, Sarah, she had seemed able finally to set aside the quest for religious emotions and "signs and wonders" and place her confidence in the act of believing the "word of God" recorded in the Bible. She would "take God at his word, whatever her emotions might be."[58] Since "faith is believing God," she would believe what "Infinite truth has uttered" even "though human probability should pronounce it impossible."[59] Thus, faith for her was essentially an intellectual exercise-- believing certain propositions to be true--although a dimension of it was trust, since the purpose of the propositions ("promises" Palmer liked to call them) was to instill confidence in the seeker and lead to action. Responding to a correspondent who fears his faith is mere intellectual effort, Palmer dismisses this as a temptation of Satan and observes, "Perhaps if the faith of believers in general were more intellectual, it might be more efficient in its operations."[60] To another in- quirer she insists that God does not "require that I believe, without a thorough foundation for my faith," adding, "Why, it is hardly of faith, but rather of knowledge; it is so easy."[61]

The ease she found was in the "objective" nature of God's "plan" for entire sanctification and what seemed to her its perfect logic. The Christian's "textbook" made plain that God demanded holiness or spiritual per- fection. It also revealed that he had provided a way for it to be obtained and mapped it out (it is through the merit of Christ but requires that the seeker act upon conviction [i.e. knowledge], leading to entire consecra- tion and faith). It further promised results, should the requirements of "the way" be complied with (e.g. "the altar sanctifieth the gift"; "come out from among them, and be ye separate, touch not the unclean thing; and I will receive you"--2 Corinthians 6:17). "Faith" in this scheme was not difficult--at least so it seemed to Phoebe in retrospect, once she had comprehended the "system" in its entirety--since such a "thorough foundation for...faith" had been "so explicitly given" by God in "his written word."[62] "The ground of faith," she explained, is "the immutable promises of the Lord Jehovah."[63]

Grasping this, the seeker of holiness has nearly completed the journey--but not quite. One thing remains. Still to be done is to verbally profess "the blessing" in the strongest terms. One must do this in order to both fully secure and, once secured, retain the blessing.

In the first instance holiness is not fully grasped until such profession is made, because this act is the ultimate demonstration of "naked faith" upon which the reception of the blessing hinges. Until one "steps out on faith" and publicly "claims the blessing," in the absence of any verification save the "naked word" (i.e. the requirements and promises of God in the Bible), full consecration has not in fact been made, nor has sanctifying faith been fully exercised. The "thus saith the Lord" to which Palmer appeals for support of the idea is "For with the heart man believeth unto righteousness; and with the mouth confession is made unto salvation" (Romans 10:10). "Do not forget," she tells a seeker after holiness, "that believing with the heart, and confessing with the mouth, stand closely connected, and 'What God hath joined together, let not man put asunder.'"[64] She admonishes another: "Your heart has believed, but your lips have not fully . . . made

confession. And thus your part of the work has been left
in part unfulfilled."[65]

As for retaining the blessing, regular public testimony is mandatory. Just as verbal testimony is a
necessary concomitant of faith in attaining the blessing, so is it in maintaining it. The faith which does
not lead to explicit, habitual confession of being "entirely sanctified," "saved from all sin," "perfected in
love," or "in the enjoyment of holiness" is deficient
and is thus not truly "sanctifying faith." The one who
initially "claims the blessing," but who does not persevere in regular testimony, loses the blessing. So Palmer
explains to a troubled correspondent, "when you lost the
blessing, you...proved the faithfulness of the Lord
Jehovah. You were warranted from his word in anticipating just the loss you sustained. It was the necessary
result of the course you pursued," that being that "you
became 'cautious in professing the blessing,'" and hence
"ceased to comply with the condition" laid down by
God.[66]

Once again this teaching is a reflection of
Phoebe's own struggle and the manner in which she eventually resolved it. The Way reveals the process. Pushing
doggedly toward holiness, she believed the Spirit of God
suggested to her that if she were to achieve it, she
would have to "declare it." And if she were to retain it
she would be "called to profess" it "before thousands!"[67] Significantly, this was the very thing she
feared most to do and which she had little success in
doing in the past. "The enemy directed her mind most
powerfully to what her former failures had been, in
reference to making confession with the mouth."[68] She
reluctantly acknowledged that "in few duties had she
more frequently brought condemnation on her soul than in

this," believing that for years she had "been hindered from rising in holiness, by a neglect to comply with the order of God [in Romans 10:10]."[69] She feared that of all the requirements of God, a failure in this was "precisely the ground on which she should lose the blessing...."[70]

Sensing this to be a crucial "test" of her resolution to give up literally everything to God, she determined that a "shrinking of the flesh" in this matter would not prevent her from reaching her goal. She would go forward, "however formidable the circumstances," and even "if it literally cost life in the effort."[71] Explicit public testimony would be a central requirement of the "way of holiness" for her, and she would comply unfailingly with all the requirements. "Woe is me if I do not profess this blessing [of holiness], and urge its attainableness, and reasonableness upon others," she would remind herself early in her burgeoning revivalist career.[72] So too would she come to believe that the same obligation lay upon all travellers in "the way," discovering unequivocal public testimony to be a logical and necessary step in the "shorter way" which she so carefully mapped out.

With the publication of The Way of Holiness in 1843, Palmer's reputation as a religious writer was sealed. Her "shorter way" had immense appeal to an age preoccupied with "perfection" and notions of how to achieve it. Notables commended the book. The president of Oberlin College, Asa Mahan, considered it to be next in value to the Bible. The editor of the Ladies' Repository thought it the best practical guide "of all that has been written on the blessed theme of entire sanctification."[73] An exception apparently was the one who thought its author "had been better engaged in washing

her dishes, than in writing."[74] Eventually the work
would be published in Canada and England and translated
into French and German for circulation in Europe.[75]
Wherever Palmer went after 1843 she would be known as
the author of The Way of Holiness.

She did not rest on her laurels, however. Within
two years she published Present to My Christian Friend,
On Entire Devotion to God. Although this book really
contains no new ideas, it makes more explicit some of
the things implied in the Advocate series and The Way,
and thus gives a fuller picture of Palmer's thinking. It
also weds her new personal-autobiographical style with
the didactic style of the 1841 holiness articles. In
fact, the first five chapters are only slightly amended
versions of the Advocate pieces, while sixteen other
chapters mix generous portions of story-telling and
personal experience with instructions on how to keep
holiness once it has been won by the "shorter way."

Two things in particular are noteworthy about
Entire Devotion. First, there is considerable elabora-
tion of the concept of covenant in connection with
holiness. The idea that holiness rests upon a covenant,
or "contract" between two parties--God and the Christian
seeker--mutually obligating them to one another according to stipulated terms, is present in the earlier
writings, but Palmer further explains it here.[76] The
"altar principle," already noted, is the touchstone
since the central obligation of each "party" intersects
here: the seeker makes the sacrifice of "entire consecration" and God renders the sacrifice holy, sanctified,
or perfect. Palmer includes a chapter on "The Altar."

So does she entitle a chapter "A Covenant," but
significantly the content concerns almost exclusively
what the seeker after holiness covenants to do. God is

called upon to accept the seeker as his forever and to
"penetrate soul and body" with the "consuming energies
of the Holy Spirit."[77] The seeker, meanwhile, covenants
to "consecrate body, soul, and spirit, time, talents,
influence, family, and estate--all...near or remote, to
be forever, and in the most unlimited sense, THE
LORD'S."[78] The implications of this are enumerated far
more specifically than before. They include the need to
be attentive to one's dress that it be appropriate to a
profession of "holiness to the Lord"; the obligation to
give at least a tenth of one's income to religious work;
the obligation to train one's children "for the self-
sacrificing service of God"; a commitment to "search the
Scriptures daily" and to be "regulated by the unadulterated WORD OF GOD"; a pledge to "profess the blessing"
openly, "irrespective of emotions," relying only on "the
exceeding great and precious promises" tying God to this
contractual arrangement. All of this is actually cast in
the formal terms of a contract concluding with
signature, seal, and date.[79]

    A second noteworthy characteristic of Entire Devo-
tion to God is the amount of attention given to retaining a state of holiness. Whereas her earlier writing
focused almost exclusively on the means of getting to
the goal, Palmer in this work is much concerned with
giving clear counsel as to how to stay, once there. One
source of her concern is the conviction that this
"second work of grace" which she teaches is the only
entrance to "holiness" and holiness is the "only fitness
for admission to the society of the blood-washed in
heaven."[80] Thus to lose the state of holiness or "perfection" is to ultimately lose heaven. Another concern
is her belief that holiness entails a growing spirituality after one has undergone the "crisis" of conviction,

entire consecration, faith, and public testimony which brings purging from all sinfulness. Though the main purpose of her publications and her preaching career was clearly to guide persons into and through this stylized experience, it is not correct to assume that Palmer's interest went no further. In The Way she had referred to holiness as a "highway" of "interminable progression" and in Entire Devotion the idea is enlarged and given specific content.[81] Though the "soul" that has entered the state of holiness is "saved from all sin at present," it is also to recognize that it is "not saved to the uttermost." In "the entire surrender of the world," it has "but 'laid aside every weight,'" enabling it now to run "with increasing rapidity and delight in the way of [God's] commandments" with "undeviating purpose and unshackled feet." This will result in "gaining new accessions of wisdom, Power, and love, with every other grace, daily."[82] That is, entire sanctification is only the beginning of an unhindered development of Christian character.

As might be expected, an important piece of advice Palmer offers for retaining holiness is to cling to that which first brought the blessing. Entire consecration and "naked faith" must be carefully maintained. Do not "let go thy grasp on the promises," she warns, nor "cease to comply with the conditions on which the promises are made."[83] The "sacrifice" of oneself must be "ceaselessly presented."[84]

In addition, Palmer explains, there is a growing set of responsibilities which increase as knowledge and spiritual strength increase. These are thus "proportionate to the light" one has, and must be met in order for entire sanctification to be retained. These responsibilities "requisition yet more and more of the spirit of sacrifice."[85] The way of holiness is "the way of the cross." In fact, "the entire way to Heaven is narrow" and demands "entire compliance" with the strict conditions of "discipleship," which are progressively revealed.[86]

As Palmer spells out these responsibilities demanding greater and greater degrees of sacrifice, a central concern, to be met with time and again in her writings, is shunning "conformity to the world," particularly in the way one dresses, but also including one's possessions generally and how time is spent. "The pursuits, the equipage, and the whole exterior, serve as an index to the mind," she maintains. One may be quite sure that a profession of entire sanctification is "questionable" if a person is careless in these areas. One may assume that "to the degree conformity to this world is practiced, is the default in regard to worldly renunciation evident."[87]

Other responsibilities to be met in maintaining a state of holiness include the continual sacrifice of "time, talents and reputation." Certainly the duties enumerated in the "covenant" will be carried out, but in addition to these literally everything must be watched.[88] One might well forefeit the blessing through refusing to profess it, indulging in "love of reputation," refusing to enter the ministry when "called," or even through "foolish talking and jesting."[89] Entire sanctification can only be retained by "the most careful circumspection in all things."[90] Indeed, warns Phoebe, "If you shrink from any duty, you will take the offering from off the altar, and then you will fall from a state of entire sanctification." And, she adds ominously, "If you begin to fall, the Lord only knows how low your fall may be."[91]

Still, as serious as this business of retaining and growing in a state of holiness might be, and as subject to careless loss as such a state might appear to Palmer, the main problem for those attracted to her teaching seemed to be something else. The exercise of heroic faith necessary to even entering a state of holiness, much less retaining it, was the difficulty. Letters from numerous correspondents evidence confusion and anxiety about the nature of "sanctifying faith." In response Phoebe wrote Faith and Its Effects; or Fragments from My Portfolio, gathering up the substance of her advice to dozens of troubled seekers after holiness. Published in early 1848 and dedicated to Methodist bishop Edmund Janes and his wife, the book elaborated at length on one of the crucial "steps" in "the way of holiness" outlined by Palmer in her previous writings and through her increasingly far flung travels.[92] Discerning exactly the concern of the book, Zion's Herald, the paper of New England Methodism, noted that, by Palmer's explanations, "such light is thrown upon the precise point of transit from condemnation to favor, from bondage to liberty, from partial to full salvation, as is not perhaps done in any other human composition."[93]

As with Entire Devotion to God, there is little in Faith and Its Effects that is not at least implied in The Way of Holiness and the even earlier Advocate articles. The new element is simply the single-mindedness with which Palmer examines this concept which was so pivotal to her own religious experience and which binds the various other elements of the "shorter way" to holiness together.

As might be expected, among the things which stand out in the volume is that in setting forth faith as the sine qua non of entire sanctification, the validity of

feelings or emotions is strongly denied. Palmer had
taken pains from the very beginning to sunder the journey to spiritual perfection from dependence upon emotional states, and here that effort is underscored. Her
own decision to be guided exclusively by the Bible
without regard to her emotions is recounted, along with
the admonition that "there is no positive standard for
feeling in the Scriptures."[94] She has, she declares,
been guided in holiness not by "extraordinary internal
or external manifestations," or "extraordinary emotion," but by a "solemn conviction that God cannot be
unfaithful" to "fulfill his promises to the trusting
one."[95] Those who look to feeling as a barometer of
spirituality are set right. To the correspondent who
suggests he has a "destitution of holiness" because joy
and peace have waned, Palmer replies: "A destitution of
joyous emotion...is not a destitution of holiness."[96]
Because "holiness is a state in which all the redeemed
powers are given up to God through Christ," the only way
a "destitution of holiness" can occur is for the "offering" to be consciously removed from the "altar." If the
offering remains in place, then faith, rather than feeling, affirms that a state of holiness is maintained.[97]

Also, not surprisingly, the obligatory nature of
faith is pressed repeatedly in this book. The seeker
after holiness must believe. Palmer presses this in two
directions. The one is the simple matter that the exercise of sanctifying faith is something done by the
seeker. Even though the ability to exercise such faith
is technically a gracious gift of God, the burden is on
the human agent since God never "withholds the power to
exercise faith from the sincere inquirer."[98] Thus, the
seeker, if he or she will, may exercise faith.

The second thrust is suggested by the first. If a seeker may exercise faith if he or she will, then also may he or she exercise faith when he or she will. That is, one is obligated to exercise faith at a precise momentary point in the way to holiness, that being at the very point of entire consecration. To hesitate even a single moment here is to question the integrity of God to fulfill his promise to accept the sincerely offered "sacrifice" ("How presumptuous to doubt God!").[99] Such doubting ("unbelief") constitutes sin which deprives one not only of a state of holiness but also the forgiveness of sin which one received in the "first blessing" of "conversion" or justification.[100]

So crucial is the faith which the seeker after holiness must exercise that Palmer at one point calls it--rather than God--"omnipotent." "O the omnipotence of faith!," she declares, "the want of it may even stay the hand of the Almighty."[101] On the other hand, the presence of faith instantly achieves the goal of holiness. It is the cord which binds all the other steps of "the way" together and makes them efficacious. It is by faith that one is "enabled, momentarily, to realize the entire consecration, and purification, of body, soul, and spirit."[102] Faith is the "key" which "opens the door, and brings the soul into the actual possession of full and complete redemption...."[103]

Now all of this may seem to suggest that Palmer set forth a "mechanistic" understanding of holiness. The whole process seems to be governed by a system of laws or principles which have been established and which are utterly predictable. Both God and human beings are bound by the system. Certain actions trigger guaranteed responses. Actions must occur in a fixed sequence in order for the desired end to be achieved. In fact, Palmer is

quite outspoken at this point in Faith and Its Effects.
The very title indicates the direction of her thought.
There are laws which govern God's "moral universe" just
as there are laws governing the physical universe. This
structure of moral or spiritual cause and effect is
revealed primarily in the Bible, but also to some extent
through rational reflection on human experience.[104] If
one understands these laws and acts in accordance with
them, it is certain that the designated means will
achieve the desired ends. Conversely, the ends can be
achieved by no other than the designated means. Thus it
is that Palmer can say that a lack of faith can confound
the power of God--"He cannot work where unbelief prevails, consistently with the order of his government"[105]--while an act of faith can momentarily achieve
holiness. Faith's "effects must of necessity follow"
faith, Palmer writes. "I say must of necessity follow,
because the principles by which the kingdom of grace is
governed are unchangeable."[106]

Not only holiness, but all aspects of religious
life are governed by this structure of law of spiritual
cause and effect. Anticipating a charge which would be
levelled against her own teaching before very many
years, Palmer criticizes those whom she understands to
teach a kind of "faithism," telling others to "only
believe you have it, and you have got it."[107] Though
Palmer's own "way of holiness" might seem to border on
this, faith being "omnipotent" in her system, her teaching is quite different since for her the exercise of
faith is hedged round with conditions which govern its
effectiveness. Though faith is the "key," it can only
open doors when it is used in its proper context of
divine requirements and promises, that which forms what
Palmer calls "continuous chain of gospel privilege."[108]

To omit any of the links of the chain--or even to arrange them improperly in relation to one another, it would seem--is to forfeit the whole of it. In seeking anything from God, the petitioner must possess the "qualifications" (i.e. be meeting the conditions and utilizing the means) which "according to the principles of God's law, entitle him to favorable hearing." [109] If the "qualifications" are possessed, then the petitioner is assured of success. Using now the language of personal relationship rather than law, a mixing of idioms not uncommon in Palmer, she asserts that "a promise fully credited does in itself convey the thing promised," and since the promises of God are all conditional, meeting the conditions ipso facto secures the promised thing.[110] "The act, on your part, must necessarily induce the promised result on the part of God."[111]

In pressing these ideas about faith, Palmer elaborates one area of her thought that was becoming increasingly prominent and which would eventually dominate her whole system. This was her understanding of the work of the Holy Spirit in achieving and retaining holiness. In the earliest writings the main focus is on God the Father as the one who graciously establishes the "plan of salvation" embodying his laws of spiritual cause and effect, and Jesus the Son as the one who bears the sins of humankind, thereby becoming the Christian's "altar" or mediator who effects reconciliation between God and humanity. The Holy Spirit plays a somewhat subordinate role as the one who helps one to understand the "plan of salvation" and hence to follow it. The Spirit mainly enlightens, convinces, prompts, and urges, working in and through the written word of God, the Bible. There is a reference in the Advocate articles to the "renewing of the Holy Ghost" which occurs when entire consecration has been made and sanctifying faith exercised, but this is not developed.[112] There is virtually no reference at all to the Holy Spirit in Entire Devotion to God.

In The Way of Holiness, however, Phoebe had begun to wrestle with the classical Wesleyan doctrine of the "witness of the Spirit" which held that assurance of being in both the "first" and "second blessings" was available to the sincere believer by way of a direct testimony or "witness" of the Holy Spirit to the individual's spirit. John Wesley had described this as "an inward impression on the soul of believers whereby the Spirit of God directly testifies to their spirit that they are children of God."[113] For many of Wesley's heirs this was an elusive experience which came and went, bound up as it was with subjective states of emotion--joy, peace, confidence, "sensing God's presence," and the like.[114] As we have already seen, Phoebe was wary of religious emotion and constructed her system of thought in such a way as to minimize, if not altogether eliminate, the role of feeling. However, child of the Wesleyan religious tradition that she was, she could not simply jettison the doctrine of the witness of the Spirit even though she might find it troublesome. What she did in The Way of Holiness was to recast it a bit to fit her system. She called it the "witness of entire consecration" and tied it to the act of entire consecration required of the seeker after holiness and to the urging, convincing work of the Holy Spirit in and through the Bible. That is, in the Way of Holiness, the "witness of the Spirit" is described as being mediated through the Bible and deduced from a human act of willing. The terms of the divine-human covenant are clearly set forth in the "written word of God" which is given "by the express dictation of the Holy Spirit."[115] Thus,

the Spirit "witnesses" through the written word when it
is read and its meaning apprehended. More specifically,
in the matter of holiness, when the "terms of the covenant" are fully complied with, the Holy Spirit "witnesses" through "the declaration of the written word"[116]--
and the seeker's own certainty that all has been placed
on "the altar"--that the provisions of the covenant are
now all fully operative. One thus has "assurance" of
being entirely sanctified. This appears to be quite
different from Wesley's "direct inward impression on the
soul."

In Faith and Its Effects Palmer returns to the
doctrine of the "witness of the Spirit" and in elabor-
ating it confirms the impression that she was in fact
creating something new. She also evidences a growing
preoccupation with the role of the Holy Spirit in holiness. In one place she refers to her own pursuit of the
"witness of entire holiness," which she defines as "the
seal of consecration on all my powers."[117] This she
eventually finds in a "simple and rational" resolution
to set herself apart from God and be wholly his and the
insight "appealingly applied" by the Holy Spirit that by
this act she is in fact "wholly sanctified."[118] This
very closely echoes The Way of Holiness.

To "Mr. P--" who asks in good Wesleyan fashion,
"when shall I be enabled to testify, that I have the
direct witness of the Spirit, that I am wholly sanctified?," Phoebe replies, "this I am sure you will have
the moment you unwaveringly rely on the promises of your
faithful God." She also adds, "you may not have any
sensible manifestation, by way of assuring you of the
acceptance of your offering, as the immediate consequence of your faith," explaining that, "To the degree
manifestations addressed to the senses are given, the

necessity of faith is precluded...."[119] This seems to leave the door slightly ajar for some later "sensible manifestation," yet Phoebe very nearly closes it in reminding her questioner that "it is written, 'The just shall live by faith; not by sight,'" and urging him to "be an example to believers in faith...."[120]

In what is her most extended exposition of the "witness of the Spirit," Phoebe answers the inquiries of a "Rev. Mr. M--." Among other things he asks simply, "What is the witness of the Spirit?" Interestingly, Phoebe apologizes for taking so long to reply to his letter, noting, "it is hard to find words, in the language of men, to explain the deep things of God."[121] She begins by trying Wesley's language, paraphrasing loosely his definition of the "witness." She then tries her own words, suggesting that it is in the act of believing in the written word of God that one "has the witness." Here she appeals to the Bible verse, "He that believeth, hath the witness in himself" (1 John 5:10). It is in "the internal consciousness that we do believe" the "communication of the Holy Spirit through the written word" that one has the "witness of the Spirit."[122] "But is there not an evidence apart from the word?" one may ask. Palmer replies, "The Holy Spirit always speaks to my heart by the word...."[123] Is this "work of the Spirit" then nothing more than the seeker's own awareness of their resolve to devote themselves entirely to God and believe with a "holy unyielding violence" of will that their offering is accepted according to the Scriptural promise? Admits Palmer, "[The Spirit's] silent operations on the heart may not always at once be discerned as distinct from the testimony of our own spirit." Yet, "we should ever bear in mind, that whatever revelations...are made to the believing heart, they are all the work of the Holy Spirit."[124]

Still, there is a sense in which Phoebe is not fully satisfied with this understanding. She refers in one place to her desire for a "sealing of the Spirit," an "establishment in grace" beyond the "witness of the Spirit" which will bring with it a profound stability, a "resting place" in God. She does not claim to have received this blessing, though she holds it to be a "privilege included in the believer's inheritance."[125] In another place she mentions one who received "a gracious baptism of the [Holy] Spirit" which enabled her to testify "in the full assurance of faith," "O I am sanctified; glory be to God!"[126] Though Palmer does not elaborate here, this "baptism" does not seem to be exactly synonymous with the "witness of the Spirit" as she has explained it. It seems to be a more "sensible manifestation." She notes of one correspondent that he has "not yet received the full baptism of the Holy Ghost."[127] She urges him to wait for this, but "with earnest wrestlings" seek the "witness of the Holy Spirit." She acknowledges that he has placed his "offering" on the "hallowed offering" but awaits the descent of "the hallowed fire." This seems to imply that he has made an entire consecration of himself, but is lacking the "naked faith" that appropriates and internalizes the "witness of the Spirit" in the "naked word" of the Bible. It also implies that he should expect a "full baptism of the Holy Ghost" at some point subsequent to entire consecration and the exercise of faith which brings with it the witness of the Holy Spirit.

"Spirit concerns" are also evidenced in a letter to the members of an unidentified church. Phoebe encourages these to "look for the full baptism of the Holy Ghost" to enliven their moribund fellowship. "This full baptism," she writes, "may be regarded as the act of ordination on the part of God, by which he empowers his disciples with the might of his Spirit, in order that they may bring faith much fruit, and that their fruit may remain."[128] She does not appear to be equating this with entire sanctification. Yet, in still another place, in the context of disputing the teaching that justification and full sanctification occur in the same moment, and quoting Wesley on there being two distinct "works of grace," she refers to the day of Pentecost and the changes the "full baptism of the Holy Ghost" given on that day wrought in the disciples of Jesus, appearing to see in this the original "second blessing" or "full sanctification" event.[129]

Whatever new directions Palmer may be hinting at here, it is clear that faith, defined as, "God hath said it, and I believe it," is the act which marks the "precise point of transit from condemnation to favor...from partial to full salvation" and is that upon which all other attendant phenomena or considerations relating to holiness hinge.

While this is the main theme of Faith and Its Effects, there are introduced some other notable subordinate themes as well. One is Palmer's belief that the special, aggressive advocacy of holiness for which she is becoming noted ought to characterize Methodism in general. "Our responsibilities before God relative to the doctrine of Christian holiness are tremendous," she reminds a correspondent. "A dispensation of the gospel has been committed to us" alone among the churches, distinguishing Methodists as those who ought to stand before the world "under the banner, 'HOLINESS TO THE LORD.'"[130] Yet she decries what she judges to be the failure of the church to measure up to its calling and lays the blame at the door of the clergy: "That there are so few comparatively among the membership who profess to enjoy the blessing [of full sanctification] may be attributed to the fact, that there is little explicit and experimental testimony among the ministry on this point."[131]

Another, though not unrelated theme, is the matter of the terminology of holiness. On the one hand, her views here appear "ecumenical." She is delighted that Christians of many theological persuasions and denominational loyalties are coming together on the "common ground of holiness." She finds it interesting that John Wesley's theology--at least his doctrine of Christian perfection or "full sanctification"--should be the point of convergence. This she ascribes to the fact that Wesley was "a man eminently taught of God" through his devotion to the Bible. His theology has appeal and rings true because it is faithful to the Bible.[132]

Even though Palmer here intends to celebrate the unity of Christians, and by no means intends to suggest that such unity means absorption by "Methodism" in all its particulars, a sectarian note is clearly audible. Those who adopt "holiness" are adopting John Wesley's exposition of it. His views are correct because "biblical." The ramifications of this are made apparent where Phoebe chides a ministerial correspondent who is not a Methodist for dissembling at the point of terminology. Why can't he proclaim the fact of holiness in his denomination, he wonders, a denomination whose creed differs from Wesleyan teaching, but use language less dissonant with the creed and less "Methodist" than the terms "perfection," "holiness," or "entire sanctification"? Her answer is that these terms are scriptural (and hence, as has been seen, "dictated" by the Holy Spirit). They are the very words of God. She cites Mark 8:38--"Whosoever therefore shall be ashamed of me and <u>my</u> <u>words</u> in this adulterous and sinful generation; of him also shall the Son of man be ashamed"--as biblical proof that hesitating to use specific biblical language alienates one from God and forfeits one's state of grace. Also, such efforts to not offend are attempts to escape the "offense of the cross" which is inescapable if one is to be a "true disciple" of Christ, and show that a person is more concerned about reputation than serving God. In fact, Palmer warns her correspondent, even though "You may in sincerity have thought that you were living in a state of entire consecration," until "you have laid your reputation, as well as everything else upon the altar, you are not thus living before God."[133] If truly sanctified he will use the biblical (i.e. Methodist) terminology and gladly suffer persecution on that account.[134]

Strong as this defense of "Wesleyan" concepts and terminology may appear, it is interesting to note that elsewhere in the book Phoebe admits to something less than complete familiarity with Wesley's <u>Works</u>, though she does demonstrate the willingness and ability to use his writings as a theological resource when it seems necessary to do so. Challenged by those claiming Wesley's support in their teaching that justification and full sanctification are not separate "works of grace," Palmer sets out to pin Wesley down on this point. "I have just been at pains to get his precise words," she tells "Miss S--." Quoting Wesley at some length, she observes, "I believe I have not read the portion here given myself for years," noting, "I have been glad of the opportunity of again refreshing my own

mind." She then adds, "Had I known that my views of
Scripture on this point so nearly accorded in word with
his, I might before have given his in place of my own."
This is a significant admission that her own theological structure was uniquely her own, though, she would
certainly argue, "Wesleyan" in its basic orientation.[135]
This is reinforced by other comments in this same letter
where Palmer remarks, "I very much venerate the opinions
of Mr. Wesley, the founder of Methodism, under God. But
I am so constituted, that it seems to be a habit which
the law of my nature demands, to analyze sentiments let
them come from whom they may, before I can really receive them as my own."[136] Recounting her turning away
from "all mere human opinions" to the "teachings of the
Spirit through the word" during her spiritual struggles,
she expresses "no small satisfaction" that the truth she
has discovered in this way is "so fully in accordance
with Mr. Wesley's views...." What is quite clear here is
that what gives validity to Wesley's veiws is their
agreement (as Palmer interprets them) with her own,
which have no "mere human" basis, but are "the things of
God" which have been "revealed" to her by the Holy
Spirit.[137]

This identification with Wesley coupled with a
declaration of independence from "all mere human opinions" strongly stamps Phoebe's next major publication,
Incidental Illustrations of the Economy of Salvation,
Its Doctrines and Duties, which appeared in 1855. Seven
years had elapsed since Faith and Its Effects, and
things were changing. Writing three major books in the
forties, Phoebe had seen her star rise and the demands
on her time multiply. As has been seen, the 1850s were
to be the apex of her career as revivalist and author.
It was in these years that she would begin travelling

regularly in Canada, pour much energy into the "Laymen's Revival" of 1857-58, and embark for a tour of Britain. Understandably her literary output fell. The only really important things to come from her pen during the decade were Incidental Illustrations, a potpourri of essays, excerpts from letters, and brief "musings" on assorted subjects, and the provocative The Promise of The Father, which was published at the very end of the period. Her several periodical contributions during this time were virtually echoes of some of the essays in Incidental Illustrations.

Not only was Phoebe busier in these days, but she was confident in her success. Gone is the hesitating, diffident tone she sometimes adopted in earlier years. Though always dogmatic to a degree, she evidences an even stronger sense of assurance of the correctness of her views in the 1850s writings. The many anecdotes in Incidental Illustrations showing Phoebe in conversation with others, many of them seekers after holiness, depict a woman who has complete confidence in both her message and her methods. She will not alter or compromise any detail. Her principles are fixed, and she is fearless in defending them, and in attacking those who do not share them.[138]

This new confidence, even militancy, discernible in Incidental Illustrations points up another change occurring in the 1850s which is also reflected in the book. This is the emergence of the "holiness crusade" centering around Palmer as an identifiable movement within the American churches (principally, but not exclusively the Methodist Episcopal) generating in its wake controversy and the taking of sides. It will be recalled that Palmer's teaching was debated openly for a time in the mid-1850s in the pages of the Christian

<u>Advocate and Journal</u>. Phoebe's followers were coming by
this time to be known as "Palmerites" and their fervent
advocacy of "second blessing holiness" perceived as a
divisive "speciality" by some.[139]

Much in <u>Incidental Illustrations</u> exhibits this
growing "partisan" mentality and points up the conflict
that was brewing. There are many barbed comments aimed
by Phoebe at the Methodist Church which evidence a
widening gulf between "holiness" people and other Methodists not identifying with the movement.

The Methodist ministry is coming to be dominated by
"younger or less pious" ministers who "court popular
applause" more than true spirituality and orthodox
belief.[140] They flaunt their "ability for profound
biblical criticism, and pulpit oratory."[141] There are
few "in comparison with the mass" who "from personal
experience" can "testify that, 'The blood of Jesus
cleanseth from all sin'!"[142] The "want of prosperity"
(i.e. numerical growth and spiritual well-being) in some
quarters of the church is due to ministers failing to
hold up holiness as "the crowning doctrine of the Bible"
and "The distinguishing doctrine of Methodism."[143] A
piece entitled "Secular Business and a Call to the
Ministry" laments the tendency of ministers to "devote
themselves to the cause of education, or to fill many a
situation which clergymen now fill connected with
dollars and cents...." Things would be otherwise if more
ministers felt it "an imperious and divine injunction"
to receive the "baptism of the Holy Ghost."[144] A section
entitled "The Old Landmarks" points the clergy (and
laity) back to Wesley who, it is argued, taught what
Palmer now teaches.[145]

Other things about the Methodist Church do not
measure up to the standard of holiness besides its

clergy. There are too few missionaries to the "perishing
heathen." The reason? It is "Because entire devotedness
to God does not more generally prevail."[146] There is too
much preoccupation with the trappings of wealth. Methodists should be like the Quakers who have maintained
their primitive simplicity rather than deeming it
"necessary to build churches with lofty spires, stained
windowglass, and fresco paintings."[147]

Palmer also reflects the growth of a distinctly
holiness "party" in her allusions to a minister in the
cause being labeled by another minister "a man of one
idea" who has holiness as "his hobby." Her judgment is
that the one idea man is the true Methodist.[148] A group
of "true" Methodist ministers, she reveals, meet monthly
at a New York church for a special holiness meeting.
These are "family gatherings" which furnish "a triumph
for truth and holiness on a large scale."[149]

Aside from these indications of some of the changes
taking place in Palmer's own career and in the movement
growing out of it, most of the content of Incidental
Illustrations of the Economy of Salvation is familiar.
There is the mechanistic "spiritual universe" with its
fixed laws of cause and effect.[150] There is the appeal
to the Bible as the sole ground of faith.[151] "Naked
faith" is "omnipotent" as the key to spiritual attainment.[152] Assurance is anchored in entire consecration
upon the "altar which sanctifieth the gift."[153] The
"witness of the Spirit" is described as residing in the
"revealed word" and being appropriated through faith,[154]
while the duty of testifying to the blessing of full
sanctification is pressed as a mandatory "condition" for
obtaining and retaining the blessing.[155]

Not quite so familiar is the pervasiveness of
"Spirit concern." Such concern is certainly not absent

from the earlier writings, surfacing quite prominently in Faith and Its Effects, but nowhere in Palmer's previous work is there the frequency of "Spirit language" or the tendency to describe the end of spirituality in terms of an "enduement with power" which equips one for zealous "soul winning" that one meets in Incidental Illustrations. Routinely, individuals and groups of people are described as needing "the full baptism of the Holy Ghost," and model "saints" are said to have received such a "baptism." Most interestingly, the primary result of Spirit or "Holy Ghost baptism" is a burden for "lost souls" and intense striving for their salvation. For the fully sanctified, "Every thing sinks into insignificance in comparison with the great work of saving sinners."[156] A specific portion of each day should be set apart for this very purpose.[157] Since saving sinners was the "object of Christ's mission to earth," we may be sure it is the central calling of his holy people.[158] Just as the disciples of Jesus received "far greater power" to persuade others to become Christians after they "received the full baptism of the Holy Ghost," so do modern day disciples.[159] Palmer was to press this theme of "Spirit baptized" activism more and more passionately during the last twenty years of her life. It would provide the motivation and rationale for a host of holiness-oriented camp meetings, charitable agencies, city missions, and foreign missionary enterprises, all having the "saving of sinners" as their ultimate purpose, and all staffed by a dedicated cadre of entirely sanctified, "Holy Spirit baptized" Christians.

B. Sanctified Feminism

A lively argument could be joined over what area of Phoebe Palmer's life and work has been most influential in the long run. Certainly her ideas about holiness caught the imagination of religious Americans in her day, making her a widely read author and much sought after "preacher." These ideas gave shape to the "holiness movement" which would command considerable interdenominational attention and support for a time in the mid-nineteenth-century before taking a schismatic turn and producing numerous new "holiness churches." These churches would continue to perpetuate Palmer's ideas on holiness well into the twentieth century. The same could be said of her methods of holiness revivalism. Her Tuesday Meeting, "holiness campaigns," camp meetings focused on holiness, holiness paper (The Guide to Holiness), and the various expressions of her "spirit baptized activism," all gave the holiness movement concrete identity and focus. While they lent to it what strength and influence it had, they also in an ironic way contributed to its departure from the mainstream and its tendency to create holiness "sects," most of which went on propagating themselves by those same methods.

Most recently attention has been directed toward Palmer's connection with the roots of feminism in the nineteenth century. Prompted by the maturing of feminist consciousness and the development of "women's studies," scholars have begun to discover important roots of the feminist impulse in religion.[160] Methodism, and the holiness movement in particular, have been found to be especially fertile ground for "feminist" convictions and practices.[161] Needless to say, Phoebe Palmer looms large in this picture. Typical is the conclusion of Donald Dayton, who writes:

it was...the denominations produced by the
mid-nineteenth-century "holiness revival" that
most consistently raised feminism to a central
principle of church life. This movement largely emerged from the work of Phoebe Palmer.
This neglected figure played a major role in
the Revival of 1857-58 and its extension to
the old world....But in the midst of these
revival efforts she published a 421-page defense of the right of women to preach entitled
The Promise of The Father. This work argued
from the account of Pentecost and became the
fountainhead of innumerable such arguments
developed through the remainder of the nineteenth century and into the twentieth.[162]

The book mentioned, The Promise of the Father, is
different from any other book Phoebe ever wrote. Not
only longer than any other (except for Four Years in the
Old World), it has less to say about "the way of holiness" so carefully detailed in the other writings. It is
a "holiness work, to be sure, but it develops at length
the "Spirit concern" Palmer had been evidencing since at
least the late 1840s, and employs almost exclusively
"Spirit language" in place of the terminology she had
favored in her earlier writings. It also reflects a
completely different way of handling the Bible from the
other works. As has been seen, her typical style of
"exegesis," if it can be called that, was "proof-
texting" with little regard for literary type, context,
or any other consideration that might have a bearing on
interpretation. In The Promise, however, Phoebe employs
some quite sophisticated biblical criticism to undergird
the lengthy argument she develops. The "word of God"
"dictated" by the Holy Spirit to which she has appealed

so often, is now a word <u>conditioned</u> by time and culture
and in need of discriminating examination.

<u>The Promise of the Father</u> articulates convictions
that had been a long time developing as Palmer wrestled
with her own growing prominence in religious circles.
It is apparent that she began her work with no real
rationale for a woman to be doing what she was doing,
except that God seemed to be directing her, opportunities were being given, and she was experiencing "success." But clearly, this was not enough in a time when
women were given very little voice in American churches.
Opposition was bound to arise and to demand sooner or
later some kind of reasoned defense. As Phoebe personally encountered some resistance to her ministry, and came
into contact with other women who told her stories of
being forbidden to give expression to their religious
faith in any significant way, she began to move in the
direction of formulating a clear justification for herself and for these other women.[163] She began to read
with the issue in mind, to collect materials relating to
it, and to take stabs at addressing it in public from
time to time.

By late 1856 she was well on her way to developing
her case, recording in her journal the seed ideas which
would shortly grow into the book. At this time she
intended only an article:

Last night I wrote, as the caption of an
article which I intended to write today, "Has
the spirit of prophecy fallen on woman?"...The
promise of the Father has either been fulfilled, or has not..."And it shall come to
pass, after those days, that I will pour out
my Spirit upon all flesh, and your sons and
your daughters shall prophesy" [Joel 2:28-29;

cf. Acts 2:17-18]. And did one of that waiting
company wait in vain; or did the cloven tongue
of fire appear to all, and sit upon "each"
waiting disciple, irrespective of sex? Surely,
this was that spoken by the prophet Joel; and
thus has the Holy Spirit expressly declared,
through Peter [referring to the account of
Pentecost, Acts 2].

The dispensation of the Spirit was now
entered upon,--the last dispensation previous
to the last glorious appearing of our Lord and
Saviour Jesus Christ.... Male and female were
now one in Christ Jesus. The Spirit now de-
scended alike on all. And they were all filled
with the Holy Ghost, and began to speak as the
Spirit gave utterance...etc., etc.[164]

The "etceteras" were responsible for expanding the
proposed article into a full-fledged book whose publication less than three years later added significantly to
Palmer's already sizeable reputation. Having by then
developed some six different lines of argument, all
leading to the conclusion that it is the intention of
God that women, whom he has equipped to minister in his
Church, be given the right to express their spiritual
gifts, the "Pentecostal argument," sketched here, still
anchored her case.

As Phoebe explained it, the present age is the
"dispensation of the Spirit" which was inaugurated with
signs and wonders (Acts 2), the chief being the power to
"prophesy," which Palmer understood to mean to "herald"
the "glad tidings [of Jesus] to others" or to proclaim
"to every creature...the love of God to men through
Christ Jesus."[165] This power was given to all, both men
and women. In fact, this gift of power and its extension

to female as well as male is "a marked specialty of the Christian [i.e. Holy Spirit's] dispensation."[166]

The presence of female "disciples" at Pentecost and their "baptism by the Holy Ghost" along with male disciples was not accidental. Phoebe makes much of the fact that numerous female "disciples" had gathered in response to Jesus' command to tarry (Luke 24:49), demonstrating once again their exemplary faithfulness to Jesus, a faithfulness which was also shown in his final hours when male followers had all but abandoned him. It was as a reward for such faithfulness that Jesus gave to his female followers the privilege of first carrying the news of his resurrection. She writes,

> Behold the first heralds of the gospel of a risen Saviour! The first commission ever given to mortals, directed from the newly risen Head of the church, is now being given to these affectionate, unflinching female disciples, who, with undaunted step, had followed the Man of Sorrows through all his weary pilgrimage here on earth. Blessed daughters of the Lord Almighty! now is your constancy rewarded.[167]

Subsequently these faithful women, along with the male disciples, were endued with power for the purpose of bearing witness, and Palmer has no doubt that they "preached" and were instrumental publicly in the conversion of three thousand people on the Day of Pentecost. "Not alone did Peter proclaim a crucified risen Saviour, but each one, as the Spirit gave utterance, assisted in spreading the good news...Unquestionably, the whole of this newly-baptized company...male and female, hastened in every direction, under the mighty constrainings of that perfect love that casteth out fear, and great was the company of them that believed."[168]

If this was so then, should it be different now?
she asks. And her answer is a firm "No"; the Pentecostal
pattern is the pattern established for the duration of
the "Spirit's dispensation." Yet things are different,
and because they are the contemporary church is enfee-
bled and condemned. Palmer registers her opinion that
"the attitude of the church in relation to this matter
is most grievous in the sight of her Lord, who has
purchased the whole human family unto himself, and would
fain have every possible agency employed in preaching
the gospel to every creature."[169] Still, given the model
of Pentecost as normative, "If the Spirit of prophecy
fell upon God's daughters, alike as upon his sons in
that day, and they spoke in the midst of that assembled
multitude, as the Spirit gave utterance, on what authority do the angels of the churches restrain the use of
that gift now?" she wonders.[170]

This, of course, leads her into the whole matter of
biblical interpretation since those who oppose female
ministry are bound to throw up biblical passages which
appear to argue against the example of Pentecost. Palmer
must show that such passages are misunderstood. Thus,
she opens her second line of argument, which is argument
from exegesis of specific biblical passages. Palmer
seeks to show that rightly understood, portions of the
Bible typically appealed to by opponents of female ministry, especially parts of certain Pauline letters, do
not conflict with the example of Pentecost. In addition,
she digs for evidence of endorsement of women ministering, even by St. Paul.

Typical is her treatment of 1 Corinthians 14:34-35
("Let your women keep silent in the churches....") which
she insists must be interpreted in the context of its
historical setting. It must also, in accord with a basic

interpretive principle which she holds to tenaciously here (but not elsewhere in her writing), be set alongside all other passages having any bearing on the matter of women ministering, "comparing scripture with scripture," rather than wresting two or three passages out of context and holding them up as normative. "What serious errors in faith and practice," she writes, "have resulted from taking isolated passages dissevered from their proper connections to sustain a favorite theory!"[171] Handled in this way, 1 Corinthians 14:34-35 may be understood as dealing with specific "unseemly practices" in the local congregation which Paul intended to proscribe for that congregation at that time. It was not meant as a general prescription for all, and certainly not for all time. Palmer writes, "Surely it is evident that the irregularities here complained of were peculiar to the church at Corinth, and in fact, we may presume, were not even applicable to other Christian churches of Paul's day, much less Christian churches of the present day, as no such disorders exist."[172] Similarly, 1 Timothy 2:12 ("But I suffer not a woman to teach....") is interpreted as meaning "I suffer not a woman to teach by usurping authority over a man," a state of affairs which apparently existed in some churches in Paul's day, but which Palmer is quite sure exists nowhere in her day, though she does not define what "usurping authority" might mean.[173]

"Comparing scripture with scripture," Phoebe surveys those other passages which seem to relate to female ministry and finds that most all acknowledge and affirm it. There is, for example, Romans 16 where Paul himself recognizes women workers in the church, commending Palmer's namesake, "Phoebe," who is a "servant (or "deacon") of the church." There is also Acts 18:26 where

Priscilla is described as teaching a man, Apollos, the Christian faith. There is the "prophetess," Anna, referred to in Luke 2:36-38. Taking all together, Phoebe concludes that there is no biblical warrant for denying women a place of ministry in the Church. Such has been done only because of the influence of the "Man of Sin" and ignorance.

In deploying this line of argument, Palmer displays considerable awareness of contemporary biblical scholarship and uses her sources in an impressive way. Though she does not know Greek and Hebrew, she does not hesitate to turn to those who do, and uses their insights with care and effectiveness. Her turn to the linguists and commentators seems to be the result of her not being able to sustain the thrust of her "Pentecostal argument" by appeal to the same proof-texting method of most of her holiness treatises. In this she is following the lead of numerous anti-slavery activists who in the couple of decades prior to the Civil War were experimenting with new methodologies for interpreting the Bible which could help them over those sticky passages which appeared to condone slavery. Their tendency was to raise as many technical (historical and linguistic) questions as possible over the historical setting and meaning of the problem passages, and then push to illuminate general "gospel principles" found throughout scripture which were said to condition or even overrule the most intractable isolated passages.[174]

Once this grounding of her case in the Bible is done (always her starting place even though this time the Bible demands considerably more than "common sense" for proper interpretation), Palmer opens a third line of argument, her argument from history. Simply put, God has historically used women to do his work and his people (i.e. now the Church) have, at least at times, recognized and approved this. Among those examples cited by Palmer are the Old Testament "judge" Deborah and prophetess Huldah; the New Testament female disciples of Jesus; the "Samaritan woman," called by Palmer the "first apostle for Christ in Samaria"; "deaconesses" like Phoebe (Romans 16:1), commended by St. Paul; references in sources like Justin Martyr to women bearing witness in the Christian Church in its earliest centuries; and even Palmer's contemporary, Queen Victoria of Britain, the head of the Church of England, as well as the political sovereign of a great empire.

Not surprisingly, in this connection much is made of John Wesley's "conversion" to the practice of women ministering. Initially resistant to the "prophesying" of women despite the model of his own mother who sometimes preached in his father's absence, he became an advocate of women ministering when he saw the practical results garnered by a number of very gifted women in the British Methodist movement.[175]

A fourth line of argument pursued by Palmer is the argument from inconsistent practice in the churches. She holds that the churches which, because of their understanding of the Bible, deny women a voice do not consistently practice what they preach. That is, if women were truly to "keep silent," they could participate in no public worship expression whatsoever, and yet no church goes that far. With evident relish she observes,

> If the apostle intended to enjoin silence in
> an absolute sense, then our Episcopalian
> friends trespass against this prohibition at
> every church service, in calling out the responses of women in company with men in their
> beautiful church liturgy, and when they repeat

our Lord's Prayer in concert with their
brethren. And thus do they trespass against
this prohibition every time they break silence
and unite in holy song in the church of God of
any or every denomination.[176]

There is also an argument from authority in which
Phoebe marshalls the opinions of various church leaders
and scholars, past and present, to show their support of
women in ministry. In part this helps her develop her
other lines of argument which depend upon exegetical and
historical data, but it also serves an independent function in showing that many highly qualified and eminent
persons support the cause she advocates.[177]

Finally, there is the practical or pragmatic argument which forms a central thrust of the book. Phoebe
argues that God is now using women to great effect in
ministry where they are given opportunity or make their
own opening. The largest portion of the four hundred
plus pages, in fact, is taken up with summaries, or
verbatim accounts copied from various sources, of women
effectively conducting ministries of all sorts in
Palmer's day (her own activities not excepted) or the
accomplishments of women in times past. Clearly she
believes that this is one of the strongest cases that
can be made. When one has lifted the model of Pentecost,
debated scripture, and all the rest, the final "proof"
that the "promise of the Father" is being fulfilled by
the Holy Spirit being "poured out upon God's daughters"
enabling them to "prophesy," is "to lay before the
reader instances in confirmation of the fact."[178]

Now, as intensely as Palmer pushes her multi-
faceted case for the ministry of women, it would be easy
to overestimate the scope of her "feminism." Her convictions are strong, but hers is a "sanctified feminism"

which has as its chief concern the right of women to share with men in "churchly" activities, especially the work of evangelism. Even in this, however, though she passionately holds to the equality of women--and even in some sense to the spiritual superiority of women to men--she does not advocate ordination for women or their holding of ecclesiastical office, or even of their filling the role of pastor. "Ordinarily, these are not the circumstances where woman can best serve her generation according to the will of God," she asserts.[179] Woman has a "legitimate sphere of action" which "differs in most cases materially from that of man."[180] The woman is normally to be homemaker and mother, a role that is best "suited to her predilections and her physical and mental structure."[181] Nevertheless, Palmer allows that woman may "occasionally be brought out of the ordinary sphere of action" and assume positions of "high responsibility" in church or state. She is certain that in such cases "the God of Providence will enable her to meet the emergency with becoming dignity, wisdom, and womanly grace."[182]

While Palmer pushes vigorously for churches to allow women to do significant religious work, and for them to recognize the essential equality of women and men before God, she has almost nothing to say about the status of women in society generally. Writing at a time when the "woman issue" was just heating up in the United States, the Seneca Falls meeting which inaugurated the organized women's movement having been held less than a dozen years before the publication of The Promise, Palmer is quick to disassociate herself from it. In the first few sentences of the book she assures her readers that her concern is not "Women's Rights." At the end of the first chapter she underscores this by insisting that she is not an advocate of "change in the social or domestic relation" of women, being "not disposed to feel that she is burdened with wrong in this direction." Still, the wary reader might have cause to wonder about Palmer's assurances, given the caveat, "Yet we do not doubt that some reforms contemplated in recent movements may, in various respects, be decidedly advantageous."[183] By this Palmer establishes the fact that her book is not a brief for the women's movement, that on that matter her own sympathies lie in a conservative direction, yet that she feels that the movement is not altogether without merit. Her concern is religious, but even here she will not take up the volatile issues of women preaching "technically so-called" (i.e. women serving as "preachers" or designated clergy) or the ordination of women, leaving these "for those whose ability and tastes may better fit them for discussions of this sort."[184]

The "feminism" she proposes, then, is a carefully circumscribed "feminism." However, it is clear that her ideas, cautiously hedged around though they may be in The Promise of the Father, have revolutionary possibilities, and did in fact contribute to an expanded role for women first in the church and the eventual opening up of the very issues Palmer herself skirted. This in turn strengthened the hand of women seeking feminine equality in the larger society. It should be remembered, however, that her overarching concern was not any sort of "feminism" per se, but rather a "laity for the times," men and women together, entirely consecrated to God and endowed through the "baptism of the Holy Ghost" with power to "spread the good news," make converts, and carry on myriad sorts of religious work.

C Holiness in Action

It is quite clear that for Phoebe Palmer holiness was not simply an abstract ideal of "perfection." It was a tangible experience one has, datable in its concreteness and specificity. It is also a way of life, equally concrete, which grows from experience and the divine-human "covenant" which is central to it.

The shape of the life of holiness is suggested by Palmer's earliest definition of "Gospel holiness": "That state of the soul which is attained by the believer when...body and soul, with every redeemed faculty, are ceaselessly presented, a living sacrifice to God." It is also "entire salvation from sin; a redemption from all iniquity" which brings to the believer "wisdom, power, and love, with every other grace...."[185] According to this, the life of holiness will need to continually demonstrate one's presentation to God of body and soul-- i.e. that one is entirely consecrated to God and his purposes. It will also need to display one's separation from sin ("entire salvation from sin") and possession of wisdom, power, and love. Though Palmer nowhere comes near articulating a full system of ethics, she does often enough address certain specifics pertaining to the life of holiness to give a fair idea of the way in which she believed each of these areas should be discharged.

1. Body and Soul Ceaselessly Presented

For one, the entirely consecrated person will devote time and energy to good works of every description. Palmer's "activism" and the fact that it grows out of her system of religious thought has been referred to already. Here is one of its sources. Entirely sanctified persons are those who have given up every claim of control over their own lives and have placed it at God's

disposal. Because this dedication typically takes place
in a churchly context, it is not surprising that an
important expression of it will be unselfish devotion to
church work. Here Palmer advocated conscientiously
attending and participating in worship services, teaching Sunday School, leading classes (in Methodism), inviting people to church, actively supporting all evangelistic and missionary efforts, and in general being
willing to serve in whatever way one is asked. She
herself, as has been seen, did all of these things, and
so provided a ready example of what she advocated for
others.

A another source of Palmer's "sanctified activism" is
her belief that "holiness" brings with it divine power
which enables one to be "useful." Entire consecration is
a "preparation for usefulness." The "full baptism of the
Holy Ghost" thrusts the believer out to do "the work of
establishing [God's] kingdom on earth." Holiness is "the
promised endowment of power" which, above all else, pre-
pares believers "for the work of bringing sinners to
Jesus."[186]

A special concern of Phoebe's was missions, both
"home" and "foreign." Blessed with abundant means, she
and Walter contributed generously to mission work, even
initiating at least one pioneer missionary effort
through their promise to partially underwrite costs.
This was the first Methodist mission to China. Interested for some time in seeing a Methodist presence
there, Phoebe had agitated among the Board of Managers
of the General Missionary Society with little success,
when she hit upon the idea of pledging money for the
project herself, and challenging twenty others to match
the pledge. The idea caught fire and the first missionaries were sent out in 1847.[187] The Palmers also tried

the same tactic in pushing for a mission in Palestine,
believing that the "pure uncompromising principles of
Methodism" ought to be planted in this "once so favoured
portion of God's vineyard."[188]

This special interest in foreign missionary work by
the Palmers stemmed from Walter's early consideration of
employing his medical skills as a foreign missionary (he
had at one time also considered a career as a clergyman), and Phoebe's initial resistance to the idea. This
eventuated in a kind of "agreement" with God in which it
seemed to her that she was given important work to do in
America in return for a pledge that she would execute
that work with missionary zeal and always be diligent in
supporting the efforts of those whom God did choose for
foreign service. Recounting this, she wrote, "my career
has ever since been influenced by these resolves."[189]

These resolves found some expression in Phoebe's
support of "home missions," that branch of evangelism
concerned with starting new churches at "home" which was
so vitally important to the welfare of all of the American denominations in the nineteenth century as they
tried to find ways to cope with population growth, the
opening of new territories, immigration, and urbanization. Phoebe was active in the Ladies' Home Missionary
Society of the Methodist Episcopal Church from early
adulthood and continued her participation even after
becoming a nationally known revivalist. She was at the
center of a number of projects undertaken by this voluntary religious female association, including the founding of the Five Points Mission, and the establishment of
a mission to Jews.[190] In addition, the Palmers in 1848
transferred their membership from the prominent Allen
Street Methodist Episcopal Church to the Norfolk Street

Church, a struggling "home mission," to lend "hands on" aid.[191]

The "Jewish Mission" Phoebe crusaded for is an especially interesting case. Sharing the belief of most American Christians of the time in a literal second coming of Christ, she thought this event to be imminent, though it could not be predicted with exactness. Preceding it, however, would be a great conversion of Jews to Christianity (a "removing of the vail [sic] from the heart of Israel"), a sign of which she thought she saw in the crowds of Jewish immigrants thronging into New York City, ripe for "harvesting" by religiously awakened and mobilized Christians.[192] To reach these potential converts she organized a "Ladies Jewish Association and Industrial Tea Meeting" and set about raising funds and laying plans, using her imposing influence (this was 1854 at the very height of her revivalist career) to gather support. After debating such questions as whether to employ a "converted Jew" or a "converted Gentile" as missionary (a Gentile was chosen), the mission commenced in the Palmers' home, using facilities vacated by the Tuesday Meeting for the Promotion of Holiness scant hours before. In spite of Phoebe's backing, however, the "mission" lasted less than one year, though it was later resuscitated under other leadership.[193]

As part of the effort, the Palmers actually "adopted" a Jewish youth, Leopold Solomon Palmer, whom they referred to as "our Jewish boy," and whom they intended to train to be a Christian minister. Evidencing no awareness of the difficulties involved in such a move, they took him into their home for a time before sending him away to school. Returning after one term for vacation, he was "enticed" by his relatives who had been "lurking around" the Palmers' home trying to see him,

and went away with them, never to return. In all, this
"adoption" lasted less than three months, leaving the
Palmers disappointed and somewhat bitter. Phoebe wrote
to friends: "He never returned. Doubtless he apostasized
from the Christian faith....He left his Bible and his
God." She also voiced her fear that the incident, if
widely known, might "detract from the sympathy enlisted
for the Jewish cause."[194]

The Five Points Mission was a much happier story
for Phoebe than the Jewish mission. Developing a concern
for the slum area known as Five Points, and convinced it
was an ideal spot for the efforts of the Ladies' Home
Missionary Society, Phoebe began a three year long campaign to sell her idea. Rebuffed by those who felt that
money spent in the area would be money thrown away, she
kept up her agitation until the needed funds were made
available and a mission undertaken. From the beginning
its scale was considerable, the first large building
housing a chapel, facilities for the minister/director,
schoolrooms, baths, and apartments for twenty needy
families to be let free of charge. This was eventually
augmented by a Five Points House of Industry employing
five hundred persons, a day school, and various other
social welfare programs. Phoebe writes in 1853 of having
attended a Thanksgiving dinner at Five Points at which
donated toys and clothing had been distributed to "between three and four hundred...children of the poor and
vile." Another time she mentions the nightly religious
services held at the mission and the "dozen to twenty"
persons who typically responded to the minister's invitation to pray for salvation "in that place which so
recently was the heart of Satan's den." Begun in 1850,
this mission was almost certainly the starting place for
American Protestant institutional work in the slums.[195]

Other areas that received Phoebe's attention and
energy were tract distribution, visitation of the poor
and sick, visitation of prisoners, and orphanage work.
Tract distribution was the earliest of these involvements, beginning in the late 1830s and continuing into
the 1850s by which time she was a revivalist of national
repute. This work brought her into contact with assorted
Deists, "skeptics," "Romanists," inebriates, and "wholly
backslidden" professors of religion, whom she sought to
convert.[196]

Tract work, since it took her into the heart of the
city, also exposed her to numerous indigents and poor
families whose material needs could not be met by a
religious tract. Always primarily interested in saving
souls, her encounter with the poor sensitized Palmer to
their other needs and drew a compassionate response. She
began taking gifts of money, food, and clothing on her
rounds, and eventually affiliated with the New York
Female Assistance Society for the Relief and Religious
Instruction of the Sick Poor, for whom she served as a
"visitor," and whose corresponding secretary she became
in 1847, filling that office until leaving for England
in 1859.[197]

Despite her advocacy of ministry to the poor, even
her contention that such was "primarily the glory of
Methodism" in its founding days and ought to remain its
"object of highest ambition," Palmer was quite conservative in her social views.[198] She believed that poverty
could not be eliminated: "There are gradations in society which always have been, and doubtless always will
be, till the end of time."[199] Some are divinely appointed as masters and some as "servants," else "why
were advices suited to those in these different relations given by the express dictation of the Spirit?"[200]

In a sense, the poor exist as an occasion for the rich to express their beneficence, for "the Dispenser of all good could say, Be ye warmed and be ye clothed, to every destitute being throughout the world, or could feed them by the hand of angels...if it were not to test the fidelity of those to whom he has intrusted a sufficiency to meet this object."[201]

Riches are "a blessing," if "rightly used." Right use means holding them "as sacred responsibilities, for which an account of stewardship must be rendered." Those who are "ever denouncing the rich, merely because they are so," are simply those who are envious because they are "not possessed of the same means."[202]

Unlike her visitation of the poor and sick, Phoebe's visitation of female prisoners in the infamous Tombs prison was carried out without benefit of any organization. She often went alone. Beginning in the 1840s, she continued this work until at least the late 1850s. She thought the inmates to be generally more receptive to her exhortations to turn to God than "the gospel hardened sinners which we often meet within our fine city churches."[203]

If all of this, combined with frequent travel, writing, overseeing the Tuesday Meeting, and caring for a family were not enough, there was always orphanage work to look after. Phoebe helped to support a "Home for the Friendless," putting her substantial reputation to use in securing permanent homes for many orphans. In at least one instance the Palmers took a homeless infant into their own home (Phoebe was 45 years old at the time), hoping for a time to keep the child. They finally thought better of it, however, and placed the child elsewhere. Named "Johnny Palmer N--" by his new mother, Phoebe was still keeping track of him in 1868, by which time he was sixteen years of age and "a fine, healthy boy, in his young manhood."[204]

Phoebe's thoughts on orphanage work are indicative of her view of charitable or benevolent, as well as church work, generally. It is the Christian's--especially the entirely sanctified Christian's--duty to carry on such work since it is explicitly commanded in the Bible. Reflecting on her efforts to place orphans she wrote, "The fact is, few really look upon it as a religious duty to adopt fatherless children, and when addressed on that subject, act, and speak with as little idea of religious responsibility, as though the Scriptures were wholly silent on the theme...God surely says, He will preserve these fatherless ones, but by whom will it be done? He does not send angels here to nurse them."[205]

2. Redemption From All Iniquity

Not only does the life of holiness entail for Palmer the devotion of time, energy, and money to good works, and a divine empowering for the task, but it also demands that one demonstrate one's "entire salvation from sin" by avoiding evil of every sort. As the examination of her major publications has shown, this tends to mean for her eschewing certain personal habits like drinking alcoholic beverages, and "fashion" in the way one dresses.

At the top of the list is dress and the obligation of the entirely sanctified Christian to dress with modesty and simplicity in a way which does not ape the "fashionable exterior" valued by the "world." Even the sincere seeker after holiness who has not yet attained "the blessing" is to put aside "fashion" as a part of the process of renunciation which leads to entire consecration.[206] Her general views are well stated in a posthumous piece in The Guide to Holiness:

> The wearing of gold, when the object is mere adornment is wrong. The Bible plainly forbids it. "Whose adorning let not be the wearing of gold and pearls and costly array" [a combining of 1 Timothy 2:9 and 1 Peter 3:3]. The Bible also forbids conformity to the world, which I conceive to mean a fashionable exterior, which, certainly, ill becomes the gravity which should distinguish the Christian lady....In treating on this subject, I wish to be governed by the Bible mode. If we may only succeed in getting the heart right, then we may hope to see dress, and every other particular, transformed by the renewing of the mind. But if the heart be not fully transformed, to the degree it is not, then all these minor matters are looked at through the wrong medium. But after all within is made conformable to the will of God, then we may hope to see all without conformable to His will; for "out of the heart are the issues of life" [Proverbs 4:23]. Dress may be considered an index to the mind. And how unseemly in the eye of God, angels, and men, that a hallowed temple, which, through the Spirit, has been made a habitation for a God, should be adorned as though it were set apart as a heathen temple for the God of this world, with gold and pearls and costly array. The body of the believer is a temple for the Holy Ghost. And what agreement hath the temple of God with idols? [2 Corinthians 6:16].... A lovely,

pure, simple and uncostly attire, to my mind, answers the Scriptural idea of dress.[207]

As usual, her authority is the Bible, and the whole paragraph is laced with biblical language.

Phoebe applied the principles set forth here without compromise. She would frequently approach the seeker after holiness, or one professing holiness, whose dress did not seem to her to properly express sanctity, and attempt to convince them of their error. On at least one occasion, which one suspects may well have been duplicated many times over, a pious mother requested Palmer to talk to her daughter about her jewelry. In this particular case, at least, she was not able to get the girl to give it up and she concluded that by this act the girl had refused to "serve the Lord with a perfect heart and a willing mind."[208] Another time she confronted a close friend who had been entirely sanctified under her ministry years before, but who had begun to "walk a little after the fashion of the world" as "the high noon of worldly prosperity began to beam upon her."[209] Though always concerned about dress as an "index to the mind" (it is an important issue already in the 1845 Entire Devotion to God), from the late 1850s on Phoebe began to make this, along with teetotalism, a more prominent theme in her revivalistic preaching. A curious result was that the offering plates passed at her meetings sometimes contained items of jewelry placed there by women brought under conviction by her explicit condemnations.[210]

Though dress drew the greatest attention from Phoebe as an area in which the entirely sanctified believer must be careful not to compromise with sin, other things were matters of concern with her as well. The growing popularity of "church fairs" or "festivals" in her day troubled her. She believed the background music commonly played at such events conditioned young people to want to dance, another activity she considered sinful, and that the fairs generally expressed too much "conformity to the spirit and usages of the world."[211] She disapproved of "religious fiction," holding it to be essentially a lie, mixing the truth of religion with a fictitious garb. This she saw, as undermining trust in the truthfulness of any religious literature. She also saw it as a "halfway house" leading to theater attendance, another proscribed habit. Phoebe's views on this led to the rupture of what appears to have been quite a promising friendship with Harriet Beecher Stowe, who along with her sister, Catherine Beecher, had read appreciatively Palmer's The Way of Holiness. Disapproving of Stowe's Uncle Tom's Cabin and the fact that it became a play, as well as the writings of her brother, Henry Ward Beecher, Palmer became a harsh critic of the pair, eventually accusing them of "aiding the kingdom of Satan, amazingly."[212]

"Entire salvation from sin" also meant for Palmer complete abstinence from alcohol. This did not create much friction for her with American Methodists, who along with many other American Protestants were enthusiastic supporters of the growing temperance/abstinence movement in the nineteenth century, but it did cause her problems in Britain, as has been seen.[213] In America Palmer applauded the success of the Temperance Crusade and promoted the use of Dr. Welch's "unfermented wine" for communion, an innovation for strictly teetotal Christians.[214]

Other areas of temptation demanding careful vigilance from those professing holiness might include being impatient with one's children (one will "gather its bitter fruits in eternity"), "unkindly chiding the ser-

vants," living ostentatiously ("making a display of
folly and fashion"), evidencing an "unhallowed haste to
be rich," gossiping and backstabbing, or, for the minister, calling attention to himself and his abilities.[215]

In all of this Palmer is for the most part simply
reinforcing traditional standards of Methodism which
held that those seeking after holiness were to be cir-
cumspect in all things. Even in her strong views on
dress, she was echoing John Wesley who laid down specific guidelines for his followers in his Advice to the
People Called Methodists With Regard to Dress.[216] More
significantly, perhaps, Palmer was not alone in her
concerns even in nineteenth-century American Methodism,
although her single-minded advocacy of holiness and her
unique "way" set her apart from many of her co-religion-
ists. Her chief doctrinal critic, Hiram Mattison, no
appreciator of Palmer's views on holiness, was indistin-
guishable from her in the matter of personal ethics, as
indicated by both the content and title of his 1867
tract, Popular Amusements: An Appeal to Methodists in
Regard to the Evils of Card-Playing, Billiards, Dancing,
Theatre-Going, Etc.[217]

3. Sanctification, Society, and Politics

As intensely concerned with "consecrated usefulness" and individual morality as Phoebe Palmer was, it
would be natural to suppose that she also entertained
strong views on social and political issues of her day.
In fact, however, she rarely commented at all on the
public issues of her time. When she did, her comments
were usually cast in terms of individual morality. A
vivid example is her reflection on the assassination of
Abraham Lincoln, which occurred not long after her return from England. She refers vaguely to the "lessons

which we must not fail to learn, if we would not have
something more terrific befal (sic) us," but is most
explicit at the point of questioning the propriety of
Lincoln's having visited the theater. For her, that was
the central issue. She writes, "Would that our dear
President had not received his death wound in the
theater.... What a noble good man was our dear President, but I fear he was not abiding under the shadow of
the Almighty, when he went to the theater that sad
night....Had he remained at the 'White House,' might he
not have been shielded by the shadow of the Almighty?
from the attack of the assassin? So we are prone to
think."[218]

On slavery and the Civil War, Phoebe had very
little to say. Wheatley holds that she abhorred slavery,
and clearly she did, but yet she never raised her hand
to combat it in any concrete fashion. While her fellow
perfectionists at Oberlin, Asa Mahan and Charles Finney,
were in the thick of the abolitionist movement along
with many other American evangelicals, Palmer was silent
on the issue. Even Timothy Smith, in his helpful study of
the relation of nineteenth-century revivalism and social
reform in which Palmer is a central heroine, has to
confess that the only major revivalists who did not join
the abolitionist march were the "Methodist perfectionists surrounding Phoebe Palmer," and that these were
"the architects of the policy of silence which later
became the regret of Northern Methodism." He is quite
right in asserting that the "other-worldly and spiritual
aspects" of Palmer's quest for holiness won out over any
impulse actively to engage social evils and that, "Although early to take part in the relief of the widowed,
orphaned, and imprisoned or in any other task which
required the exercise of compassion," she and her fol-

lowers "were laggards in whatever demanded stern attacks on persons and institutions."[219]

Phoebe's obviously strong feelings on slavery may be seen in her few comments on the Civil War, which are interesting for another reason as well. While one might expect her to manifest a narrow, Northern partisan view of the war as did many Northern religious leaders, she actually comes much closer to the "transcendent" view of the war articulated notably by Lincoln, Philip Schaff, and Horace Bushnell, which saw no party as innocent and the whole nation as suffering together under a wise and just Providence.[220] From England to her confidante, Mrs. Bishop Hamline, she wrote,

> I do not doubt but the God of nations has long
> had a controversy with us on account of this
> national sin [of slavery], and an awful con-
> viction has rested on my mind that thousands,
> if not tens of thousands, of those who are
> flesh of our flesh, and bone of our bone, may
> yet fall, if we do not, as a nation, hasten to
> do the thing that is right before God and
> man....If God has had a controversy with [the
> South] for rejecting the right, He has always
> had a controversy with [the North], in so long
> winking at, and often participating in the
> wrong. How cruel was the passage of the Fugi-
> tive Slave law bill, and what atrocities have
> been permitted by the North under its sanc-
> tion. It makes my heart sick to dwell on the
> sad details of this war, and the thought of
> how much longer we may keep the hand of God
> upon us by our tardiness as a nation....[221]

It would seem that Palmer's profound sense of guilt for "injustice winked at" may reflect her own regret for being absorbed with other causes and issues and failing to speak out in any way against slavery.

A part of the slavery controversy and the events leading to Civil War was the fragmenting of many American religious bodies, Palmer's Methodist Episcopal Church among them. This splitting of the churches, which occurred during the 1830s and '40s, was a significant harbinger of the political division of the nation which was to follow. For the Methodists, the General Conference of 1844 was one of the most important of their entire history, as it resulted in a nearly century-long division between Northern and Southern Methodists. yet to read Palmer, one would never know that such momentous events were transpiring, much less very nearly in her own parlor! During the conference several prominent clergymen who were in the middle of the battles raging in the sessions at Green Street Church either boarded with the Palmers or were entertained in their home. The issues of the conference could hardly have escaped such an interested observer of the affairs of the church as Phoebe was, and yet, she only thought it important to mention that the atmosphere created by so many clerical notables was "impregnated with love and holiness."[222] Her main interest in the conference was the fact that two of her close confidants, Leonidas Hamline and Edmund Janes, were elected bishops of the church. She saw their election as a major victory for the perfectionist cause.[223]

As for the role of the sanctified in politics generally, Palmer again has little to say, though what she does say tends to strengthen the "otherworldly" at the expense of concrete involvement in the political process. She urges Christians to vote for "God-fearing" candidates (though she gives no criteria for determining who these may be), but at the same time also cautions against "engaging in political strife." She seems to be suggesting that Christians support "God-fearing" candidates, but that they not be such candidates themselves. The appropriate activity for sanctified Christians is not to wield power, but to pray for those who do.[224]

CHAPTER V
PHOEBE PALMER AND THE DOCTRINE
OF CHRISTIAN PERFECTION:
CONTINUITIES AND DISCONTINUITIES

The Phrase "entire devotion to God," which became
the title of one of Phoebe Palmer's books, appropriately
describes her life and work. The pivotal event in
Phoebe's personal history was the attainment of "holiness" through the entire devotion of herself to God and
his purposes. By this definite, datable act she believed
she was set apart to God in an unconditional sense; she
was "entirely sanctified" and hence freed from intentional sinning and filled with perfect (unadulterated,
pure) love for God and humankind. Convinced that such a
state was the ultimate goal of Christian spirituality,
she had sought it with great intensity, and, once finding
it, protected and nurtured it with a passion some might
regard as obsessive. Convinced also that holiness was
not optional, some sort of supererogatory achievement
for a spiritual elite, but the obligation of every
believer here and now, she gave herself unstintingly to
helping others find it. Her efforts took her from sitting room and parlor into the public arena and a pioneering career as an author, preacher, and effective
champion of religious causes. Her whole life from 1837
on was thus wrapped up with "holiness" and all that she
understood it to involve.

This passionate commitment to the pursuit and
attainment of holiness is best understood in terms of
the theological and ecclesiastical tradition in which

Palmer's religious sensibilities were molded. A child of Methodism, which had been organized as a church less than twenty-five years at the time she was born, Phoebe was a very near heir of John Wesley, who, delineating "The Character of a Methodist," had described him as one who "continually presents his soul and 'body a living sacrifice, holy, acceptable to God'; entirely and without reserve devoting himself, all he has, all he is, to His glory."[1] Wesley's ideal "Methodist" was shaped by his own religious pilgrimage which took on focus and energy when in young adulthood he became convinced "of the absolute impossibility of being half a Christian," renounced a simply birthright religion, and began to pursue "scriptural Christianity" which he conceived of as something demanding and transforming of all of one's energies and faculties. "I resolved to dedicate all my life to God," he wrote, "all my thoughts and words and actions; being thoroughly convinced, there was no medium; but that every part of my life (not some only) must either be a sacrifice to God, or myself, that is, in effect, the devil."[2] The end result of this, Wesley believed, would be the attainment of "Scripture perfection," which he sometimes also called "entire sanctification," "holiness," or "the second blessing," a state of spirituality marked by "pure love filling the heart, and governing all the words and actions."[3] The "Methodist" societies and bands Wesley organized all over Britain during the middle and late decades of the eighteenth-century were made up of Christian believers who desired to join Wesley in his quest for the "perfection" held out by "scriptural Christianity."

The quest for perfection given impetus by Wesley in eighteenth century England was transplanted to North America early on by Methodist lay immigrants who were

part of the general British and European migration
across the Atlantic to the "new world." Set in North
American soil by the 1760s, Methodist societies matured
quickly and bore fruit. Planted initially under the
aegis of the Church of England, as were Wesley's first
British societies, they were numerous and vital enough
by the time of the Revolutionary War to have acquired a
life of their own. With the near demise of the Church of
England through the war years due to its close identification with the English Crown, the societies cut themselves adrift from it and forged a new link among themselves, bringing into being the Methodist Episcopal
Church in 1784. Like the parent societies, the new
church flourished in American soil and soon outstripped
not only the British movement but all other American
religious bodies as well, becoming before 1850 the
single largest American Protestant denomination. Even in
its early success, however, Methodism was a church with
the soul of a society. Its self identity was shaped by
its origins as a small movement for elevated piety
within a national church. This is reflected in Bishops
Coke and Asbury who in 1798 declared the purpose of the
church to be "to raise a holy people," adding "we will
have a holy people or none."[4]

This Methodist quest for perfection, though perpet-
uating the central concern of Wesley and his British
societies, could not long remain unaffected by the distinctive American environment in which it was now growing. Transplanted from one environment into a new one,
as were all seventeenth-and eighteenth-century American
churches, Methodism inevitably, along with them, came to
be shaped by the new environment. In responding to
different forces and reflecting different experiences,
the American movement took on an identity quite separate

from that of British Wesleyanism. In common with other
American churches it developed an "American style" which
set it apart.[5] Using a different metaphor, Thomas A.
Langford has described the Wesleyan movement as a stream
which, flowing through different terrain, has taken on
the coloration of that particular terrain.[6] American
terrain resulted in American coloration.

This is important for understanding Phoebe Palmer's
significance as a religious leader and her special
contribution to the Methodist quest for perfection. The
fact that she was an American Methodist living in the
nineteenth century fashioned her understanding and
articulation of holiness, and even her public career, in
substantial ways. Hers was an innovative and, one might
say, uniquely American contribution to the Wesleyan
tradition. Melvin Dieter has described the American
holiness movement as a "wedding of the American mind,
prevailing revivalism, and Wesleyan perfectionism...."[7]
It is argued here that it was Palmer who presided over
this wedding and that an examination of her relationship
with the involved parties is necessary for a full understanding of Palmer herself, as well as the tradition
which nurtured her and the movement she helped to
launch.

A. From Wesley to Palmer:
The Methodist Theological Heritage
1. The Formulators
Since Palmer was not a theologian in the general
sense, but rather a preacher of one idea who preached
that idea--holiness--in both word and in print, it is
not necessary to survey the whole of the Methodist
theological heritage. It was the concept of Christian
Perfection which captured her.

Of course Christian Perfection was a central theme running through the Wesleyan tradition from the beginning. Several commentators have in fact identified it as the distinguishing feature of that tradition.[8] Wesley himself traced the beginnings of Methodism to the time in 1729 when he and his brother, Charles, "saw they could not be saved without holiness, followed after it, and incited others so to do," and he always held that the concept of Christian Perfection which grew from the following after holiness was "the grand depositum which God has lodged with the people called Methodists."[9]

As Wesley developed his idea of "perfection," he described it as being related to sanctification. He taught that in justification one receives divine forgiveness for sin and is "accounted as righteous" before God, while in sanctification one is actually made righteous by the grace of God. In stating this much Wesley was saying nothing with which the Reformed Protestantism of his day could not agree. However, Weslely said much more than this. It was his contention that not only did a process of sanctification occur gradually throughout the life of a Christian from the time of justification, but that the process could be "entire," or completed in some sense, at a particular moment in life prior to the point of death. Early on he thought this moment would be very near the end of one's life, but later taught that it might occur at any time after justification.

The "completion" point would simply be that moment in which, by faith, believers would trust God to expel the remains of sin from their heart by imparting Godlike love, which would bind them unreservedly to God as well as expressing itself through them as a holy affection toward humankind. In late career Wesley summarized his view of the matter by maintaining "(1) That Christian perfection is that love of God and our neighbor, which implies deliverance from all sin. (2) That this is received merely by faith. (3) That it is given instantaneously, in one moment. (4) That we are to expect it, not at death, but every moment; that now is the accepted time, now is the day of this salvation."[10]

Despite the fact that Wesley definitely stressed the instantaneous quality of Christian Perfection, he did not ignore or deny the role of process. He believed that a steady growth into holiness began at the moment of justification and continued throughout life so long as the believer strove earnestly to acquire and express Christian graces. He also held that after the "crisis" of entire sanctification there continued to be growth in grace, but now even more rapid and marked than before due to the purity of intention made possible by the absence of sin.[11] Thus for Wesley, Christian Perfection was both instantaneous and gradual.

Though he declared "all our preachers should make a point of preaching perfection to believers, constantly, strong, and explicitly; and all believers should mind this one thing, and continually agonize for it," Wesley did not hold that a believer who lacked this "second blessing" was a second-class Christian or no Christian at all.[12] He cautioned against considering the justified but unperfected to be "merely justified," and dismissed the notion "that every one is a child of the devil, till he is thus renewed [made perfect] in love." "On the contrary," he wrote, "whoever has 'a sure confidence in God, that, through the merits of Christ, his sins are forgiven,' he is a child of God, and, if he abide in Him, an heir of all the promises."[13]

As to attaining "perfection," Wesley taught that just as for justification, the _sine qua non_ is faith.

This was a major discovery of Wesley's own pilgrimage in which he moved from seeking after holiness by works to accepting holiness by faith. "Faith is the only condition of sanctification, exactly as it is of justification."[14] By "faith" Wesley meant "both a supernatural 'evidence' of God and the things of God, a kind of spiritual 'light' exhibited to the soul, and a supernatural 'sight' or perception thereof." By "supernatural" Wesley meant that this did not arise naturally from fallen human nature; it resulted instead from God awakening otherwise moribund human spiritual capacities in order to rouse human beings and draw them to him. Thus, faith is for Wesley a "supernatural faculty" given to the seeker after God and also a "conviction" concerning the things of God which arises from the exercise of that faculty. The primary conviction which faith receives or "produces" is that "God was in Christ reconciling the world unto himself" (2 Cor. 5:19) and that "Christ loved _me_ and gave himself for _me_." This conviction brings with it another aspect of faith which is "confidence, trust, reliance, adherence, or whatever else it be called" in the object of faith; namely the Christ.[15] By the operation of this faith one comes both to justification (being declared right with God, which is the first step of "salvation") and sanctification (being made holy or God-like, which is "full salvation").

But the exercise of sanctifying faith would not just "happen," according to Wesley. It would occur in the context of faithful "waiting" upon God, involving "works of piety" like public and private prayer, receiving Communion, searching the scriptures, attending preaching, and fasting, and "works of mercy" such as feeding the hungry, visiting those that are in prison, and instructing the ignorant.[16] This "faithful waiting" would eventually lead to a conviction of one's "proneness to evil," even though justified, of "the still continuing tendency of the flesh to lust against the spirit," and hence to a "repentance consequent upon justification" and the exercise of sanctifying faith, which brings "pur[ity] from every spot of sin." "This is the way wherein God hath appointed his children to wait for complete salvation."[17]

For the sincere seeker after holiness, then, Wesley thought that perfection would come in due time. His study of the Bible and careful attention to the experience of persons testifying to having been "made perfect in love" convinced him that there was a certain sequence to the process, and that certain means were helpful in negotiating the path, but the pattern he prescribed was always general, rather than specific, and always open to revision on the basis of experience. John L. Peters is quite right in asserting that "while Wesley was insistent on the pursuit of a definite goal--'holiness of heart and life'--he held no brief for orthodoxy of method.... With Wesley the manner of attaining perfect love was as a ladder the nature and length of which might well vary with the differences which are inescapable in human personality. It was not a Procrustean bed into which all believers must be forced."[18] Thus, "while it may be possible to discover and prescribe certain aids to spiritual progress, Wesley felt that it was also wise to remember that 'God is tied down to no rules'....He concluded that 'there is an irreconcilable variability in the operations of the Holy Spirit on the souls of men."[19]

The same flexibility also marked Wesley's use of terminology to describe the "second work of grace." He

employed various terms, many of them interchangeably, to
refer to different aspects of the experience, causing no
little confusion among his critics, and even his followers on occasion."[20] Advising the Methodists on properly
testifying to holiness, Wesley wrote, "Avoid all magnif-
icent, pompous words; indeed, you need give it no general name; neither perfection, sanctification, the
second blessing, nor the having attained. Rather speak
of the particulars which God has wrought for you."[21]

Along with John Wesley, a major architect of the
Methodist theological heritage was Wesley's contemporary
and designated successor, John Fletcher (1729-1785).
Called by some "the Theologian of Methodism," Fletcher
was the first to develop a distinctively "Wesleyan"
theological position, one which went considerably beyond
Wesley's assorted sermons, tracts, and letters. Also,
Fletcher was a man of exemplary character, being widely
considered a "saint" and an outstanding model of the
Christian Perfection he and Wesley taught. Wesley considered him unequalled in piety, describing him as "one
so inwardly and outwardly devoted to God; and I scarce
expect to find another such on this side of eternity."[22]
Joseph Benson's _Life_ of Fletcher was widely popular in
both England and America for many years following its
first appearance in 1804.[23]

In his _Checks to Antinomianism_ (1775), Fletcher
addressed the relationship between grace and human freedom. Arguing against those in the Methodist camp who
espoused Calvinist-Augustinian views of the matter, he
articulated a "Methodist Arminianism" which attempted to
balance affirmation of salvation by grace with an affirmation of human freedom to respond to divine grace with
either acceptance or rejection.[24] In the minds of many,
Fletcher succeeded so well in this that he "settled

forever all the questions of the Calvinian controversy
...for many a long year, Methodist preachers drew their
arguments and illustrations from his invaluable
Checks...."[25]

Though Fletcher's concerned himself with much more
than Welsey's distinctive doctrine of Christian Perfection, he did write at some length on it, fashioning his
last Check to Antinomianism as a "Polemical Essay on the
Twin Doctrines of Christian Imperfection and A Death
Purgatory" (usually referred to as his "Treatise on
Christian Perfection.")[26] In this he essentially reiter-
ated Wesley's views, but also added a few new twists.
One of these was his strong defense of the word "perfection" to describe the state of holiness Wesley and his
followers believed to be attainable in this life. Wesley
had defended the word, too, believing it to be biblical,
but allowed considerable flexibility. Fletcher, on the
other hand, filling the role of controversialist for the
Wesleyans, insisted on the word as a kind of "test" of
faithfulness to the cause. Citing Mark 8:38 and Luke
9:26 he wrote, "Now the words...'Be ye perfect,' etc.,
being Christ's own words, we dare no more be ashamed of
them, than we dare desire him to be ashamed of us in the
great day [of judgment]. Thus much for the word perfection."[27]

Fletcher also added to the Wesleyan scheme a new
cluster of ideas centering on the biblical account of
the day of Pentecost and relating sanctification (especially the aspect of "entire sanctification") to the
experience of Jesus' disciples on that day. He held that
in being "filled" or "baptized" with the Holy Ghost,
they were in fact entirely sanctified. He was the first
to make this identification.[28] Wesley, though he never
actually repudiated Fletcher's new way of regarding

sanctification, did not find it to his liking and continued to use other images and terms. Though this does not appear to have been an important issue in the eighteenth century, it did suggest some subtly different implications in each man's view of sanctification.[29] Fletcher, although he taught that sanctification had both a gradual and an instantaneous aspect, as did Wesley, in his development of "Pentecostal" images and concepts, tended to shift the balance toward the instantaneous. This is so even though he clearly believed one might have multiple "baptisms with the Holy Spirit," for while one might have a succession of "effusions of the sanctifying Spirit," each of these would be an instantaneous, momentary event.[30]

Closely related to Fletcher's use of Pentecostal images for sanctification is his development of a doctrine of "dispensations." According to this, there are three major epochs in God's dealings with humankind, that of the Father (covered by Old Testament history), the Son (illustrated by the "transitional" nature of John the Baptist), and the Holy Spirit, the latter inaugurated at Pentecost. Each successive age is significantly superior to the one preceding it. Only the last brings the "perfect Gospel of Christ." Besides describing a kind of progressive revelation of God through history, Fletcher also held that this scheme was paralleled by actual stages in an individual person's experience of God, as he or she might move from being outside Christianity, to being a Christian but an "imperfect" one, to being initiated into the "dispensation of the Holy Spirit" and made perfect through a "baptism of fire," which fulfills "the promise of the Father."[31]

Fletcher also introduced some new ideas of the nature of faith into the Wesleyan tradition. Whereas

Wesley had described faith as a divine gift, a supernatural faculty given so that one might apprehend "divine
things" and be able to "trust" in Christ, Fletcher saw
faith as more an act of human will. He tended to describe it as a strenuous believing in propositions, or
"promises" given in the Bible. To a "Mr. Vaughn" he
wrote concerning holiness:

> To aim aright at this liberty of the children
> of God requires a continual acting of faith--
> of a naked faith in a naked promise or declar-
> ation, such as, "The Son of God was manifested
> to destroy the works of the devil [1 John
> 3:8]:--The law of the spirit of life, in
> Christ Jesus, hath made me free from the law
> of sin and death [Romans 8:2]:--I can do all
> things, through Christ, who strengtheneth
> me"[Philippians 4:13]. By a naked faith in a
> naked promise, I do not mean a bare assent
> that God is faithful, and that such a promise
> in the book of God may be fulfilled in me; but
> a bold, hearty, steady venturing of my soul,
> body, and spirit upon the truth of the prom-
> ise, with an appropriating act. It is mine,
> because I am a penitent sinner; and I am de-
> termined to believe, come what will. Here you
> must stop the ear of the mind to the sugges-
> tions of the serpent; which, were you to
> reason with him, would be endless, and would
> soon draw you out of the simple way of that
> faith by which we are both justified and
> sanctified.
>
> You must also remember that it is your
> privilege to go to Christ by such a faith
> now....[32]

To another he wrote of the "unhappy medium of corrup-
tible flesh and blood" which "stands much in our way" of
"enjoying God," but which at the same time provides
occasion for "giving more glory to him" through "believing his naked truth."[33]

In this connection Fletcher took some important
steps toward stressing free will at the expense of
grace. Partly this was due to the fact that his thought
was forged in the heat of controversy with Calvinists
who emphasized absolute divine sovereignty, predestination, irresistible grace, and the like. He thus tended
to state his own views of free will in the strongest
possible terms, actually initiating the turning in Methodism from "free grace to free will" which Robert E.
Chiles traces to Richard Watson.[34] John L. Knight even
argues that Wesley himself in his later years actually
changed his views under Fletcher's influence, coming to
emphasize "works and free will almost to the exclusion
of grace."[35] This emphasis made it easy for Christians to
think of the work of God and the "works" of human beings
in salvation as divided into discrete compartments.

One other new twist given to the Methodist theological heritage by John Fletcher was his view of the
obligation of the entirely sanctified believer to testify to "the blessing." Fletcher did not write formally of
this, but rather related it in his preaching. In fact,
his ideas here came into circulation not through anything of his own but through the Journal of Hester Ann
Rogers, the wife of a Methodist preacher, and friend of
Fletcher and his wife, Mary Bosanquet. Rogers recorded
an account of a gathering in 1781 where Fletcher expounded on Acts 2, relating being "renewed in love" to
Pentecost and being "filled with the Holy Ghost," and
exhorted those present to seek "the blessing." He also
confessed:

But I am ashamed....I have dishonored my
God, and denied my Saviour, by not confessing
him....I have been ashamed and afraid to declare what he hath done for my soul....

Last Wednesday evening [God] instructed
and commanded me by his word, "Reckon yourselves, therefore, to be dead indeed unto sin,
but alive unto God through Jesus Christ"
(Romans 6:11). I obeyed the voice of God, and
now obey it, by declaring, to the praise of
his love, I am freed from sin...

I have received this blessing four or
five times before, but I grieved the Spirit of
God by not making confession, and as often I
let it go. I lost it by not observing and
obeying the order of God, who hath told us,
"With the heart man believeth unto righteousness, and with the mouth confession is made
unto salvation (Romans 10:10)"; which latter I
neglected.

Now, my brethren...I have confessed in
your presence, and now I resolve in your presence also, henceforth I will confess my Master
to all the world. And I declare unto you...I
am now "dead indeed unto sin."[36]

Fletcher then added:

You who are hungering and thirsting after
righteousness, what wait you for? Delay not.
Unite yourselves to Jesus your holiness by
believing; take to yourselves this great salvation; take it now. You must receive it by
faith; faith lays hold, and says, "It is
mine...." Reckon thyself indeed dead to sin
and alive unto God, now, this moment. O reckon

now! Fear not; <u>believe</u>, <u>believe</u>, <u>believe</u>! and
continue to believe every moment...for it is
retained as it is received, by faith alone.
Whosoever thou art that wilt perseveringly
believe it will...constrain thee to <u>confess</u>
<u>with thy mouth</u>....[37]

Fletcher here also refers to the unsanctified as "half
believers," telling them, "you are only in an improper
sense called believers, who reject this!"[38]

Another notable shaper and transmitter of the Methodist heritage was Adam Clarke (1760?-1832). Clarke was
a transitional figure who became a Methodist in the
1770s under Wesley, but who outlived the founder by some
forty years, helping to lead the movement into a new
era. A man of enormous energies, Clarke contributed to
his times as preacher, three-time president of the
Methodist Conference, Bible translator and commentator,
organizer of efforts to feed the hungry, educate women,
and provide for retired preachers and widows, and archi-
vist for the British government, among other things.

Busy with so many projects, Clarke was never able
to produce the theological "Institutes" or "Systematics"
that he desired to write, but he did leave, along with
his massive <u>Commentary</u>, a collection of jottings on
various topics, which were arranged and published by
Samuel Dunn in 1835 as <u>Christian Theology</u>.[39] This
collection provides a helpful view of the Wesleyan tradition in the early nineteenth century.

On the critical concept of Christian Perfection,
Clarke largely perpetuated Wesley's understanding of the
nature of "the blessing," although, like Fletcher, he
stressed some things Wesley had not. For one, he almost
totally eliminated the gradual dimension allowed by both
Wesley and Fletcher in attaining and growing in holi-

ness. "In no part of the Scriptures are we directed to seek holiness gradatim," he declared. "We are to come to God as well for an instantaneous and complete purification from all sin, as for an instantaneous pardon. Neither the seriatim pardon, nor the gradatim purification, exists in the Bible."[40]

Interesting here is the reference to the Bible as the final arbiter of the matter. This is characteristic of Clarke's approach to religious knowledge generally, and to sanctification specifically. While Wesley also considered the Bible to be the final source of authority for religious belief and practice, he believed it needed to be tested and confirmed in the experience of Christians, as well as interpreted in light of human reason and the whole sweep of historic Christian tradition, these things together forming the so-called "Wesleyan quadrilateral" of religious authority. This meant that for Wesley doctrine was shaped by the Bible operating in life. On the matter of Christian Perfection he even said that, "If I were convinced that none in England had attained what has been so clearly and strongly preached ...I should be clearly convinced that we had all mistaken the meaning of those scriptures" pertaining to holiness.[42] Clarke, by contrast, allowed experience no role when he declared, "The truth is, no doctrine of God stands upon the knowledge, experience, faithfulness, or unfaithfulness of man; it stands on the veracity of God who gave it." As for sanctification, "suppose not one could be found in all the churches of Christ whose heart was purified from all unrighteousness, and who loved God and man with all his regenerated powers, yet the doctrine of Christian perfection would still be true..." "In all cases of this nature," Clarke wrote, "we must

forever cease from man, implicitly credit God's testimony, and look to Him...."[42]

Clarke also had some revealing things to say about
the nature and operation of faith which placed him close
to Fletcher's views. He carefully draws distinctions
between what God does in salvation and what humans do.
Faith is something humans do. God gives the power in
some sense to exercise faith, but the actual exercise is
a human willing to believe, "the act of faith is a man's
own." Otherwise, why are we commanded to believe and
condemned for not believing?: "[God] commands us to
believe; reproaches us for our unbelief; tells us that
if we believe not, we shall not be established; asserts
that he who believes not, has made God a liar...and
finishes the confrontation of our infidel speeches with
'He that believeth not shall be damned' [Mark 16:16]."[43]
In fact, God's commandment is central to eliciting
faith, for "The highest, the most sovereign reason that
can be given for believing, is, that God has commanded
it."[44] Does one require "signs and miracles" in order to
exercise faith? That is a "weak faith." "God has a right
to be believed on his own word alone [cf. Fletcher's
"naked word"]; and it is impious...to demand" any
more.[45] Also, since holiness comes by faith, and faith
is a work which is commanded and possible now, holiness,
according to Clarke, may be attained in the present
moment.

As for terminology, Clarke for the most part used
Wesley's vocabulary of "perfection," "entire sanctification," "holiness," "to be full of the love of God," and
the like. He did not embrace Fletcher's "Pentecostal
language" and imagery, although he did refer to entire
sanctification as an "effusion of the Holy Ghost."[46] The
word "perfection" he held to be biblical and useful,

although he did not recommend it with quite the inflexibility of Fletcher. The reason he did not was not because the word was likely to be misunderstood as implying too much about the state of "holiness"--a concern of Wesley's--but that it implied too little. He considered it hedged with "so many qualifications and abatements that cannot comport with that full and glorious salvation recommended in the gospel" as to be inadequate. "Had I a better name, one more energetic, one with a greater plentitude of meaning...I would gladly adopt and use it," he proclaimed.[47]

Whatever term one might use to describe it, Clarke was quite sure that the "second work of grace" most certainly involved abstaining from evil of any sort. His Theology thus includes specific exhortations about dancing, tobacco and dress. He judged that dancing had been for him personally a "downfall," involving him in a whole way of life characterized by "worldly-mindedness," immorality and crass materialism. He condemned dances as, "snares for souls; destructive of chastity, modesty, and sometimes even of humanity itself; and a pernicious invention to excite the most criminal passions."[48]

Tobacco, he held, leads to "dried and shriveled brains." It is a "sin" because it destroys the God-created body, and it creates a dependency which makes it in effect the tobacco user's "god." Use of tobacco is also often accompanied by other forms of "dissipation" including drunkenness.[49]

As for dress, sanctified persons should dress with modesty and simplicity. "New creatures" should appear new on the outside, as well as the inside, and be readily distinguishable from "old creatures." Dress also gives occasion for the sin of pride, so it should be plain and humble.[50]

2. The Popularizers

In surveying the development of the Methodist heritage of religious thought from John Wesley into the nineteenth century, one gains only a partial view of things if attention is limited to just the major formulators or interpreters of doctrine like Wesley, Fletcher, and Clarke. Though the Methodist preachers learned their theology from these, the laity was much more likely to learn its theology from what might be called the "popularizers" of Methodism. These were laypeople themselves for the most part, who were widely revered as the "saints" of Methodism. Accounts of their lives were published and read avidly by the pious. Most of these were identified with the pioneering phase of the Methodist movement and a good number of them were women.

One of the best known of these was Hester Ann Roe Rogers (1756-1794), a contemporary of Wesley, Fletcher, and Clarke. Rogers was known for her unusual degree of religious sensibility ("She was followed by divine impressions from her childhood") and her dedicated promotion of the Wesleyan movement in its pioneer days.[51] Largely self-educated, she became a student of the Bible, a religious counselor to many via her prolific letter writing, a class leader, and a comforter of the poor and sick. Single for most of her life, she married Methodist preacher James Rogers ten years before her death and shared his work in Ireland and England. She was acquainted with the major Methodist leaders of the day, especially Wesley and Fletcher, and was one of the few persons present when Wesley died in 1791. This, together with the facts that she kept a rather complete journal of her thoughts and activities, and died young "in the cause," propelled her to prominence as an almost martyr figure in Methodist imagination.

Like Phoebe Palmer, whom she greatly influenced, Rogers was not a "theologian" in the formal sense, but rather a "preacher" of "holiness" who absorbed and expounded a rather consistent body of religious ideas relating to the pursuit and attainment of that coveted "blessing." These ideas evidence a blending of Wesley and the unique perspectives of Fletcher and Clarke, especially Fletcher. Quite close to Fletcher, and an admirer of his piety, as were most Methodists, she found his ideas on many topics to be very attractive.[52]

For instance, Rogers habitually mixes Wesley's language of "perfect love" with Fletcher's "pentecostal language," as when she recounts her reception of the "second blessing." "Lord, cried I, make this the moment of my full salvation! Baptize me now with the Holy Ghost, and the fire of pure love."[53] In a letter to Wesley himself, she writes of believing herself led by God to pray "for a universal and pentecostal outpouring of His divine fullness."[54]

Rogers also tends to view faith, along with Fletcher, as a human act and as belief in rational propositions, as when she instructs her cousin that "Faith believes the record true, without staggering at the promise," and counsels him to believe "the word of God that cannot lie." She also explains to him that though "the power given [to exercise faith] is of grace," the "use of that power is the act of man."[55] "You must embrace the promise, believe it, hang upon it, rejoice in it as your own" in order to be fully sanctified, she declares to him another time.[56]

In pressing this view of faith, Rogers also emphasized the instantaneous nature of sanctification, a

strong note in Fletcher and the only dimension of sanctification allowed by Clarke. She records her conviction
"that whenever sin is totally destroyed, it is done in a
moment," and her husband remembered that she "saw it her
duty to bid those who felt the burden of indwelling sin,
to look for the total destruction of it in one moment;
ever pressing them to believe for the blessing; to
believe now...."[57] A correspondent is questioned about
her experience "of inward, instantaneous sanctification...."[58]

In all of this, Rogers both reflected and contributed to the development of the Wesleyan tradition on
the popular level along those paths marked out by
Fletcher and Clarke on the more scholarly level. In
other areas, however, Rogers contributed some more or
less original elements to the popular tradition, elements which were potent influences upon Phoebe Palmer.

For one thing, Rogers was almost certainly the
source of Palmer's "altar principle." To her cousin in
1776 she wrote: "I feel I am very unworthy, yet offering
up myself and my services on that altar which sanctifieth the gift, my God accepts a worthless worm, through
his beloved Son."[59] Though Rogers did not elaborate the
idea to the lengths Palmer later would, this phraseology
and its unexplored implications were no doubt a seed
which was planted when Phoebe as a girl read Rogers, and
which was nurtured and flowered in the hothouse of her
adolescent and early adult religious pilgrimage. For
both Phoebe and her sister, Sarah, it would bring resolution to their struggle with the matter of assurance,
and would blossom into Phoebe's most characteristic
teaching about holiness.

Another idea of Rogers' which impressed itself upon
Palmer's consciousness was that giving witness to a

particular level of spirituality confirms one's faith that such a state has in fact been attained. Referring to her entire sanctification, Rogers noted, "I soon found that repeating [the Lord's] goodness, confirmed my own faith more and more. And so did the Lord bless me in declaring it...."[60] Together with her account of Fletcher's claiming to have lost "the blessing" four or five times by not declaring it publicly, this concept furnished material for Palmer to develop her "theology of testimony" which linked public witness integrally with the operation of faith, making it mandatory for the attainment and retention of holiness.

Palmer was also influenced by a view appearing in Rogers' Memoir which was expressed not by Hester Ann herself, but by her husband, James, after her death. In an eulogy to Hester Ann included in the Memoir, James Rogers stated his belief that God had taken his "all of earthly treasure" to heaven and that he was bound to God and heaven as never before.[61] This concept would be found by Palmer to be personally applicable in the midst of trauma over the deaths of three of her children, and would furnish her with the phrase which she used often and to which she gave almost biblical authority, "God takes our treasure to heaven that our hearts may be there also."[62]

One could go on documenting other specific ideas Palmer absorbed from Rogers' Memoir, but probably as important as these ideas was the model of religious experience and piety which Rogers provided. This is reflected all through Palmer's writings and public career. As Rogers was known for her "out of the common" literary abilities, so Palmer early on wrote religious poetry and essays.[63] Rogers carried on a vast letter-writing correspondence throughout her life; so did

Palmer. As a leader of Methodist classes, a compassionate visitor to the poor and sick, one committed to
"employing every talent for God," and a confidante of
noted religious leaders, Rogers was a prototype for
Palmer. Palmer's journal and spiritual autobiography,
The Way of Holiness, exudes a "Rogerian" style. The interior warring with "the Tempter," the spontaneous suggestion of scripture to the mind to combat him, the
poring over the Bible on one's knees, the "venturing on
the promise in spite of reasoning and unbelief," the
dreams of warning or comfort from God, which are a part
of Rogers' spiritual odyssey are all found in Palmer as
well. There are even events recounted by Palmer which
sound as if they were almost deliberate copies of experiences described by Rogers, such as her composed singing
of hymns on a steamboat whose boiler had burst as a
testimony to frightened passengers--in Rogers' case it
was a yacht in high seas off the coast of Ireland.[64]

Another who popularized the Wesleyan tradition
through his widely read Life was William Carvosso (1750-
1834).[65] A contemporary of Rogers, though he outlived
her by some forty years, he too represented the "pioneering" era of the Methodist movement. Also, like
Rogers, he was a layperson who developed a significant
"ministry" without benefit of clerical credentials. For
a time he was a "disciple" of Wesley who "followed him
from place to place, and mingled among the overwhelming
crowds that hung upon his lips...."[66] Not formally educated, he did not even learn to write until the age of
sixty-five, producing the numerous letters and accounts
of his experience from which the Life was compiled only
during the last twenty years of his life.[67] He was,
nevertheless, adept at farming, and it was his success
there that made it possible for him to give his later

years to traveling about as an unofficial lay "evangelist" for the Wesleyan movement.

Carvosso's special concern was the nature of faith.
His reflections on faith overshadow all else in the
Life, constituting very nearly an obsession. In his
understanding of faith, Carvosso was guided by John
Fletcher and Hester Ann Rogers, though he added to them
some "improvements" of his own.[68] Though Phoebe Palmer
never credited Carvosso--or Rogers or Fletcher for that
matter--for her views on faith, she was immensely
indebted to him, as can be seen in a quick overview of
his teachings.

Carvosso held that faith is an act of human willing, graciously aided by God to be sure, but in its very
essence more a human response to the grace of God. He
wrote, "God imparts the power or grace [to believe]; but
he requires us to use it. He commands us to believe."[69]
Regularly he pressed upon persons their duty to believe
if they would obtain salvation, as he did a woman seeking both entire sancitification and physical healing:
"'And now,' said I, 'it is a duty which God requires of
you to believe in Jesus Christ, and the truth of his
promises.'" Another was assured that "his ransom was
already paid, and that the duty which remained for him
was to believe with all his heart."[70]

Such faith is reasonable, according to Carvosso,
and rests upon "objective" grounds, i.e. the Word or
promises of God. "Faith is an act of reason, and
believing is a kind of knowing" based upon the
"testimony of Him whom we believe," wrote Carvosso.[71]
One who had been helped by him to better understand
faith noted that "his remarks on the nature of [faith]
were clear and forcible in an extraordinary degree,
commending themselves to my reason...."[72]

Such reasonable faith, when dutifully exercised, is very nearly omnipotent, according to Carvosso. "Faith subdued all his evils, repaired all his breaches, supported and solaced him under all his trials and sorrows, made the fullness of Christ all his own, and impowered him with an ability to become an immense blessing to multitudes."[73] Faith is the "root from which all the branches of holiness grow."[73] "It is faith alone which is the foundation of all our holiness, strength, and happiness."[75] Faith "clears the apprehension, impresses the affections, determines the will, and governs the life."[76] Faith can even move or inhibit God. Describing his prayers for the salvation of his children, he recorded his belief that

> [God] has gone so far in encouraging us to ask
> the fulfillment of his promises, that he has
> condescended to say, "Put me in remembrance";
> as if he had said, "When you pray, be sure to
> bring the promises with you." Hence, I con-
> clude, if I have faith to give full credit to
> God's word, that promise which I lay hold of
> is mine, and all that it contains, so far as
> my wants are concerned [cf. Palmer's teaching
> that the "promise conveys the thing pro-
> mised"]. On the other hand, if I entertain a
> doubt, or stagger at the truth of God, I
> consider I have no claim, and my prayers will
> not find access. Such is the dreadful effect
> of unbelief, that speaking after the manner of
> men, it binds the hands of God.[77]

Naturally, such "omnipotent" faith can get what it seeks now. "In receiving the salvation of the Gospel," Carvosso "had no opinion of delays, exceptions, or limits," his charge being "come; for all things are now ready [Luke 14:17]."[78] Faith lays hold of the promised blessing," whether justification, or sanctification, without hesitation or delay...."[79] His own attainment of the "second blessing" occurred when he "began to exercise faith, by believing I shall have the blessing now." "Just at that moment" he was "emptied of self and sin, and filled with God."[80] Typical of his counsel to others is the advice given to his niece to "at once, 'reckon yourself to be dead indeed unto sin, and alive unto God, through Jesus Christ.'"[81]

The faith that Carvosso commends is a "naked faith," a belief which stands bare upon the word of God, with nothing else to sustain it. He quotes with approval Fletcher's comments on "naked faith" (independent of all feelings) in a "naked promise," and often applied them to his own situation. In an unusually intense bout with temptation, he found that "naked faith was my only defense; the only weapon with which I could maintain the fight."[82] Another time he observed, "After fifty-six years spent in the service of God, I find I have nothing to keep my soul in motion but faith...."[83]

In addition to these ideas on the nature of faith, Carvosso contributed much else, along with Hester Ann Rogers, to Phoebe Palmer's thought and career. There is the fear of declaring publicly one's reception of the "second blessing" and the teaching that this must be done in order to attain and then keep it.[84] There is the "pentecostal" or "Spirit" language originated by Fletcher and used by Rogers, though as in Rogers, it is mixed with more "Wesleyan" terminology and not applied to entire sanctification with any real consistency.[85] In this connection Carvosso may have been the inspiration for what is perhaps Palmer's best known poem, set to music by her daughter Phoebe Palmer Knapp as the gospel

song, "The Cleansing Wave." Words like "Oh, now I see
the crimson wave, the fountain deep and wide...I see the
new creation rise...Polluted nature dies! Sinks 'neath
the cleansing flood...The cleansing stream, I see, I
see! I plunge, and, oh, it cleanseth me!" echo
Carvosso's petition, "Lord, I want a fresh baptism of
thy Spirit, a deeper plunge into the crimson flood, in
order to rise more and more into all the life of God."[86]

There is also the style of Carvosso's work as a
"lay exhorter" which strongly marks Palmer's career. It
was noted of Carvosso that he freely used illustrations
to "help the understanding and the confidence of the
seeking soul," especially in relation to the nature of
faith. His goal was to simplify religious truth that it
might be grasped by the common person. His success in
this is attested to by one who wrote to Carvosso's son,
"Until I saw your excellent father, it seemed to me I
never met with anyone whose exposition of faith came
within the reach of my understanding...."[87] Palmer declared in her book (not unintentionally titled), Incidental Illustrations of the Economy of Salvation, her
desire to "present old truths, newly dressed, with, perhaps originality of conception" and to "set forth Bible
doctrines and duties as simplified to her own perceptions...and made tangible by every-day illustrations and
experiences."[88] In this same book there is even an
account of an incident in Palmer's experience which is
an almost exact duplication of one in Carvosso's, both
involving the persuasion of persons that they were in
fact entirely sanctified when they had not believed this
to be the case.[89]

In his work of "simplifying" religion, Carvosso
could often be confrontational and aggressive. Perhaps
an extreme example was his pursuit of a young girl out

of her house into another, and the delivering of a
sermon in a loud voice up the stairs when she took
refuge in a locked room![90] Short of this, however, he
was continually confronting apathetic churchgoers and
"backsliders," and the unsanctified with their obligation to be fully conformed to the will of God, accepting
no compromise or excuse. It can hardly be doubted that
Phoebe Palmer found inspiration for her public career in
Carvosso's example.

B. Palmer and the Nineteenth-Century American Milieu

Already noted is M.E. Dieter's description of the
American holiness movement as a "wedding of the American mind, prevailing revivalism, and Wesleyan perfectionism." The foregoing discussion has attempted to
unpack the character of the "Wesleyan perfectionism" to
which Phoebe Palmer was exposed as she was growing up.
As has been seen; the tradition was an evolving one. It
was developing along two tiers, a formal theological
one, represented by Wesley himself, John Fletcher, and
Adam Clarke, and a popular one, represented by Hester
Ann Rogers and William Carvosso, among others. Palmer
absorbed much from the tradition, especially as it was
molded and perpetuated by its "popularizers." In fact,
her own career may be seen as an extension of this
"popular Wesleyanism" with its distinctive emphases into
the American context. She also heightened certain of its
characteristics and made some creative additions to it
in keeping with her own individual religious journey and
the larger "American experience" of which she was part.
Her popularity and succcess can be taken to represent
the triumph of "popular Wesleyanism" in a society in
which during Palmer's heyday the "common man" was as-
cending in all areas of social, political, and religious

life. That this development did not go unchallenged will
be seen, yet it was almost inevitable, given the nature
of American Methodism and American culture generally in
the nineteenth century.

Palmer came along at a fortuitous time. The Wesleyan movement, always strongly dependent upon lay support even in Britain, was actually initiated in America
as a lay movement without clerical supervision. Until
Wesley sent his first missionary "preachers" in 1769--at
American request--the movement was totally lay directed
and "popular" in the extreme. The fact that it generated
some of the roots of the democratic and anti-creedal
Disciples of Christ/Christian movement is easily understandable, given these beginnings and orientation.[91]

Its theological structure, often underestimated by
students of religious history, was considerable. It had
been formally set out by Wesley, Fletcher, Adam Clarke,
and Richard Watson, the latter's Theological Institutes
(1828) representing the first real Wesleyan "systematic
theology." It was, however, a British structure; American Methodists were dependent upon these early British
formulators for their religious ideas. This situation
could not prevail for long though, since the Americans
were certain to eventually flex their own doctrinal
muscles and begin to respond to the challenges and
currents of their own environment. This happened first
in connection with American Methodism's encounter with
the prevailing Calvinism of American Protestantism, and
with emerging Unitarianism and Universalism.[92]

Phoebe Palmer came to maturity in these early years
during which the British doctrinal authorities still
prevailed on most issues, but in which the first tentative efforts were also being made to give American
Methodism its own voice. There were the makings of an

educated elite, but this was slow to develop in a movement which stressed practical piety over everything
else. The first permanent Methodist college was not
founded in America until around 1830, and even a formal
"course of study" for ministers was not standardized
until 1848. The situation was thus ripe for creative--
even if not formally trained--laypersons, to wield considerable influence. Such persons could draw upon the
tradition of lay initiative in the American movement,
and the stream of "popular Wesleyanism" well established
in Britain and well-known in America.

Given this situation, Palmer was able to emerge
from what might well have been a life of relative obscurity as the wife of a New York physician into national and even international prominence as an articulate
and forceful spokesman for a central element of the
Wesleyan tradition, Christian perfection. Of course, had
that doctrine not become a source of considerable anxiety for nineteenth-century American Methodists, Phoebe
might still have remained "Mrs. Doctor Palmer." But as
it happened, American leadership became fearful of losing the religious intensity and rigor associated with
the pursuit of "second blessing" holiness, and sought to
promote its "revival" in the church by various means.[93]
At least two persons wrote treatises on the subject as
early as the 1820s.[94] These were essentially compila-
tions of material from Wesley and Fletcher. In 1841
Phoebe Palmer published her anonymous articles in the
Christian Advocate, and in 1843 produced The Way of
Holiness, calling strongly to mind the "popular Wesleyanism" of Rogers and Carvosso. In between George O. Peck
brought out the most thorough and systematic American
treatment of Christian Perfection up to that time, The
Scripture Doctrine of Christian Perfection Stated and

Defended, based on a series of lectures he had presented
in New York area churches during 1840-1841.

At about the same time, Timothy Merritt began publishing The Guide to Christian Perfection, mainly to
circulate the testimonies of persons claiming to have
been made perfect in love. In this he was strongly
encouraged by Walter and Phoebe Palmer, and Phoebe's
sister, Sarah Lankford, all of whom had recently made
such testimony themselves.

Concern about the state of holiness in Methodism
also called forth the Tuesday Meeting for the Promotion
of Holiness, of which Phoebe became the leader, and out
of which came many of the most enthusiastic promoters of
a "holiness revival" in Methodism.

Thus Phoebe, both by thrusting herself, and being
thrust by circumstances, into the very center of this
effort to retain the primitive spirit of Methodism,
became a force to be reckoned with. Identifying strongly
with Methodism's heritage of reverence for the concept
of holiness or spiritual perfection, she also could call
upon its tradition of lay initiative, and the theological legacy of "popular Wesleyanism"--a potent combination.

In all of this, as has been noted already, Palmer
was much more than simply a transmitter of other persons' ideas. Though she drew much from the tradition,
she also shaped and added to it in important ways. And
here "prevailing revivalism" and the "American mind"
made their impact.

Revivalism influenced Palmer in two quite different
ways. She was, on the one hand, a revivalist herself in
the mold of Charles Finney and the other well-known
revival preachers of her day. Religious life in America
throughout the nineteenth century was to a great extent

shaped by the traveling evangelists, their protracted meetings, and their calls to repentance and virtuous living now. Palmer's Methodism was an especially enthusiastic exponent of revivalism, domesticating the rugged frontier camp meeting of early century into a regular feature of Methodist life, thereby providing periodic opportunity to stir the already pious to even greater devotion, and call sinners to forsake their sin.[95] By Palmer's day, a network of permanent or semi-permanent camp meeting sites linked Methodists throughout North America. These were augmented by periodic protracted meetings, sometimes of many weeks, duration, in city and village churches, which paralleled the camp meeting in style and substance.

A chief feature of revivalism was its single-minded focus upon bringing about conversions, and its compression of the journey from sin to salvation into a few weeks, a few days, or even a few hours. The revival preacher's opportunity to awaken the "lost" was limited to the meeting or meetings in which he might command their fleeting attention to his warning of divine judgment and offer of escape. The appeal must be gotten across quickly, vividly, and with immediate opportunity for response.

Phoebe Palmer, in her effort to reawaken Methodism to its perfectionist heritage, and to bring all other Christians into the perfectionist camp as well, quite naturally adopted revivalistic machinery to accomplish her goal. In the process she wedded revivalism and perfectionism in a more complete union than had before been seen.[96] Her presentation of the doctrine of Christian Perfection was tailored to the exigencies of camp meeting and protracted meeting. Where the average revivalist pressed for conversion now, Palmer pressed for entire sanctification <u>now</u>. Where the general revivalist developed a stylized and much compressed "morphology of conversion" to simplify the process and provide a "foolproof" path to salvation, Palmer developed a stylized, "foolproof" way of holiness to guide the seeker after "full salvation."[97] Thus, the instantaneous nature of entire sanctification was strongly underscored, pivoting on the act of a free human agent in the "crisis" of entire consecration. Process, or growth in holiness, though not denied, took a decided backseat to immediacy.

This was, of course, not a wholly unanticipated development. Wesley himself had pressed the "instantaneous blessing" strongly in his later life. Fletcher with his "baptism of the Holy Ghost" conception, and Adam Clarke with his denial of gradual sanctification, had gone far toward weighting the scales on the instantaneous side. The "popularizers" of Wesleyanism like Rogers and Carvosso appear to have taught only an instantaneous sanctification. Nevertheless, some balance seems to have been maintained in early American Methodism, J. L. Peters concluding from his study of colonial Methodist preaching that it "included the concept of an experience attainable 'now and by simple faith' and...at the same time made ample provision for corporate Christian nurture."[98] Under the perfectionist revivalism of Palmer, however, this balance was significantly altered.

Also, in the context of pressing for immediate sanctification, the matter of faith became critical. Stressing that sanctification came by "simple faith," as did justification, the perfectionist revivalist needed to make sanctifying faith something concrete and subject to decisive human action. Revivalists not of a perfectionist bent were of course faced with the same need, and the tendency, even among those in the Calvinist doctrinal tradition which strongly held saving faith to be a divine gift, was to cast it more as an act of human will, of belief in a set of doctrinal propositions or statements of scripture. Charles Finney, perhaps the pre-eminent revivalist of the century, and a product of Calvinistic Presbyterianism (although he repudiated many elements of that tradition), described faith as "the will's reception of truth," and as "something to be done--a solemn duty" which "we are commanded to do upon pain of eternal death." It is "the will's closing in with the truths of the gospel."[99]

Methodists--"Arminians" in this matter to begin with--were better equipped than Calvinists to deal with the faith issue in the atmosphere of revivalism, and by the nineteenth century had built up a considerable body of thought about the nature of faith, most of it echoing Adam Clarke's "the act of faith is a man's own." But here lies a problem. In the literature of late eighteenth-and early nineteenth-century Methodism, one senses struggle over the nature of faith. It is discernible in both "learned" circles and at the popular level. For Wesley, as we have seen, faith was a gift from God, a "supernatural" faculty, a kind of spiritual "eye," with which to receive and appropriate spiritual truth. The human agent could close off this "eye" and ignore its existence, thus rendering it impotent, or allow it to function as intended. Thus, for Wesley, the human agent is morally responsible for <u>using</u> faith, but does not "create" faith.

Essential for Wesley's view is his contention that faith is bound up with a "mystical" relationship with Christ; that it is finally trust in Christ, or God, whose "presence" is somehow palpably felt or sensed by the believer. Faith is "a sure trust and confidence in

God that, through the merits of Christ, my sins are forgiven and I am reconciled to the favour of God."[100] Albert Outler comments: "The essence of faith [for Wesley] ...has always to do with man's immediate and indubitable assurance of God's living and loving presence in his heart."[101]

Thus, for Wesley, "saving faith" (both "justifying faith" and "sanctifying faith") would seem to be a dynamic flow of belief and confidence in the direction of God from a person whose divinely given "eye" of faith is open and receiving the spiritual "light" radiating from God.

What one finds in Fletcher, Clarke, and the Wesleyan popularizers, however, is quite different from this. Fletcher writes of a "naked faith"--stripped of something, apparently--the object of which is not God or Christ, but a "naked promise or declaration." Clarke is even more emphatic in planting faith upon "God's word alone" and declaring that the highest reason for exercising faith is not one's "immediate and indubitable assurance of God's living and loving presence in his heart," but the fact that God "has commanded it." He belittles those who require "signs and miracles" to accompany faith. Similarly, Rogers, and Carvosso especially, speak of faith as "believing the record true," and as "an act of reason" and a "duty which God requires," which ultimately turns alone upon some "objective" body of "evidence." All seem almost defensive about faith.

There are probably several reasons for this shift in emphasis. For one, the controversy with Calvinism, in which Fletcher was the main Wesleyan defender, pushed the Wesleyans to define their own position in the most uncompromising terms. This led to the nearly exclusive stress on the human role in salvation noted before. In this atmosphere, Wesley's way of describing faith likely seemed almost too "Calvinist."

Also, the increasing stress on the instantaneous dimension of entire sanctification seen in those after Wesley necessitated a different conception of faith. If sanctification is attained by faith, and is also an instantaneous and momentary event, then faith must be something which occurs momentarily. It must be an act of precise description and operation. "Naked faith" in "naked promises," defined as a willing obedience to divine commands, fit the bill better than Wesley's more "relational" conception.

In addition, one must consider the influence of rationalism in the eighteenth and early nineteenth century. Wesley, in much of his work, was reacting against rationalism's influence on religion. His advocacy of "heartfelt" religion was at odds with the currents of Deism and Unitarianism in his day. Yet it can be argued that his movement did not escape rationalism's influence in its attempts to organize and articulate a coherent doctrinal position. Wesleyan thinkers, when they began to explain their movement to the world, found themselves forced to borrow rationalistic categories of thought, at least to the extent of demonstrating that their views were coherent and rested upon rationally defensible foundations.[102] As this happened, faith came to be expressed more and more in a rationalistic fashion as belief in "rational" propositions of divinely revealed truth, and less as trust and confidence in an unseen, but "felt," supernatural presence working in one's "heart."

Phoebe Palmer found this view of faith to fit perfectly with her perfectionist revivalism. The definition of faith suggested by Fletcher and Clarke, and taken up by Rogers and Carvosso, whom she knew so well, provided her (along with her "altar principle" and stress on entire consecration) with the key with which to unlock the door of holiness in her own personal religious journey, making possible the assurance of her salvation for which she sought so long. And it fit the need for an immediate response to God's command, "Be ye holy."

Yet revivalism influenced Palmer in a quite different way as well. While in her view of the instantaneous nature of sanctification and the nature of sanctifying faith she appropriated those elements of the Wesleyan tradition which meshed with nineteenth-century American revivalism, in another way she rejected both Wesleyanism and revivalism, reacting against an element in both for which she had no sympathy. This was the prominent role given to emotions, affections or feelings.

Throughout Methodism from Wesley to Palmer, there was a marked emphasis on true religion as something "heartfelt." Wesley's quest for "perfect love" was a quest for a state of such rapturous devotion to God that divine love would overwhelm the believer and flow almost unimpeded through him or her.[103] Wesley taught that persons justified or entirely sanctified would know themselves to be such, largely through an interior conviction--a feeling--that God had forgiven or cleansed their sin. This was his doctrine of assurance which rested on the concept of the "witness of the Spirit."

Throughout eighteenth- and early nineteenth-century Methodism one finds intact this stress on feeling. It is not a pure subjectivism, something Wesley regarded as "enthusiasm" and guarded against by hedging "holy feelings" around with scripture, reason, and the accumulated tradition of the Christian Church--even though some outside the Methodist movement considered Methodists to be "enthusiasts" or fanatics.[104] It is, however, "subjective," and the expected emotions could either wax or wane, being overwhelming and potent one moment, weak and elusive the next.

Rogers and Carvosso reflect much of the popular regard for religious feelings. Rogers wrote:

> I went to bed last night so full of the love of God, I could not sleep for several hours.... At preaching this morning I was so overcome with the love and presence, and exceeding glory of my triune God, that I sunk down unable to support it! It was long before I could stand or speak! All this day I have been lost in depths of love unutterable! At the love-feast I was again overwhelmed by his immediate presence! All around me is God![105]

Echoing this, Carvosso described several of his experiences of strong religious emotion:

> I was one night in bed, so filled--so overpowered with the glory of God, that, had there been a thousand suns shining at noon-day, the brightness of that divine glory would have eclipsed the whole! I was constrained to shout aloud for joy. It was the overwhelming power of saving grace....I was so visited from above, and overpowered by divine glory, that my shouting could be heard at a distance. It was a weight of glory that I seemed incapable of bearing in the body....This is a morning without a cloud; all is calm, and joy and peace....I cannot express what I feel. It is "joy unspeakable and full of glory"; a sinking

into nothing at the feet of Christ; a feeling that he is "all in all."[106]

American Methodism was thoroughly in tune with this stress on feeling. The Methodist preacher expected even the unconverted to have religious feelings, including a "sense of guilt, feeling of separation from God, apprehension for the future," and near despair, "which would lead to groans and tears," while the converted would experience "an assurance of forgiveness and being... among the saved," a "sense of relief, of joy," which might well "overflow into exclamations of delight."[107]

It is, of course, well-known that American revivalism, from the time of its first stirrings in the eighteenth-century Great Awakening, placed a premium on religious emotions. Revivalists argued that strong feeling was an essential part of genuine conversion, while revival critics tended to focus on some of its more extreme manifestations, dismissing revivalism as a whole as dangerous emotionalism.[108] Emotional expression became especially prized by the frontier revivalists of the early 1800s.

Phoebe Palmer grew up in this setting. The Methodism of her day perpetuated the "shouting Methodist" image of the movement held by many, and Methodists were major participants in the frontier camp meetings, an involvement which tended to heighten even more their already substantial concern for the affective content of religion. Not only conversion but sanctification as well came to be understood and articulated at the grass roots largely in terms of emotional states and processes. The barometer of the emotions was a key element in gauging one's level of spirituality.[109]

Palmer, for whatever cause, her self-diagnosed "proneness to reason" being part of it, was not able to find sufficient assurance of her acceptance with God according to the subjective criteria offered her by her Methodist mentors. As has been seen, she often "wept because she could not weep," and felt herself left out of the emotional "exercises" she witnessed at the Methodist mourner's bench. She could not point to a definite conversion experience because she had never undergone the deep anguish and emotional release associated with such a "crisis."

In frustration she cast about for a more concrete, "objective" way to religious certainty. This she found in: 1) taking the Bible--for her, the "dictated word of God"--as her "textbook";[110] 2) the "rationalistic" view of faith beginning to emerge in Fletcher et al.; and 3) the two ideas of her own creation, these being the "altar principle" which guaranteed instantaneous holiness to the sincere, obedient seeker, and the virtual equation of entire sanctification with the believer's act of entire consecration of herself or himself to God.

This is not to say that Palmer did not teach that genuine conversion and holiness involve a "mystical," felt relationship to Christ. Her understanding of Christianity was too much suffused with pietism for that to occur. And in her writings one can find many examples of the language of religious emotion, some of them paralleling the strongest statements of Rogers and Carvosso. Yet, these are somehow less "convincing," and appear more like deliberate recitations of a familiar formula than spontaneous expressions of religious rapture.

While strong religious feeling may not have been unknown to Palmer, it is clear it was a limited part of her experience, and her system of religious thought

reflects this in its distrust of feeling and its exalta-
tion of the "objective" and verifiable.[111]

Though thousands of people found this simple,
shorter system of Palmer's appealing and helpful in
their own religious pilgrimages and adopted it, there
were critics. Though some of these were outside of
Palmer's Methodist tradition, and thus saw the whole
idea of a present perfection to be an "enthusiastic"
notion, the most outspoken and persistent were Methodists who considered Palmer's revivalistic popular Wesleyanism to be an "un-Wesleyan" system of "new measures."

Chief among these was Hiram Mattison, a minister/
teacher who dogged Palmer throughout the 1850s. In 1855
he managed to place several articles in the Christian
Advocate and Journal before the Palmers pressured the
editor to close its pages to further discussion on the
subject.[112] The thrust of the Mattison articles is instructive in determining the concerns of those Methodists who were not in sympathy with Phoebe's teaching.

The earliest article does not mention Palmer by
name, but plainly is targeting her views. Entitled
"Deceived Professors of Sanctification," it tries to
damn Palmer and her admirers by associating them with
the fanatical George Bell and Thomas Maxfield, two
preachers who stirred up controversy in British Methodist Societies in the 1760s. These two, who eventually
caused a schism in the Wesleyan movement, came under
Wesley's censure because of what he considered their
extravagant notions about sanctification. According to
Mattison, their chief error was persuading persons to
believe themselves sanctified when they were not. This
they were able to do because they dismissed Wesley's
doctrine of the witness of the Spirit and taught that

persons "<u>received</u> [sanctification] while they prayed, whether they <u>felt</u> they were cleansed or not" on the strength of their faith.[113] Anyone familiar with Palmer would immediately recognize in this her stress on "naked faith" and the altar "which sanctifieth the gift."

Furthermore, says Mattison, Bell and Maxfield disparaged those who were unsanctified and even rejected Wesley's counsel when they decided he too was "wanting in holiness." They considered themselves as having nothing to learn from those not enjoying the "second blessing." Here one could see Palmer's stress on the absolute necessity of a second work of grace, and her tendency to consider those not in the blessing as either spiritually deficient or willfully sinful.

The troublemakers also considered all those who did not share their views to be "persecuters." They "disparaged the doctrine of growth in grace," established separate meetings for the promotion of holiness ("as if Mr. Wesley's meetings were for some other object"), severely condemned their critics, and finally split off to form their own sect. Concludes Mattison, even though these such were considered heretical and disruptive teachings and actions by Wesley, "these very doctrines are being reproduced and circulated in our own times, as the very essence of Methodism!," a thinly veiled allusion to Palmer's work.[114]

Phoebe did not respond right away, choosing instead to put a prudent distance between Mattison and herself, and, when she did respond, did so in an indirect fashion. Appearing nearly three months after the first article, Palmer's piece, entitled "Believe that Ye Have It and Ye Have It," referred only to unnamed "theological discussionists" and the "many and continuous cautions" issuing from "periodicals and pulpits" which had misrepresented and caricatured her as teaching that one needs only to believe that one is sanctified in order to be sanctified. She argued that she taught no such thing, but held sanctifying faith to be possible only when all the divine requirements preparatory to faith have been fully met. She did not respond to any of the other charges made in Mattison's article.[115]

Mattison was back in the very next issue of the Advocate with an open frontal attack on Palmer, citing chapter and verse of her writings in support of his contention that she in fact taught--as he also entitled his article--"Believe that Ye Have It and Ye Have It." Here he argued that her view of faith, her "altar theology," and her insistence on public testimony on the basis of nothing but faith constitute a "new theory" of holiness which is "erroneous" and "calculated to mislead and do harm," and again raised the specter of Bell and Maxfield. He held that her system confuses the act of entire consecration with the "great work of sanctification," of which it is a part, but only a small part, the greater part being the work of God in expelling sin and filling the human heart with divine love.

Mattison also delivered some ad hominems. He suggested that Palmer "leave the teaching of Christ's flock where God has left it--with the CHRISTIAN MINISTRY," and asked, "With our good Bibles, and the writings of Wesley, and Fletcher, and Watson, and a score of others, are we so ignorant as to require a sister to travel from conference to conference to instruct us upon this subject?" Also, clearly chafing at Palmer's protectors in high places, he wonders, "Is error any the less mischievous because propagated by a female? Shall the tares be allowed to grow unmolested because planted by the hand of a woman?"[116]

The next issue of the Advocate carried an almost point by point rebuttal by an anonymous defender of Palmer using the pseudonym "Equity."[117] Mattison answered, once again underscoring his contentions with the heading, "Believe that Ye Have It and Ye Have It," and offering additional "proof" that Palmer had originated an un-Wesleyan "new theory of sanctification," which is "at variance with the Holy Scriptures" and "calculated to promote fanaticism and strife, and division..."[118] This time he attempted to tie Palmer not with Bell and Maxfield of a bygone day, but with the contemporary non-Methodist "New Divinity" advocates of perfection at Oberlin College. There Charles Finney, Asa Mahan, and Henry Cowles had linked the strongly modified Calvinism or "New Divinity" of Nathaniel William Taylor with a doctrine of perfectionism inspired largely by Wesleyan sources, but nuanced according to Taylor's heavy stress on the free moral agency and moral accountability of human beings. Finney, for example, defined sanctification as "nothing more nor less than entire obedience, for the time being, to the moral law."[119]

Even though stressing heavily moral responsibility and free will themselves, many Methodists considered that "New Divinity" exponents had gone so far in this direction as to be "Pelagian"--i.e. denying that human beings not renewed by God's grace are "totally depraved," and holding that divine grace is not necessary for human salvation. Mattison was one of these, for he charged that what Palmer taught was not the real "purification of the heart by the Holy Spirit," but "the mere consecration of ourselves to God--the New Divinity sanctification taught by Professor Mahan at Oberlin." This he held "ignores the idea of the purification of the moral nature by the Holy Spirit" and is hence "NOT

METHODISTIC," but is a "Pelagian theory of sanctification."[120] He also suggested that Mahan's printed
endorsement of Palmer's writings sealed his case.

The charge was denied by another of Palmer's de-
fenders in the next issue of the Advocate, who cited
several Methodist publications' support of her teaching
as "eminently Scriptural and Wesleyan." This issue also
carried the editorial note closing off further discussion of Palmer's views and the editor's own assertion
that "sister Palmer is essentially correct in her views
of...Christian Perfection," though admitting that her
peculiar modes of expression were unique, and possibly
subject to misinterpretation.[121]

If Phoebe thought the controversy had been put to
rest by the Advocate's refusal to accept further articles, she must have been rudely jolted by new opposition from a wholly unexpected quarter. The venerable
Nathan Bangs, the virtual patriarch of American Methodism in Palmer's day, and a "regular" at her Tuesday
Meeting, joined Mattison in publicly condemning aspects
of Phoebe's teaching barely a year after the Advocate
flap. Bangs, who had taught her as a child and who had
earlier defended her, putting down criticism to "misap-
prehension of her opinions," in early 1857 choose the
forum of the Tuesday Meeting to level his own criticism.[122]

Like Mattison, Bangs was troubled by Palmer's view
of faith and her recasting of Wesley's doctrine of the
witness of the Spirit. He charged that her altar theology, her view of "omnipotent faith" as a "holy violence"
which infallibly realizes the promises of God, and her
locating of the "witness of the Spirit" in scripture
alone were all in error. Seeing her emphasis upon "naked
faith" as likely to lead to self-deception (Palmer

thought the contrary emphasis upon feeling to be the root of self-deception), he cited Wesley and Fletcher in support of his teaching that the believer must have internal evidence that the work of sanctification is done. Arguing that faith is more properly confidence in God than a belief which accounts a promise to be the thing promised, as Palmer taught, he expressed the heart of his concern:

> Now, it is most manifest that Mr. Wesley considered that the faith by which we are sanctified is inseparably connected with a divine evidence and conviction that the work is done; and hence the theory which teaches that we are to lay all upon the altar or surrender up our hearts to God by Faith in Christ and then without having any evidence of the Holy Spirit that it is accepted, or having any change in our disposition, or any emotion of joy and peace, more than we had before, is not sound, is unscriptural, and anti-Wesleyan....[123]

Bangs further underscored the gravity of his concern by declaring, "the error at which I aim is not a mere incidental error. It is, in my judgment, a fundamental one, as it strikes at the root of experimental religion ...."[124]

Phoebe, curiously, never acknowledged Bangs' rebuke. Perhaps she was too stung by the assault of one so close, or maybe she was simply embarrassed to admit that one so eminent, and previously a supporter, had differences with her. Whatever the case, she was soon to be swept up into the revival excitement of 1857-58, would leave for England in 1859, and not return to the U.S. until 1863, by which time there would be new problems to be addressed. However, it appears that Palmer did in fact respond--at least implicitly--to the concerns of both Bangs and Mattison by highlighting an element of her thought which seemed to strengthen the area in which they found her weak. This is at least one way to understand her very marked turn to the concept of the baptism of the Holy Ghost in the middle and late 1850s.

It will be recalled that already by the late 1840s she was evidencing a growing interest in the role of the Holy Spirit in sanctification, though this was still rather tentative. By 1855, when Incidental Illustrations was published, very near the time of the Mattison articles, this was becoming a major concern and the book is liberally sprinkled with "Spirit language." By 1859, after Bangs' volley, The Promise of the Father announced her almost total conversion to "Pentecostal" and "Spirit" terminology. Four Years in the Old World confirmed the impression with its myriad descriptions of the descent of "fires of the Spirit," "baptisms of the Spirit," and the "Pentecostal flame" bringing "the gift of power." It seems that here Palmer was trying to respond to the criticisms that her system limited Wesley's doctrine of a dynamic witness of the Spirit to a "lifeless" declaration of the Bible, and ignored the need for genuine sanctification to be evidenced by a changed, "holy" life. By calling entire sanctification a "baptism of the Holy Ghost" and emphasizing the power for "witnessing" and making converts which it imparted, Palmer was not only adding to her system a functional equivalent of Wesley's "witness of the Spirit"--i.e. something subjectively experienced and objectively manifested--she was also shifting the balance back toward the divine (i.e. "baptism" is what God the Holy Spirit does as a result of the seeker's entire consecration), where her critics were pushing her. In this she may have been influenced by the perfectionists at Oberlin, and their tendency to refer to sanctification as a "baptism of the Holy Ghost," although one need not look that far. Ample sources were available in the Wesleyan tradition in Fletcher and the popularizers Palmer knew so well.[125]

Palmer's critics, had they cared about such things, might well have traced her apparent departure from Wesley to a difference in philosophical bases. Though neither Palmer nor her critics evidence much self awareness about philosophical presuppositions, it appears they played an important role in the genesis of Palmer's "American revivalistic Wesleyan perfectionism."

A powerful influence on the American mind through the nineteenth century was the Scottish Philosophy of Common Sense, or Scottish Realism. Movements as diverse as the "rational orthodoxy" of Princeton and New England Transcendentalism took important cues from it.[126] While some Americans were careful students of the formulators of the school, reading after Thomas Reid (1710-1796), James Beattie (1735-1803), and Dugald Stewart (1735-1828), most simply absorbed some of the general habits of thought and outlook associated with it, as these were modeled by teachers, moralists, and preachers, among others.[127]

The Common Sense Philosophy was essentially a reaction to the more unsettling implications of the psychology of John Locke, which had been developed so explicitly by George Berkeley and David Hume as to deny the possibility of having certain knowledge of the existence of an external world of material objects. The Common Sense thinkers reasserted that the common perceptions of ordinary people actually reveal a real world "out there" as it is, and not simply "ideas" whose relation to anything besides themselves can be neither tested nor verified. In this they relied heavily upon analysis of the "structure" of the human mind, a structure they believed to be prior to and independent of experience.

Though developed in many directions, the Common Sense Philosophy was especially vital in inspiring high regard for an inductive, "scientific" approach to religion and morals, as well as to the natural sciences. The systematic observation and analysis of Francis Bacon and Isaac Newton was held up as a model for all branches of inquiry. For religious thinkers, this meant that the "facts of human consciousness, of nature, and of Scripture, all of which yielded <u>laws</u> rather than metaphysical fancies, were to provide the grounds of argument."[128]

Phoebe Palmer, though she most likely would not have recognized the names of any of the Common Sense philosophers, certainly imbibed their spirit as it pervaded American thought in her day. This can be readily seen in her "mechanical" conception of the spiritual and moral world, her view of faith as a kind of "knowledge" grounded in the objective "facts" of the Bible, and her stress on free will and one's duty to be holy without delay. Also, her controversial teaching that assurance rises out of the act of believing (as well as from the objective "promises" of scripture), dubbed by her critics "believe that you have it and you have it," reflects Scottish Realism's faith in fixed and unvarying laws of human consciousness and knowing.

By contrast, John Wesley, Palmer's somewhat distant "father in the faith," drew breath from a different intellectual atmosphere. Though a contemporary of the Scottish Realists, his views were shaped more by John Locke, whose <u>Essay Concerning Human Understanding</u> he

serialized in his <u>Arminian Magazine</u>.[129] From Locke he
learned that knowledge comes to the mind through sense
experience. Knowing is thus a matter of sensation--of
feeling. The mind <u>feels</u> what it believes. Thus, knowledge for Wesley was not so much what the mind understands, as what it <u>experiences</u>. Nothing is known that
cannot be felt.

This Lockean epistemology and psychology, along
with the influence of Pietism, thus helped to determine
Wesley's regard for feeling in religion. As we have
already seen, Wesley even held faith to be a kind of
faculty of sense which receives the "light" of God and
divine things. Therefore, the operations of faith are
felt, and they are inextricably bound up with a palpable
sense of the divine presence. Hence, for Wesley, "naked
faith" standing on nothing but a "naked promise" has no
meaning. Faith is not an assent to evidence, and it
cannot be "naked" and be faith, since faith is clothed
in the sensible "communication" of God and divine truth
to the believer, eliciting from the believer trust and
love.

Consistent with this, Wesley held that assurance of
justification or sanctification must be <u>felt</u> to be truly
known. Such assurance comes by the "witness of the
Spirit" which in its direct, and most essential dimension, is a palpable, sensible conviction of the work of
God in one's life. One could not have knowledge, and
hence confidence, of one's spiritual state short of this
perceptible experience. Thus, to testify to receiving
either a "first" or "second blessing" simply on the
basis of "promises" and a leap of "naked faith," as
Phoebe Palmer urged, would be for Wesley to claim to
know something one did not really know.[130]

In their differing philosophical assumptions, then, can be seen some of the roots of the differences between Palmer and Wesley as they attempted, each in their own historical setting, to explain and commend what they both were convinced was the privilege of all Christians, namely, perfect holiness. This also helps to explain how Palmer, though she was familiar with the writings of Wesley, and quoted him from time to time, tended to misread him on key issues such as the nature of faith, and the doctrine of the "witness of the Spirit."

C. Palmer and the Development of the "Sectarian Holiness Movement"

In 1867, several years after Phoebe and Walter Palmer returned from England to try to pump new life into the sagging holiness movement, the first "national camp meeting for the promotion of holiness" was held at Vineland, New Jersey. Though the Palmers were not workers at this camp, they supported it, carrying the official announcement in the Guide to Holiness. In part the announcement read:

> A GENERAL Camp-meeting of the friends of "holiness" to be held at Vineland, Cumberland County, N.J., will commence Wednesday, July 17, and close Friday, 26th. We affectionately invite all, irrespective of denominational ties, interested in the subject of the "higher Christian life," to come together, and spend a week in God's temple of Nature. While we shall not cease to labor for the conviction and conversion of sinners, still the special object of this meeting will be to offer united and continued prayer for the revival of the work of holiness in the Church...to strengthen

the hands of those who feel themselves comparatively isolated in their profession of holiness; to help any who would enter into this
rest of faith and love; to realize a Pentecostal baptism of the Holy Ghost; and all with
a view to increased usefulness in the churches
of which we are members. Come, brothers and
sisters of the various denominations, and let
us...furnish an illustration of evangelical
union, and make common supplication for the
descent of the Spirit....[131]

The organizing committee of ministers issuing the
call intended the meeting to be ecumenical; it would be
a show of Christian solidarity for "the higher Christian
life," as second blessing holiness was often called,
especially in non-Methodist circles. They hoped it would
bring closer the realization of the vision of interdenominational unity around the great theme of "holiness
unto the Lord" that Phoebe Palmer had been championing
for 25 years. What also peeks through their words is
their awareness that the vision was further from fulfillment than one glorious camp meeting--or even several
glorious camp meetings. The meeting is to be for those
who "feel themselves comparatively isolated in their
profession of holiness," an admission that the holiness
advocates were hardly a conquering army in the American
churches, even in Methodism, their most natural home.
They still commanded considerable support in many
places, but the tide was turning, and before many more
years "holiness people" would find themselves not "increasingly useful" in their churches, but relegated to
the sidelines and generally considered "useless," if not
positively harmful. Many would find the growing isola-
tion intolerable and would decide that a separate "holi-

ness church" was a better alternative to waging ineffec-
tive guerrilla warfare in hostile surroundings. "Crank-
tification" some would derisively call their revered
doctrine.

The National Campmeeting Association for the Promotion of Holiness which organized itself in the aftermath
of the Vineland camp meeting to sponsor further "general
holiness campmeetings," hardly intended to start down
the road toward separatism and sectarianism--quite the
contrary. However, in taking charge and giving an
organizational center to a movement that had previously
flowed in denominational channels for the most part (the
Palmer-inspired network of meetings for the promotion of
holiness being quite informal and entirely decentral-
ized), it both brought holiness people together in a
more concerted way than ever before, and also helped to
magnify the difference between them and those in the
churches who were less enthusiastic about a "second
blessing." The national association also soon sprouted
regional and local "holiness associations" which formed
to promote camp meeting-style holiness meetings, publish
holiness papers, sponsor holiness-supporting missionaries, and in some cases establish holiness schools as
refuges from denominational colleges where holiness was
not esteemed. Though the National Campmeeting Association always counseled strict denominational loyalty,
these regional and local organizations almost inexorably
became breeding grounds for separatists, and provided
ready vehicles for the creation of new "holiness"
denominations.[132]

Phoebe Palmer played no direct role in the process
begun by the formation of the National Campmeeting Association for the Promotion of Holiness. She and Walter
were never even Association members, although they did

appear at several Association-sponsored camp meetings during Phoebe's declining years, and their Guide to Holiness regularly carried news of Association activities. Their support was not as avid as one might expect, however, considering their role as the leading holiness advocates of the day. One suspects that their intense loyalty to Methodism, a loyalty which had led them to shun their ideological kin in the Free Methodist movement, and their sensitivity to the often repeated charge that promotion of holiness as a "speciality" leads to schism, made them uneasy about the divisive potential of a group like the National Association, even though they might find its successes worth applauding.

Nevertheless, the Palmers were closely identified in the popular mind with the work of the National Camp-meeting Association and the proliferating holiness associations around the country. Even the National Association itself claimed them as parents. An officer of the Association declared at Phoebe's death, "The present National Campmeeting movement for the promotion of holiness owes its inception largely to the inspiration and labors of our sister [Palmer]."[133] George Hughes, one of the sponsors of the first "general holiness campmeeting" and a business associate of the Palmers in religious publishing, found it necessary to defend their denominational loyalty when he published his "biography" of Walter in 1884. By then several separatist holiness denominations had grown out of organized holiness "associations," and numerous "unauthorized" holiness evangelists were operating outside of regular ecclesiastical channels. Lest the Palmers be judged guilty by association with this turn of events, Hughes, himself secretary of the national Campmeeting Association (and a loyal Methodist), noted pointedly, "Such was their loyalty to the church and its usages that they waited for official invitations, and so acted under the proper authority."134

Hughes was quite right, and yet so were those who considered the post-Civil War movement the child of Phoebe Palmer. Not organizationally linked to the movement, and certain to be appalled at the fragmentation of holiness forces into a host of competing sects had she lived to see it, she <u>had</u> laid the groundwork for all of this to happen.

Her aggressive crusade to reinstate second blessing holiness as the "grand depositum" of Methodism had created a distinct "holiness party" within that church. Her unique presentation of holiness doctrine aroused opposition from those favoring more traditional usages, even as it galvanized her followers into an army of dedicated "Palmerites," further spotlighting the distance between "holiness people" and others. Her attempt to find interdenominational unity in "holiness" bore significant fruit for a time, but it also helped to eventually produce a pool of non-Methodists who were frustrated and estranged from their churches because they espoused a doctrine and way of life at variance with the traditions of their particular denomination. Her development of the "Pentecostal" theme, somewhat latent in popular Methodism, provided a powerful motivation for "Holy-Ghost baptized" Christians, lay men and women, along with clergy, to initiate and support religious and charitable work of all sorts, some of which were almost certain to run afoul of ecclesiastical bureaucracies. Her special meetings for the promotion of holiness, her effort to make camp meetings centers of holiness renewal, and her use of the <u>Guide to Holiness</u> as a mouthpiece for holiness forces, all provided means

that would be used by the "sectarian holiness movement"
to pull away from its parent bodies when it discovered
it no longer had their support and approval.

One could develop nearly an entire study around
Palmer's direct impact upon the organizations and
churches that began to form in the 1870s and after. Such
a task is beyond the scope of the present effort. However, a few particulars may be noted. Aside from the
methods of holiness revivalism which she developed
during her public career, her distinctive system of
thought was that which had the greatest ongoing influence. Both her unique articulation of "the way of holiness" and her exposition of the "promise of the Father"
furnished models for large numbers of American Christians to understand and explain their own religious
pilgrimages.

In 1885, eleven years after Phoebe's death, a general convention of holiness advocates met in Chicago. By
this time there were already separate holiness churches
in existence, and the delegates included both those who
favored what was being called by this time "come-out-
ism," and denominational loyalists. Among other business
a doctrinal statement was adopted which reflected the
broad consensus of holiness forces at that conference.
Their statement on sanctification echoed Palmer at many
points. "Entire sanctification," they declared, is "that
great work wrought subsequent to regeneration, by the
Holy Ghost, upon the sole condition of faith, such faith
being preceded by an act of solemn and complete consecration...." Justified, but unsanctified persons should
"be encouraged to go up at once to the Canaan of perfect
love." Once sanctified, it "is the duty of all who are
made partakers of entire sanctification...to testify
thereof....Such testimony should be very definite, as

much as possible in the use of <u>Bible terms</u>," and should this duty be shirked, "the light of the soul will soon become darkness."[135] This statement served as a doctrinal standard for the holiness movement and informed numerous "articles of faith" produced by separatist holiness groups, as well as the expositions of many holiness preachers and teachers.

Even more vividly reflective of Palmer's ongoing influence were some of the sermons preached by evangelists which aimed at leading persons into "the way of holiness." W. E. Shephard, an early twentieth-century holiness revivalist, gained national repute with an "illustrated sermon" which followed Palmer's "shorter way" steps to sanctification almost to the letter, and which exuded her sense of "holiness ethics."

According to Shephard, the seeker after holiness could be sanctified by faith, but "before one can exercise this faith, he must put himself on believing ground" which involves an "unconditional consecration of himself to God" and the fulfillment of divine "conditions."[136] The process of consecration is likened to placing a sacrifice on the altar, Christ being that altar. As soon as consecration is made, "the Altar sanctifieth the gift." When "we do our part in the contract," Shephard declares, God necessarily does his part.[137]

To illustrate entire consecration, Shephard would then place a box upon the "altar," from which he would take cards and objects representing what was being consecrated a "living sacrifice" to God and explain the implications. For example, consecrated hands "will not be channels for wrongdoing." They won't traffic in "distilled damnation" or "handle the filthy weed." They will "write letters, give out tracts" and "help the poor

and needy, the sick and distressed."[138] Similarly, consecrated eyes will "not read the sickly, sentimental
love trash which so fills the papers, magazines, and
books" or "look upon suggestive pictures." They will
"read the Word of God" and "spiritual books and
papers."[139] Consecrated lips will abstain from gossip or
slander or "foolish talking, joking and jesting," and
give themselves to testimony, prayer, and being the
"mouthpiece of God," delivering "any message in the fear
of God...regardless of consequences."[140]

The evangelist then confronted the speaker with the
duty to testify to the blessing, Romans 10:10 underscoring the point just as it did for Phoebe Palmer. He
would ring a small bell at this point to indicate the
clarity with which testimony must be made. One must use
precise terminology and seize every opportunity. "You
will have to ring it out with unmistakable sound,"
Shephard would tell his audiences.[141]

One thing Shephard taught which was a post-Palmer
addition to holiness thought was that entire sanctification would be accompanied by "a great demonstration of
joy" in which one might "shout or jump or dance for joy"
or "in any other way act as the Holy Ghost indicates."[142] Even though this represents an understandable
interpretation of Phoebe's concept of the baptism of the
Holy Ghost bringing "fire" and an endowment with
"power," she would not have endorsed it. For later
holiness people, it seems that Palmer's "naked faith"
was as difficult a concept as it was for many of her
contemporaries, and they found more palpable assurance
that the "second blessing" was attained in exercises of
"holy joy," a reassertion of revivalism's regard for
emotion, and an ironic twist to a "way of holiness"
which had been conceived to steer clear of emotion.

Still Palmer's ideas about faith were not neglected altogether. Often times, in fact, they appeared side by side with apparently conflicting views.[143] Some even refined Palmer's concepts further and wrote books explaining in detail the "laws" which they were convinced governed faith. Such a one was J. G. Morrison, a General Superintendent in the Church of the Nazarene for a time in the 1930s. In his book, <u>Achieving Faith</u>, Morrison described faith as "governed by law" and subject to principles, which, when followed, result in the "invariable recurrence of certain results, under similar conditions." The "law of faith" is "a law which works as automatically as...the laws of chemical affinity," Morrison declared, or as "automatically as the wire delivers electric current when properly connected."[144]

So invariable and "automatic" is this "law of faith," according to Morrison, that Christians can even use it to get things God does not desire them to have, and which are not for their good. A story of a sick child healed according to the "law of faith" only to grow into crime and be hanged, illustrates the point. Even non-Christians can "use" faith in a sort of "power of positive thinking" way to bring "desired things to pass."[145]

Reviewing the achievements of the Christian Church through the ages, Morrison put them all down to the power of faith:

You will find that it was faith, <u>faith</u> FAITH, that brought victory, secured every advance, toppled the walls of hoary superstitions, translated the Bible into hundreds of languages, inaugurated missionary enterprises, founded holiness churches, and brought us to the present hour with every thing we know of

God, His salvation, and His Book, that is precious to our hearts![146]

In Morrison's formulations, Palmer's "omnipotent faith"--with perhaps a new twist or two--is plainly being taught to a new generation.

But it was not only Palmer's concept of "the shorter way" of holiness and its associated ideas which influenced the "sectarian holiness movement." Her brief for women in ministry was embraced by the new holiness churches with the consequence that scores of women became pastors and evangelists in these groups, as well as missionaries, deaconesses, and directors of the many charitable and social service efforts which the holiness bodies launched.

The movement produced numerous tracts defending its practice. One of the most comprehensive of these was Women Preachers by Fannie McDowell Hunter, a minister in the Holiness Church of Christ which operated in the southern United States.[147] The book is a veritable compendium of exegesis and arguments provided by Phoebe Palmer's The Promise of the Father. The Bible passages that suggest that females "ministered" in Old Testament and New Testament settings are examined. The women "prophets," "judges" and disciples of the Bible are duly noted. Much is made of the fact that a woman was the first to carry the news of Jesus's resurrection. And, of course, Pentecost is held up as the pre-eminent model for the Church, men and women together receiving "the promise of the Father." Hunter even deduces from data given in the book of Acts that at least 105 of the 120 disciples present on the day of Pentecost were women![148]

She also wrestles with the difficult Pauline passages, and finds, along with Palmer, that these refer to specific conditions of Paul's day and have no general applicability. Moreover, one finds the "argument from history"--including this time Phoebe Palmer--and fully half of the book given over to the "practical argument" --i.e. testimonies from nine contemporary women preachers whose lives and experiences are offered as validation of the claim that women, as well as men, are endowed with power for ministry by the "baptism of the Holy Ghost."[149]

However, whereas Phoebe Palmer meant her argument to support wide ranging "lay ministry" by women, her daughters in the holiness churches pressed it to its logical conclusion, and claimed full ministerial rights, including ordination, which almost all holiness churches granted. Thus, even though her example and views were slow to make much of an impact on the "mainline" American churches, her own Methodist Church not granting full clergy rights to women until 1956, she sparked a mini-revolution through the holiness bodies, with the result that women participated fully in these groups a quarter of a century before Federal woman-suffrage and nearly three-quarters of a century before the modern feminist movement.

CHAPTER VI
CONCLUSION

Phoebe Palmer's contemporaries waxed eloquent in their efforts following her death in 1874 to fix her place in the firmament of religious achievement. She had made a significant impact upon their lives. Her work and teachings had helped many to think religiously in new ways, to imagine and experience a kind of spirituality which was appealing and personally fulfilling, and to conduct their lives according to new values. For those whose lives had been so rearranged, the one to whom they owed so much could not be simply a mere mortal. She was, they thought, a giant of history. The "Columbus of the Higher Life," the Rev. Talmage called her, "Synonym of holiness unto the Lord!"[1] "Among all the 'elect ladies' whom Christianity has produced, none have excelled Phoebe Palmer," declared the editor of the Christian Standard.[2] Another eulogizer concurred, confessing to having "no recollection of any record of usefulness by a female in the entire history of the church that will at all compare with hers."[3]

The historian must, of course, handle such plaudits carefully. Recognizing that assessments like these certainly point to a more than ordinary individual, even when allowance is made for nineteenth-century sentimentality and the possibility of self-serving on the part of those associated with aspects of Palmer's ongoing legacy, one must yet ask finally, what in fact did Phoebe Palmer accomplish during her thirty-five years of activity in the public eye? What will the evidence allow one to say about her importance as a nineteenth-century religious notable? Our study would seem to support several conclusions.

First, Palmer was a major force behind the renewed focus on "holiness" in American Methodism in the mid-nineteenth century. Whether it was as near being forgotten as some Methodists believed or not, the concept of Christian Perfection was vividly spotlighted by Palmer's multi-faceted efforts. She was not the only Methodist promoter of the "second blessing" during the period in which she lived, but she was certainly the most single-minded and most widely known--and hence probably most influential--of those who sought to keep the attention of the little "society" which was fast becoming a denomination from wavering from its "grand depositum" of religious truth. Certainly no one else could match her round of visits to meetings for the promotion of holiness, churches, halls, and camp meetings, or her literary output over four decades. Well situated by family ties, personal experience, disposition, talent, and marriage to wield influence in a religious movement that was seeking its way from an association of "societies" founded for spiritual discovery and fellowship within the Church of England to an autonomous denomination operating according to the American pattern of free-for-all competition among pluralistic religious bodies, Palmer worked tirelessly to keep Methodists from straying from the "way of holiness" during the journey. It was thus largely, if not quite exclusively, due to Phoebe Palmer that "The Gospel of Christian holiness became a chief strain in the melody of mid-century Methodism."[4]

Yet Palmer's work and influence extended beyond Methodism. For her, holiness was no sectarian novelty; it was rather the chief doctrine of the "crowning dispensation" in the series of "dispensations" or epochs marking the dealings of God with humankind. She held that the Bible, revered as divine revelation by all Christians irrespective of denomination, throughout its pages set forth the need for, and the way to holiness. To be a Christian was, for her, to be confronted with a divine requirement for personal holiness and to be privy to the counsel of the "Word of God" as to how this could be attained. Thus, Palmer's "perfectionist revivalism" helped to stimulate a perfectionist zeal in American Protestantism generally in the middle nineteenth century. Her "union meetings" saw Baptists, Presbyterians, Episcopalians, Congregationalists, Dutch Reformed, and Quakers mingling with Methodists in a quest for a "higher Christian life" free from the defeating snares of sin and personal failure. "By 1870, holiness teachings of one sort or another seemed to be everywhere in American revivalist Protestantism."[5]

Other forces were at work, to be sure. The widespread religious revivals of the second Great Awakening had helped to create a climate of religious hungering and expectancy in America. Some Christians believed the revivals would wash away divisive, humanly devised creeds and polity in waves of divine power, leaving behind a body of Christians fully united in their common experience of God's grace and their commitment to the Bible alone. More than a few thought they saw the dawning of the millennium just around the corner. Others began to believe that the "ordinary" conversions occurring in the revivals were only a "warmup" for the spiritual blessings God intended to shower upon his people.

There was also the heady optimism which pervaded American culture as a whole in the first half of the nineteenth century. A nation newly freed from European domination, with expanding borders and population, and the promise of unprecedented material wealth and social and political democracy, could hardly do other than stimulate visions of individual and corporate perfectibility. These visions found varied expression in the numerous creative enterprises and crusades of Phoebe Palmer's day, an era marked by what Alice Felt Tyler has called "freedom's ferment."[6] The "holiness movement" was one of these.

Again, Phoebe Palmer was not alone in her work, although her wide-ranging ministry in promoting "holiness" was not matched by any contemporary. The "Columbus of the Higher Life" Talmage called her. He was not quite correct. Certainly not in Methodism where John Wesley's teaching of Christian Perfection antedated her work by a century. Nor even was she really the "discoverer" for non-Methodists like Talmage. Charles Finney and Asa Mahan had begun teaching perfection or "full sanctification" several years before Palmer conducted her first Tuesday Meeting or published her first book. She was perhaps more aptly the "Daniel Boone" of the "higher life"; she was a "trailblazer" who wanted to make hitherto remote areas accessible to settlement. She mapped out the lay of the land and cut roads.

In her efforts to do this Palmer created a distinctive system of thought. Consciously innovating, she fashioned her "shorter way" to holiness from several sources: the teachings of Methodist founder John Wesley; the teachings of the several British "formulators" and "popularizers" of Wesleyanism in the eighteenth and early nineteenth century; and her own experience in the

milieu of early nineteenth-century American revivalistic
religion. Typical for the time, even while she considered herself fully within the tradition of Methodist
thinking about holiness, her strongest appeal was not to
the tradition, but to the Bible as a "textbook" of
religious belief and practice, its truths plain and
"reasonable" to any inquiring mind. It was the Bible,
she believed, which was the source of her "innovative"
insights into holiness.

This distinctive system of thought sought to make
Christian Perfection a "rational" concept and its attainment simple and "foolproof." Accordingly, three
motifs may be seen "governing" Palmer's system: the way
of holiness (there is a definite path to be followed);
the shorter way (it is not so long and wandering a path
as some hold); the simplified way (it is a path easily
understood and simple in the directness with which it
reaches the goal). The various particulars of her
thought can all be understood as contributing to and
buttressing the definiteness, the brevity, or the simplicity (or all three) of the "way of holiness" she maps
out.

Although Phoebe Palmer's assiduous efforts on behalf of holiness were vital to that theme becoming a
"chief strain in the melody of mid-century Methodism,"
so too did her "new measures" of special meetings for
the promotion of holiness, "shorter way" theology, holiness literature, and all the rest lay the groundwork for
a holiness "party" within Methodism--and other churches
as well--which, given time, would be the occasion for
suspicion, hostility, and ultimately division. Seeming
to carry the day by mid-century, within fifteen years
after the close of the Civil War the holiness heirs of
Palmer were scattering for cover. Sensing themselves no

longer welcome in the "mainline" churches as these
groped their way through the rapidly changing currents
of late nineteenth-and early twentieth-century American
life, "holiness people" carried on Palmer's single-
minded "perfectionist revivalism," enshrining much of
her theology and many of her methods, in new, separate
"holiness" denominations.

In a similar, though more roundabout fashion,
Palmer also had a part in the emergence of modern Fundamentalism and Pentecostalism. As noted, Palmer's travels
took her to Britain during the years 1859-63. Her efforts there were supplemented and built upon by several
other Americans. Among these were Charles Finney and Asa
Mahan, D. L. Moody, who experienced a "second blessing"
and adopted "perfectionist" views at the urging of some
Free Methodist ladies,[7] and the husband-wife team of
Robert Pearsall and Hannah Whitall Smith who toured
England during 1873-75. Under the Smiths especially, the
fledging British holiness interest was given organized
expression in a series of conventions not unlike the
American camp meetings for the promotion of holiness.
These were eventually institutionalized in the "Keswick
Conventions" held in the English Lake District parish of
Keswick.[8]

Due to the fact that Keswick found its greatest
support among non-Methodists, the view of holiness espoused there soon shed some of its more "Methodistic"
trappings and came to center on a "baptism with the Holy
Spirit" which did not so much free one from sin (sin was
"suppressed," rather than destroyed or "eradicated" as
most Methodists taught), as it did impart extraordinary
divine "power for service." This view had strong affini-
ties to the holiness teaching evolved at Oberlin, and
was not at all unanticipated by Phoebe Palmer herself.[9]

Such Holy Spirit-aided service would manifest itself primarily in evangelism and missions, it was believed, and Keswick Conventions usually strongly pled for greater involvement of Christians in both.

In time Keswick views were transported back to the U.S. by Moody and other members of the "transatlantic community" of revivalistic Protestantism and grafted onto the home-grown variety of perfectionist revivalism, producing a kind of hybrid form which emphasized a "full consecration" of Christians to God, which would result in a "filling with the Holy Spirit," bringing power for practical service. Along with this teaching, considerable interest in the Holy Spirit's role in the Church was generated and numerous conferences and conventions sprouted up to study the matter. Some of these "bible conferences," which stressed the need for a personal "baptism of the Holy Ghost" as well as a revival of "holy power" in the churches, and aggressive evangelism, also took a keen interest in the "bible prophecy" of the nascent "dispensationalist" movement. A number of scholars have seen the network of conferences and works which grew out of these concerns as an important "nursery" of Fundamentalism.[10]

It might also be noted that Palmer's emphasis on the bible as an infallible "textbook" of objective data, "dictated" by God, and "immutable" helps to place her in the parental line of Fundamentalism. True, she was not alone in her views; in religiously plural America, many were turning to "no creed but the bible" to find some solid grounds for religious certainty. Still, given her wide popularity and influence, Palmer must be counted as one of the major purveyors of "biblicism" to a later generation.

As for Palmer's links to Pentecostalism, one need not look far. They are to be found in some of the same emphases that tie her to Keswick, i.e. her view of "Spirit baptism" and her later preoccupation with biblical Pentecost as the original occasion of "entire sanctification." Over time, she came more and more to speak of "holiness" in terms of a "baptism of the Holy Ghost" which provided Christians with "power" for "service" to God and for holy living. In Palmer's Methodist surroundings, her holiness followers tended to mix more or less uncritically such concepts with more "Wesleyan" ideas (there was, of course, already the "pentecostal" influence of John Fletcher in Methodism, which also strongly shaped Palmer's thought through the "Wesleyan popularizers"), while in non-Methodist holiness circles such emphases became more or less normative, especially when augmented by Oberlin and Keswickian teaching.

This stress on biblical Pentecost as the occasion for a "second blessing" and as normative for the Christian (each must undergo a "personal Pentecost"), and the element of power underscored by Palmer and even more strongly by Keswick and Oberlin, together with the considerable interest in the Holy Spirit and manifestations of the Spirit in the Church which such teaching helped to generate, created a climate for the emergence of Pentecostalism. Once one began to take the book of Acts account of the day of Pentecost as a paradigm of religious experience and to emphasize the element of divine power manifested there, it was not an illogical jump to conclude that glossolalia or "speaking in tongues" was a central evidence of the reception of that power.

Of course, Palmer herself never made that jump, nor did most of the holiness people who embraced her "pentecostal" themes and images, or who were influenced by

Keswick-style teaching. Yet some did. It is interesting to note that most early Pentecostal leaders had some connection with separatist "holiness" organizations spawned by the holiness movement where they had imbibed teaching heavily indebted to Phoebe Palmer. However, as Pentecostal thought developed it divided over how to render holiness teaching into thoroughgoing Pentecostal (i.e. tongues speaking) categories. One group, trying to sort out the nature of the sanctification/pentecostal baptism with divine power (accompanied by tongues) experience, divided it into two separate experiences--a second work of grace (entire sanctification) bringing cleansing from sin and the gift of "perfect love," followed by a third work of grace, bringing power for service and evidenced by speaking in tongues. A second group tended to locate "cleansing" in the "first work" of grace, describing the "second blessing" as exclusively a gift of divine power attested by speaking in tongues.[11] In this way the ambiguities and possibilities in Phoebe Palmer's thought furnished resources for modern Pentecostalism.

Finally, Phoebe Palmer was the first woman to become widely noted--and as widely accepted--as a religious leader and thinker in America. One can of course point to earlier figures like Anne Lee (1736-1784) and Jemimah Wilkinson (1753-1819). Lee's following during her lifetime, however, was very limited. The real growth of her Shaker movement came under others after her death. Wilkinson's notoriety as "The Public and Universal Friend" was narrowly regional. Also, both women were popularly regarded as being on the very perimeter of "mainstream" religion.

Palmer's achievement was quite different. Parlaying her talents into power in a religious body traditionally open to lay initiative (including significant female participation, in Britain at least), she rode the crest of revivalism with its levelling and egalitarian tendencies (all the unconverted equally condemned before God; saving grace available to all) beyond her own shallow pool into the deeper waters of American religious life. Methodism gave her a more or less natural training ground, while revivalism--to change the metaphor--gave her the "bridge" to a national, and eventually international following. Revivalism, by upsetting traditional religious structures and patterns, opened the way for a whole host of innovative "new measures," a female itinerant evangelist/teacher not the least of these.

Also, Palmer did not mean to neglect the unique opportunity she had to keep the newly opened door ajar for others like herself. She attempted to take advantage of this by providing an explicit rationale for expanded roles for women in religion in The Promise of the Father. Though few after her quite matched her accomplishments, her work and her writing did contribute to expanded religious roles for American women and this has been an essential part of the process of women gaining larger roles in American culture generally.

Was Phoebe Palmer the most "useful" female in the entire history of the Christian Church as some claimed? Certainly to those touched by her for good and caught up in the excitement of her enthusiasm for "entire devotion to God," she must have seemed so. Her achievements were not small. She cast a very long shadow in her own day. Given the proper angle of vision, it may still be seen today.

BIBLIOGRAPHY

Works By and About Palmer

Boynton, Rev. J. Sanctification Practical: A Book for the Times. With an introduction and appendix ("The Act of Faith by which the blessing of Holiness is Obtained and Retained") by Phoebe Palmer. New York: Foster and Palmer, Jr., 1867.

Hughes, Rev. George. The Beloved Physician, Dr. Walter C. Palmer, M.D., and His Sun-Lit Journey to the Celestial City. New York: Palmer and Hughes, 1884.

Hughes, Rev. George. Fragrant Memories of the Tuesday Meeting and Guide to Holiness. New York: Palmer and Hughes, 1886.

Palmer, Phoebe. Entire Devotion to God: A Present to A Christian Friend. London: Salvationist Publishing and Supplies, Ltd., [1845] 1853.

Palmer, Phoebe. Faith and Its Effects: Fragments from My Portfolio. New York: Published for the Author [1845] 1848.

Palmer, Phoebe. Four Years in the Old World. New York: Foster and Palmer, Jr., Publishers, 1865.

Palmer, Phoebe. Incidental Illustrations of the Economy of Salvation. Boston: Henry V. Degen, [1855] 1859.

Palmer, Phoebe, editor. Pioneer Experiences; or, The Gift of Power Received by Faith, Illustrated and Confirmed by the Testimony of Eighty Living Ministers of Various Denominations. New York: Walter C. Palmer, Jr., 1868.

Palmer, Phoebe. The Promise of the Father; or, a Neglected Specialty of the Last Days. Boston: Henry V. Degen, 1859.

Palmer, Phoebe. The Way of Holiness, With Notes by the Way. New York: W. C. Palmer, [1843] 1867.

Roche, John A. The Life of Mrs. Sarah A. Lankford Palmer. New York: George Hughes & Co., 1867.

Wheatley, Rev. Richard. The Life and Letters of Mrs. Phoebe Palmer. New York: Palmer & Hughes, 1876.

Wesley and Methodism: Primary and Secondary Works

Arthur, William. The Tongue of Fire; or, the True Power of Christianity. New York: Harper and Brother, Publishers, 1857.

Baker, Frank. From Wesley to Asbury: Studies in Early American Methodism. Durham, North Carolina: Duke University Press, 1976.

Baker, Frank. Methodism and the Love Feast. London: The Epworth Press, 1957.

Benson, Joseph. The Life of the Rev. John W. De La Flechere. New York: The Methodist Book Concern, n.d.

Bucke, Emory Stevens, ed. The History of American Methodism. 3 volumes. Nashville: Abingdon Press, 1964.

Cannon, William R. The Theology of John Wesley. Nashville: Abingdon Press, 1946.

Carvosso, Benjamin, editor. Life of William Carvosso, Sixty Years A Class Leader. Cincinnati: Jennings and Pye, n.d. [first edition 1835].

Cell, George Croft. The Rediscovery of John Wesley. New York: Henry Holt and Co., 1935.

Chiles, Robert E. Theological Transition in American Methodism: 1790-1935. Nashville: Abingdon Press, 1965.

Clarke, Adam. Christian Theology. New York: T. Mason and G. Lane, [1835] 1840.

Harmon, Nolan B., editor. The Encyclopedia of World Methodism. 3 volumes. Nashville: United Methodist Publishing House, 1974.

Jackson, Thomas, editor. The Works of the Rev. John
    Wesley, A.M. 14 volumes. Kansas City, Missouri:
    Nazarene Publishing House. Reprint of the edition
    authorized by the Wesleyan Conference Office,
    London, 1872.

Ladies of the Mission. The Old Brewery and the New
    Mission House at the Five Points. New York:
    Stringer and Townsend, 1854.

Langford, Thomas A. Practical Divinity: Theology in the
    Wesleyan Tradition. Nashville: Abingdon Press,
    1983.

Lee, Umphrey. John Wesley and Modern Religion.
    Nashville: Cokesbury Press, 1936.

Lindstrom, Harald. Wesley and Sanctification.
    Stockholm: Nya Bokförlags Aktiebolaget, 1946.

Lummus, Aaron. Essays on Holiness. Boston: Timothy
    Ashley, 1826.

Mattison, Hiram. Popular Amusements: An Appeal to
    Methodists in Regard to the Evils of Card-Playing,
    Billiards, Dancing, Theatre-Going, Etc. New York:
    Carlton and Porter, 1867.

McDonald, W. and John E. Searles. The Life of Rev. John
    S. Inskip. Boston: McDonald and Gill, 1885.

Merritt, Timothy. The Christian's Manual: A Treatise on
    Christian Perfection. New York: N. Bangs and J.
    Emory, 1825.

Norwood, Frederick A. The Story of American Methodism.
    Nashville: Abingdon Press, 1974.

Norwood, Frederick A. Sourcebook of American Methodism.
    Nashville: Abingdon Press, 1982.

Outler, Albert C., editor. John Wesley. New York:
    Oxford University Press, 1964.

Peck, George O. The Scripture Doctrine of Christian
    Perfection Stated and Defended. New York: Carlton
    and Porter, 1842.

Peters, John L. Christian Perfection and American
    Methodism. Nashville: Abingdon Press, 1956.

Piette, Maximin. John Wesley in The Evolution of Protestantism. Translated by J. B. Howard. New York: Sheed and Ward, 1937.

Rogers, Hester Ann. An Account of the Experiences of Hester Ann Rogers. New York: Lane and Scott, 1850.

Rogers, Hester Ann. The Life of Faith Exemplified; or, Extracts from the Journal of Mrs. Hester Ann Rogers. New York: Carlton and Porter, 1861.

Simpson, Matthew, editor. Cyclopedia of Methodism. Philadelphia: Louis H. Everts, [1876] 1882.

Sugden, E. H., editor. The Standard Sermons of John Wesley. 2 volumes. London: The Epworth Press, 1921.

Starkey, Lycurgus M., Jr. The Work of the Holy Spirit: A Study in Wesleyan Theology. Nashville: Abingdon Press, 1962.

Stevens, Abel. Life and Times of Nathan Bangs, D.D.. New York: Carlton and Porter, 1863.

Sweet, William Warren. Methodism in American History. Nashville: Abingdon Press, 1954.

Telford, John, editor. The Letters of The Rev. John Wesley, A.M.. 8 volumes. London: The Epworth Press, 1931.

Thomas, Hilah F. and Keller, Rosemary Skinner, editors. Women in New Worlds: Historical Perspectives on the Wesleyan Tradition. Nashville: Abingdon Press, 1981.

Tyerman, Luke. Wesley's Designated Successor. New York: A. C. Armstrong and Son, 1886.

Van Cott, Margaret. The Harvest and the Reaper: Reminiscences of Revival Work of Mrs. Maggie N. Van Cott. New York: N. Tibbals and Sons, 1876.

Wesley, John. A Plain Account of Christian Perfection. Kansas City, Missouri: Beacon Hill Press of Kansas City, 1966. Reprinted from the text authorized by the Wesleyan Conference Office, London, 1872.

Wesley, John. Advice to the People Called Methodists With Regard to Dress. London: John Parmore, 1780.

Williams, Colin W. <u>John</u> <u>Wesley's</u> <u>Theology</u> <u>Today</u>.
Nashville: Abingdon Press, 1960.

Wide, Rev. Daniel, editor. <u>Methodism</u> <u>in</u> <u>Earnest</u>: <u>Being</u>
<u>the</u> <u>History</u> <u>of</u> <u>the</u> <u>Great</u> <u>Revival</u> <u>in</u> <u>Great</u> <u>Britain</u>;
<u>in</u> <u>Which</u> <u>Twenty</u> <u>Thousand</u> <u>Souls</u> <u>Professed</u> <u>Faith</u> <u>in</u>
<u>Christ</u>, <u>and</u> <u>Ten</u> <u>Thousand</u> <u>Professed</u> <u>Sanctification</u>,
<u>in</u> <u>About</u> <u>Six</u> <u>Years</u> <u>in</u> <u>Connection</u> <u>With</u> <u>the</u> <u>Labors</u> <u>of</u>
<u>Rev.</u> <u>James</u> <u>Caughey</u>. Boston: Charles H. Pierce,
1850.

<u>The</u> <u>Works</u> <u>of</u> <u>the</u> <u>Rev.</u> <u>John</u> <u>Fletcher</u>. 4 volumes. New
York: Carlton and Phillips, 1854.

<u>General</u> <u>Works</u>

Ahlstrom, Sidney E. <u>A</u> <u>Religious</u> <u>History</u> <u>of</u> <u>the</u> <u>American</u>
<u>People</u>. New Haven and London: Yale University
Press, 1972.

Anderson, Robert Mapes. <u>Vision</u> <u>of</u> <u>The</u> <u>Disinherited</u>: <u>The</u>
<u>Making</u> <u>of</u> <u>American</u> <u>Pentecostalism</u>. New York: Oxford
University Press, 1979.

Barnes, Albert. <u>An</u> <u>Inquiry</u> <u>Into</u> <u>the</u> <u>Scriptural</u> <u>Views</u> <u>of</u>
<u>Slavery</u>. Philadelphia: Perry and McMillan, 1846.

Bercovitch, Sacvan, editor. <u>Typology</u> <u>and</u> <u>Early</u> <u>American</u>
<u>Literature</u>. Amherst: University of Massachusetts
Press, 1972.

Blanchard, J. and Rice, N.C. <u>A</u> <u>Debate</u> <u>on</u> <u>Slavery</u> <u>Held</u>
<u>in</u> <u>The</u> <u>City</u> <u>of</u> <u>Cincinnati</u>. Cincinnati: H. Moore and
Company, 1846.

Boles, John B. <u>The</u> <u>Great</u> <u>Revival</u> <u>1787-1805</u>: <u>The</u> <u>Origins</u>
<u>of</u> <u>the</u> <u>Southern</u> <u>Evangelical</u> <u>Mind</u>. Lexington: The
University Press of Kentucky, 1972.

Booth, Catherine. <u>Female</u> <u>Ministry</u>; <u>or</u> <u>Woman's</u> <u>Right</u> <u>to</u>
<u>Preach</u> <u>the</u> <u>Gospel</u>. New York: Salvation Army
Supplies Printing and Publishing Department, 1975.
Reprint of the first edition, London, 1859.

Bozeman, Theodore Dwight. <u>Protestants</u> <u>in</u> <u>An</u> <u>Age</u> <u>of</u>
<u>Science</u>: <u>The</u> <u>Baconian</u> <u>Ideal</u> <u>and</u> <u>Antebellum</u> <u>American</u>
<u>Religious</u> <u>Thought</u>. Chapel Hill: The University of
North Carolina Press, 1977.

Bruce, Dickson, Jr. And They All Sang Hallelujah:
Plainfolk Campmeeting Religion, 1800-1845.
Knoxville: The University of Tennessee Press, 1975.

Cagle, Mary Lee. Life and Work of Mary Lee Cagle.
Kansas City, MO: Nazarene Publishing House, 1928.

Carwardine, Richard. Transatlantic Revivalism: Popular
Evangelicalism in Britain and America, 1790-1865.
Westport CT: Greenwood Press, 1978.

Chauncy, Charles. Seasonable Thoughts on the State of
Religion in New England. Hicksville, New York: The
Regina Press, 1975. Reprint of 1743 edition.

Cherry, Conrad. Nature and Religious Imagination: From
Edwards to Bushnell. Philadelphia: Fortress Press,
1980.

Cole, Charles C., Jr. The Social Ideas of the Northern
Evangelists, 1826-1860. New York: Octagon Books,
Inc., 1966.

Conant, William C. Narratives of Remarkable Conversions
and Revival Incidents. New York: Derby and Jackson,
1858.

Cott, Nancy F. The Bonds of Womanhood: "Woman's Sphere"
in New England, 1780-1835. New Haven and London:
Yale University Press, 1977.

Cross, Whitney. The Burned Over District: The Social
and Intellectual History of Enthusiastic Religion
in Western New York, 1800-1850. New York: Harper
and Row, 1958.

Dayton, Donald W. Discovering an Evangelical Heritage.
New York: Harper and Row, 1976.

Dieter, Melvin Easterday. The Holiness Revival of the
Nineteenth Century. Metuchen, N.J.: The Scarecrow
Press, 1980.

Douglas, Ann. The Feminization of American Culture. New
York: Alfred A. Knopf, 1977.

Edwards, Jonathan. Religious Affections. Edited by John
E. Smith. New Haven: Yale University Press, 1959.

Faust, Clarence H. and Johnson, Thomas H. Jonathan Edwards, Representative Selections. New York: Hill and Wang, 1962.

Findlay, James F., Jr. Dwight L. Moody: American Evangelist, 1837-1899. Chicago: University of Chicago Press, 1969.

Finney, Charles G. Lectures on Systematic Theology. Edited by James H. Fairchild. Oberlin, Ohio: E. J. Goodrich, 1878.

Finney, Charles G. Lectures to Professing Christians. New York: Fleming H. Revell Company, 1878.

Finney, Charles G. Memoirs of Rev. Charles G. Finney. New York: A. S. Barnes and Company, 1876.

Finney, Charles G. The Promise of the Spirit. Compiled and edited by Timothy L. Smith. Minneapolis: Bethany House Publishers, 1980.

Finney, Charles G. Views on Sanctification. Oberlin, Ohio: James Steele, 1840.

Flower, Elizabeth and Murphey, Murray G. A History of Philosophy in America. 2 volumes. New York: G. P. Putnam's Sons, 1977.

Gundry, Stanley N. Love Them In: The Life and Theology of Dwight L. Moody. Grand Rapids: Baker Book House, 1976.

Handy, Robert T. A Christian America: Protestant Hopes and Historical Realities. New York: Oxford University Press, 1971.

Hatch, Nathan O. and Noll, Mark A., editors. The Bible in America: Essays in Cultural History. New York: Oxford University Press, 1982.

Heath, Merle McClurkan. A Man Sent of God: The Life of J.O. McClurkan. Kansas City, MO: Beacon Hill Press, 1974.

Hogue, Wilson T. History of the Free Methodist Church. 2 volumes. Winona Lake, Indiana: Free Methodist Publishing House, 1915.

Hudson, Winthrop S. Religion in America. New York: Charles Scribner's Sons, 1982.

Hudson, Winthrop S. The Great Tradition of the American Churches. New York: Harper and Brothers, 1953.

Hudson, Winthrop S. American Protestantism. Chicago: University of Chicago Press, 1961.

Hughes, George. Days of Power in the Forest Temple. Boston: John Bent and Company, 1873.

Hunter, Fannie McDowell. Women Preachers. Dallas: Berachah Printing Company, 1905.

James, Janet Wilson, editor. Women in American Religion. Philadelphia: University of Pennsylvania Press, 1980.

Johnson, Charles A. The Frontier Campmeeting: Religion's Harvest Time. Dallas: Southern Methodist University Press, 1955.

Jones, Charles E. Perfectionist Persuasion: The Holiness Movement and American Methodism, 1867-1936. Metuchen, N.J.: The Scarecrow Press, Inc., 1974.

Kraditor, Aileen S., editor. Up From the Pedestal: Selected Writings in the History of American Feminism. Chicago: Quadrangle Books, 1968.

Madden, Edward H., and James H. Hamilton. Freedom and Grace: The Life of Asa Mahan. Metuchen, N.J.: The Scarecrow Press, Inc., 1982.

Mahan, Asa. Autobiography, Intellectual, Moral, and Spiritual. London: Published for the author, 1882.

Mahan, Asa. Baptism of the Holy Ghost. New York: Walter C. Palmer, Jr., 1870.

Mahan, Asa. Scripture Doctrine of Christian Perfection; With Other Kindred Subjects, Illustrated and Confirmed in a Series of Discourses Designed to Throw Light on the Way of Holiness. Boston: D.S. King, 1839.

Marsden, George M. The Evangelical Mind and The New School Presbyterian Experience. New Haven: Yale University Press, 1970.

Marsden, George M. Fundamentalism and American Culture: The Shaping of Twentieth Century Evangelicalism. New York: Oxford University Press, 1980.

May, Henry F. The Enlightenment in America. New York: Oxford University Press, 1976.

McLean, A. and Eaton, J.W., editors. Penuel, or Face to Face With God. New York: W. C. Palmer, Jr., Publisher, 1870.

McLoughlin, William G. Revivals, Awakenings, and Reform. Chicago: University of Chicago Press, 1978.

McLoughlin, William G. Modern Revivalism: Charles Grandison Finney to Billy Graham. New York: The Ronald Press Company, 1959.

McLoughlin, William G. The American Evangelicals, 1800-1900: An Anthology. New York: Harper and Row, 1968.

Mead, Sidney E. Nathaniel William Taylor, 1786-1858: A Connecticut Liberal. Chicago: University of Chicago Press, 1942.

Mead, Sidney E. The Lively Experiment: The Shaping of Christianity in America. New York: Harper and Row, 1963.

Miller, Perry. The Life of the Mind in America from the Revolution to the Civil War. New York: Harcourt and Brace, 1965.

Morrison, J. G. Achieving Faith. Kansas City, MO: Nazarene Publishing House, 1926.

Niebuhr, H. Richard. The Kingdom of God in America. New York: Harper and Row, 1937.

Orr, J. Edwin. The Second Evangelical Awakening in Britain. London: Marshall, Morgan, and Scott, Ltd., 1949.

Pollock, J. C. The Keswick Story. Chicago: Moody Press, 1964.

Porterfield, Amanda. Feminine Spirituality in America. Philadelphia: Temple University Press, 1980.

Prime, Samuel Irenaeus. Five Years of Prayer, With The
    Answers. New York: Harper and Brothers, 1864.

Prime, Samuel Irenaeus. The Power of Prayer, Illustrated
    in the Wonderful Displays of Divine Grace at the
    Fulton Street and Other Meetings. New York: Charles
    Scribner, 1859.

Ravitch, Diane. The Great School Wars. New York: Basic
    Books, 1975.

Redford, M. E. The Rise of the Church of the Nazarene.
    Kansas City, MO: Nazarene Publishing House 1948.

Roberts, Benjamin Titus. Why Another Sect. Rochester:
    Earnest Christian Publishing House, 1879.

Rose, Delbert R. A Theology of Christian Experience:
    Interpreting the Historic Wesleyan Message.
    Minneapolis: Bethany Fellowship, Inc., 1965.

Rossi, Alice, editor. The Feminist Papers: From Adams to
    de Beauvoir. New York: Columbia University Press,
    1973.

Ruether, Rosemary Radford and Keller, Rosemary Skinner,
    editors. Women and Religion in America: The
    Nineteenth Century. New York: Harper and Row, 1981.

Ruether, Rosemary and McLaughlin, Eleanor. Women of
    Spirit: Female Leadership in the Jewish and
    Christian Traditions. New York: Simon and Schuster,
    1979.

Sandeen, Ernest R. The Roots of Fundamentalism: British
    and American Millennarianism, 1800-1930. Chicago:
    University of Chicago Press, 1970.

Shaw, S. B., editor. Echoes of the General Holiness
    Assembly. Chicago: S. B. Shaw, Publisher, 1901.

Shea, Daniel B., Jr. Spiritual Autobiography in Early
    America. Princeton, N.J.: Princeton University
    Press, 1968.

Shepherd, W. E. How to Get Sanctified: An Illustrated
    Sermon on Practical Consecration. Cincinnati: The
    Revivalist Press, 1916.

Sizer, Sandra S. Gospel Hymns and Social Religion: The Rhetoric of Nineteenth Century Revivalism. Philadelphia: Temple University Press, 1978.

Smith, Amanda Berry. An Autobiography: The Story of the Lord's Dealings with Mrs. Amanda Smith the Colored Evangelist Containing an Account of Her Life Work of Faith and Her Travels. Chicago: Meyer and Brother, 1893.

Smith, John W. V. Quest for Holiness and Unity: A Centennial History of the Church of God (Anderson, Indiana). Anderson, Indiana: Warner Press, 1980.

Smith, Timothy L. Called Unto Holiness, The Story of the Nazarenes: The Formative Years. Kansas City, MO: Nazarene Publishing House, 1962.

Smith, Timothy L. Revivalism and Social Reform in Mid-Nineteenth Century America. Nashville: Abingdon Press, 1957.

Stoeffler, F. Ernest, editor. Continental Pietism and Early American Christianity. Grand Rapids: William B. Eerdmans Publishing Company, 1976.

Synan, Vinson, editor. Aspects of Pentecostal - Charismatic Origins. Plainfield, New Jersey: Logos International, 1975.

Synan, Vinson. The Holiness-Pentecostal Movement in the United States. Grand Rapids: William B. Eerdmans Publishing Company, 1971.

Thomas, Paul Westphal and Thomas, Paul William. The Days of Our Pilgrimage: The History of the Pilgrim Holiness Church. Marion, Indiana: John Wesley Press, 1976.

Tyler, Alice Felt. Freedom's Ferment: Phases of American Social History from the Colonial Period to the Outbreak of the Civil War. Minneapolis: University of Minnesota Press, 1944.

Tyrell, Ian R. Sobering Up: From Temperance to Prohibition in Antebellum America, 1800-1860. Westport, CT: Greenwood Press, 1979.

Upham, Mrs. Phebe Lord, editor. Letters of Madame Guyon: Being Selections of Her Religious Thoughts and

Experiences, Translated and Rearranged from Her Private Correspondence. New York: W. C. Palmer, Jr., 1870.

Upham, Thomas Cogswell. A Treatise on Divine Union, Designed to Point Out Some of the Intimate Relations Between God and Man in the Higher Forms of Religious Experience. Boston: Charles H. Pierce and Company, 1851.

Upham, Thomas Cogswell. Principles of the Interior or Hidden Life: Designed Particularly for the Consideration of Those Who are Seeking Assurance of Faith and Perfect Love. New York: Harper and Brothers, [1843] 1859.

Wallace, Rev. Adam. A Modern Pentecost: Embracing A Record of the Sixteenth National Campmeeting for the Promotion of Holiness. Philadelphia: Methodist Home Journal Publishing Company, 1873.

Warfield, Benjamin Breckinridge. Perfectionism. 2 volumes. New York: Oxford University Press, 1931.

Weber, Timothy P. Living in the Shadow of the Second Coming: American Pre-Millennialism 1875-1925. New York: Oxford University Press, 1979.

Welter, Barbara. Dimity Convictions: The American Woman in the Nineteenth Century. Athens, Ohio: Ohio University Press, 1976.

Wolf, William J. Lincoln's Religion. Philadelphia: Pilgrim Press, 1970.

Wynkoop, Mildred Bangs. A Theology of Love. Kansas City, MO: Beacon Hill Press, 1972.

Periodicals and Articles

Ahlstrom, Sidney E. "The Scottish Philosophy and American Theology." Church History, 24 (1955): 257-272.

Clebsch, William A. "Christian Interpretations of the Civil War." Church History, 30 (1961): 212-222.

Coppedge, Allan. "Entire Sanctification in Early American Methodism." Wesleyan Theological Journal, 13 (1978): 34-50.

Dayton, Donald W. "Asa Mahan and the Development of American Holiness Theology." Wesleyan Theological Journal, 9 (1974): 60-69.

Dayton, Donald W. "The Doctrine of the Baptism of the Holy Spirit: Its Emergence and Significance." Wesleyan Theological Journal, 13 (1978): 114-126.

Dayton, Lucille Sider, and Donald W. Dayton. "Your Daughters Shall Prophesy: Feminism in the Holiness Movement." Methodist History, 14 (1976): 67-92.

Dreyer, Frederick. "Faith and Experience in the Thought of John Wesley." The American Historical Review, 88 (1983): 12-30.

Dunlap, E. Dale. "Tuesday Meetings, Camp Meetings, and Cabinet Meetings: A Perspective on the Holiness Movement in the Methodist Church in the United States in the Nineteenth Century." Methodist History, 13 (1974): 85-106.

Gabriel, Ralph H. "Evangelical Religion and Popular Romanticism in Early Nineteenth Century America." Church History, 19 (1950): 344-47.

Guide to Christian Perfection (Guide to Holiness). 1839-1901.

Hamilton, James E. "Academic Orthodoxy and the Arminian-izing of American Theology." Wesleyan Theological Journal, 9 (1974): 52-59.

Hovet, Theodore. "Phoebe Palmer's 'Altar Phraseology' and the Spiritual Dimension of Woman's Sphere." The Journal of Religion, 63 (1983): 264-280.

Howard, Ivan. "Wesley Versus Phoebe Palmer: An Extended Controversy." Wesleyan Theological Journal, 6 (1971): 31-40.

Hudson, Winthrop S. "The Methodist Age in America." Methodist History, 12 (1973): 3-15.

Keller, Rosemary Skinner. "Women and the Nature of Ministry in the United Methodist Tradition." Methodist History, 22 (1984): 99-114.

Kewley, Arthur A. "Campmeetings in Early Canadian Methodism." Canadian Methodist Historical Society Papers, 2 (1980).

Knight, John Allen. "John Fletcher's Influence on the Development of Wesleyan Theology in America." Wesleyan Theological Journal, 13 (1978): 13-33.

Mullin, Robert Bruce. "Biblical Critics and the Battle Over Slavery." Journal of Presbyterian History, 61 (1983): 70-85.

New York Christian Advocate and Journal. 1835-1875.

Roche, Rev. J. A. "Mrs. Phoebe Palmer." The Ladies' Repository, February 1866: 65-70.

Scott, Leland H. "Methodist Theology in America in the Nineteenth Century." Religion in Life, 25 (1955): 87-98.

Semple, Neil. "The Decline of Revival in Nineteenth Century Central-Canadian Methodism: The Extraordinary Means of Grace." Candadian Methodist Historical Society Papers, 2 (1980).

Sizer, Sandra. "Politics and Apolitical Religion: The Great Urban Revivals of the Late Nineteenth Century." Church History, 48 (1979): 81-98.

Smith, Timothy L. "Righteousness and Hope: Christian Holiness and the Millennial Vision in America, 1800-1900." American Quarterly, 31 (1979): 21-45.

Smith, Timothy L. "The Doctrine of the Sanctifying Spirit: Charles G. Finney's Synthesis of Wesleyan and Covenant Theology." Wesleyan Theological Journal, 13 (1978): 92-113.

Wall, Ernest A. "I Commend Unto You Phoebe." Religion In Life, 26 (1957): 396-408.

Unpublished Materials

Francis, Russell E. Pentecost 1858: A Study in Religious Revivalism. Unpublished Ph.D. Dissertation, University of Pennsylvania, 1948.

Gaddis, Merrill E. Christian Perfectionism in America. Unpublished Ph.D. Dissertation, University of Chicago, 1929.

Knight, John Allen. John William Fletcher and the Early Methodist Tradition. Unpublished Ph.D. Dissertation, Vanderbilt University, 1966.

"Letters" to Walter and Phoebe Palmer. Palmer Folder. Drew University Archives Manuscript Collection. Rose Memorial Library, Drew University, Madison, New Jersey.

"Letters" to Phoebe Palmer. Boxes 460-461. Methodist Episcopal Church Records Collection. New York Public Library, New York, New York.

Neff, Blake J. John Wesley and John Fletcher on Entire Sanctification: A Metaphoric Cluster Analysis. Unpublished Ph.D Dissertation, Bowling Green State University, 1982.

Raser, Harold E. Communitarian Images and Themes in Nineteenth Century Holiness Campmeetings. Unpublished working paper, 1980.

Scott, Leland Howard. Methodist Theology in America in the Nineteenth Century. Unpublished Ph.D. Dissertation, Yale University, 1954.

Shipley, David C. Methodist Arminianism in the Theology of John Fletcher. Unpublished Ph.D. Dissertation, Yale University, 1942.

Spicer, Carl L. The Great Awakening of 1857 and 1859. Unpublished Ph.D. Dissertation, Ohio State University, 1935.

Woods, Bruce A. The Great Hamilton Revival of 1857. Hamilton, Ontario: Stanley Avenue Baptist Church, n.d.

FOOTNOTES

CHAPTER I

[1]The Guide to Holiness, January 1875, pp. 6-7.

[2]The Guide to Holiness, December 1874, pp. 181, 186.

[3]See Winthrop Hudson's article by this title in Methodist History, 12 (1974), pp. 3-15. Hudson sees Methodist influence as predominating from as early as 1825 up until the eve of World War I.

[4]Richard Carwardine, Transatlantic Revivalism: Popular Evangelicalism in Britain and America, 1790-1865 (Westport, CT: Greenwood Press, 1978).

[5]Typical of numerous contemporary observers is the opinion of Rev. John A. Roche, writing in The Ladies' Repository, February 1866, that probably nowhere else could one find sitting "as many ministers for the single purpose of spiritual help. For successive weeks we have seen there from twenty to thirty preachers of the gospel" (p. 69). Roche notes participation by Baptists, Congregationalists, Dutch and German Reformed, Presbyterians, and Episcopalians, in addition to Methodists.

[6]Rev. Richard Wheatley, The Life and Letters of Mrs. Phoebe Palmer (New York: Palmer & Hughes, 1876).

[7]Sydney E. Ahlstrom, A Religious History of the American People (New Haven and London: Yale University Press, 1972), p. 478. He here cites Timothy L. Smith, Revivalism and Social Reform in Mid-Nineteenth Century America (Nashville: Abingdon Press, 1957).

[8]Winthrop S. Hudson, Religion in America (New York: Charles Scribner's Sons, 1982), pp. 344-345. He cites Smith's Revivalism and Social Reform and John L. Peters, Christian Perfection and American Methodism (Nashville: Abingdon Press, 1956).

[9]This renewal of interest is represented by such works as George Croft Cell, The Rediscovery of John

Wesley (New York: Henry Holt and Company, 1935); Umphrey
Lee, John Wesley and Modern Religion (Nashville: Cokes-
bury Press, 1936); Maximin Piette, John Wesley in the
Evolution of Protestantism. Translated by J. B. Howard
(New York: Sheed and Ward, 1937); William R. Cannon, The
Theology of John Wesley (Nashville: Abingdon Press,
1946); Harald Lindstrom, Wesley and Sanctification
(Stockholm: Nya Bokforlags Aktiebolaget, 1946).

[10]Emory Stevens Bucke, editor,The History of American Methodism, 3 volumes (Nashville: Abingdon Press,
1964).

[11]Typical of this type of holiness denominational
historiography is Wilson T. Hogue, History of the Free
Methodist Church, 2 volumes (Winona Lake, IN: Free Meth-
odist Publishing House, 1915); and M. E. Redford, The
Rise of the Church of the Nazarene (Kansas City, MO:
Nazarene Publishing House, 1948.)

[12]Merrill E. Gaddis, Christian Perfectionism in
America (Unpublished Ph.D. Dissertation, University of
Chicago, 1929); Benjamin Breckinridge Warfield, Perfectionism, 2 vols. (New York: Oxford University Press,
1931).

[13]See Warfield, vol. II, pp. 55-57, 66-68, 465ff.

[14]Warfield, pp. 351, 356-360, 370-71, 373.

[15]See Gaddis, pp. 375ff.

[16]See William Warren Sweet, Methodism in American
History (Nashville: Abingdon Press, 1954), pp. 341-45.

[17]Gaddis, p. 436.

[18]Gaddis, p. 438.

[19]Compare, for example, Peters with the previously
cited William Warren Sweet, Methodism in America, pp.
341-345. Sweet contends that by the time of the Civil
War "Wesley's doctrine of Christian perfection was
largely neglected...among the main Methodist bodies." He
sees a protest against this situation arising after the
Civil War, and culminating in major agitation over the
"so-called 'holiness' question" between 1880 and the
close of the century (p. 341). This was resolved by a
siphoning off of "holiness partisans" into "separate
holiness sects" in the 1890s and after, according to

Sweet. Peters, by contrast, finds a revival of interest in Christian Perfection building already in the 1830s and reaching major proportions by the 1850s. The post-Civil War interest to which Sweet points, Peters sees as the "flame out" of the earlier revival (see especially Peters, chapters 4 and 5, pp. 109-150).

[20]Peters, p. 110.

[21]Peters, p. 110.

[22]Peters, p. 112. Emphasis added.

[23]Peters, p. 113.

[24]Ernest A. Wall, "I Commend Unto You Phoebe," Religion In Life, XXVI (1957), pp. 396-408.

[25]There are over 45 separate references to Phoebe Palmer or Dr. and Mrs. Palmer in Smith's book.

[26]Smith, p. 79.

[27]Smith, p. 79. Smith's remarks in this context refer specifically to nineteenth-century revivalism and the usual way of highlighting the frontier origins and character of revivalistic practices. Smith's burden is to show revivalism on the eve of the Civil War to be a largely urban phenomenon, enlisting the energies and support of the most popular and respected religious figures of the day.

[28]Smith, p. 79. On the latter point see pp. 145-177.

[29]Smith, p. 176.

[30]Wall, pp. 403-406.

[31]Wall, p. 398.

[32]Wall, p. 399.

[33]Wall, p. 401.

[34]Bucke, History, vol. II, pp. 608-627.

[35]Bucke, pp. 610, 611-12, 615, 620.

[36]Delbert R. Rose, A Theology of Christian Experience: Interpreting the Historic Wesleyan Message (Minneapolis: Bethany Fellowship, Inc., 1965).

[37]This group grew out of the earlier National Campmeeting Association for the Promotion of Holiness, the creation of a group of prominent Methodists--some of them close to Phoebe Palmer--in 1867. It is known presently as the Christian Holiness Association. A Theology of Christian Experience is a sort of biography of Smith.

[38]Peters, p. 112.

[39]E.g. Wall, pp. 406-408.

[40]Ivan Howard, "Wesley versus Phoebe Palmer: An Extended Controversy," Wesleyan Theological Journal, 6 (1971), pp. 31-40. The Wesleyan Theological Society is a "learned association" of scholars interested in or associated with the various "holiness" denominations, primarily in the U.S., claiming to perpetuate the Wesleyan theological tradition.

[41]Howard, pp. 37-38. The exact nature and implications of this divergence will be made clear in subsequent chapters.

[42]Charles E. Jones, Perfectionist Persuasion: The Holiness Movement and American Methodism, 1867-1936 (Metuchen, NJ: The Scarecrow Press, Inc., 1974), p. xiii. This work was originally submitted as a doctoral thesis to the University of Wisconsin, 1968, under the title "Perfectionist Persuasion: A Social Profile of the National Holiness Movement Within American Methodism, 1867-1936."

[43]Jones, p. 5. Emphasis added.

[44]Jones, p. 5.

[45]Melvin Easterday Dieter, The Holiness Revival of the Nineteenth Century (Metuchen, NJ: The Scarecrow Press, 1980), especially pp. 25-45. This was originally submitted as a doctoral dissertation to Temple University in 1972 and published by the author in 1973.

[46]Dieter, p. 27.

[47]See pp. 27-32, 35-37, 42-45, 62-63 on these. All are significant concerns of the present study.

[48]Dieter, p. 62.

[49]Dieter, p. 62.

[50]See Donald W. Dayton, "The Doctrine of the Baptism of the Holy Spirit: Its Emergence and Significance," Wesleyan Theological Journal, 13 (1978), pp. 114-126; Lucille Sider Dayton and Donald W. Dayton, "Your Daughters Shall Prophesy: Feminism in the Holiness Movement," Methodist History, 14, (1976), pp. 67-92; Donald W. Dayton, Discovering an Evangelical Heritage (New York: Harper and Row, 1976). See chapter 8, "The Evangelical Roots of Feminism," pp. 85-98.

[51]Amanda Porterfield, Feminine Spirituality in America (Philadelphia: Temple University Press, 1980), pp. 66-67.

[52]Rosemary Radford Ruether and Rosemary Skinner Keller, editors, Women and Religion in America: The Nineteenth Century (New York: Harper and Row, 1981), pp. 8, 206, 217-218.

[53]Nancy A. Hardesty, "Minister as Prophet? or as Mother?: Two Nineteenth Century Models," in Hilah F. Thomas and Rosemary Skinner Keller, editors, Women in New Worlds: Historical Perspectives on the Wesleyan Tradition (Nashville: Abingdon Press, 1981), pp. 88-101.

[54]Carwardine. Revivalists examined include Phoebe Palmer and her husband, Asahel Nettleton, Calvin Colton, William Buell Sprague, Edward Norris Kirk, Edward Payson Hammond, James Langley, and Charles G. Finney, among others.

[55]Carwardine, p. 185. Pp. 182-197 contain scattered material on the Palmers.

[56]"Palmer, Phoebe" in The Encyclopedia of World Methodism, 3 vols. edited by Nolan B. Harmon (Nashville: United Method. Pub. House, 1974), vol. 2, p. 1852.

CHAPTER II

[1]Frederick A. Norwood, The Story of American Methodism (Nashville: Abingdon Press, 1974), p. 120.

[2]There is some confusion about the name of Mrs. Worrall. Wheatley, p. 16, gives the name "Dorthea," while John A. Roche, The Life of Mrs. Sarah A. Lankford Palmer (New York: George Hughes and Company, 1898), in chronicling the life of Phoebe's sister, has the name "Dorothy," p. 17. In an earlier article on Phoebe, "Mrs. Phoebe Palmer," The Ladies' Repository, February 1866, pp. 65-70, Roche had identified her mother as "Dorothea," p. 65. "Dorothea" is the form given by Rev. George Hughes, Fragrant Memories of the Tuesday Meeting and the Guide to Holiness (New York: Palmer and Hughes, 1886), p. 3. Roche, The Life of Mrs. Sarah A. Lankford, pp. 17-18, gives the information about the number of children in the Worrall family.

[3]Roche, The Life, p. 18.

[4]Cited in Bucke, vol. I, p. 294.

[5]Wheatley, p. 16.

[6]Wheatley, p. 17.

[7]According to Roche, Ladies' Repository, p. 65, he was twenty-one, while in The Life the same author gives twenty-five as his age. Wheatley, Life and Letters, p. 14, has twenty-five. Worrall was born on Nov. 15, 1771 according to The Guide to Holiness, August 1874, p. 43. That would date his arrival in America in either 1792 or 1796.

[8]Wheatley, pp. 13-14.

[9]Wheatley, p. 14. Cf. Hughes, Fragrant Memories, p. 3.

[10]Wheatley, p. 14.

[11]Wheatley, p. 14.

[12]Wheatley, p. 15.

[13]Wheatley, pp. 15-16. Presumably Worrall had been "converted" in typical Methodist fashion once before, previous to joining the Wesleyan Society as a boy.

[14]Wheatley, p. 405.

[15]Phoebe Palmer, Four Years in the Old World (New York: Foster and Palmer, Jr., Publishers, 1865), p. 140. Cf. Wheatley, pp. 206-208.

[16]Roche, Ladies' Repository, p. 65.

[17]Roche, The Life, p. 18.

[18]Wheatley, p. 18.

[19]Roche, The Life, p. 70.

[20]Wheatley, p. 86. Even so, as an adult Phoebe always had the luxury of domestic help and abundant income from a physician husband.

[21]Wheatley, pp. 40-41.

[22]Wheatley, p. 18.

[23]Wheatley, p. 159.

[24]Wheatley, p. 160.

[25]Roche, The Life, p. 18. The two sisters Phoebe and Sarah developed an especially close relationship. Less than two years apart in age, their lives were always closely intertwined; "They lived largely in one another," according to Roche, p. 162. In early marriage they and their spouses shared one house. Following Phoebe's death, the widowed Sarah wed Phoebe's surviving spouse, Dr. Walter C. Palmer.

While one might gather from Phoebe's religious ideas (see chapter 4) that home was a demanding and affectionless place, quite the opposite is true of Sarah's theology. For her God is a benevolent and beneficent "Father", like a kindly understanding mother, one who sympathizes with human frailties. E.g. Roche, pp. 26-27, 44-45, 67-68. Phoebe's own relationship with her husband exudes warmth and affection--e.g. Wheatley, pp. 144, 260-264. There is a certain "coldness" in her relationship to her children, but that may be explained by her tragic losses in this connection rather than by upbringing.

Both Phoebe and Sarah had notable public careers, as did brother, Dr. Isaac G. Worrall.

[26]Wheatley, p. 23. This was written in the context of reflections on her teenage love life. She explains that although she had three or four suitors she would have been prepared to accept, "as I did not see my parents' approving smile, I have carefully avoided their society....", p. 22.

[27]Wheatley, p. 17.

[28]Phoebe Palmer, Faith and Its Effects: Fragments from My Portfolio (New York: Published for the Author, [1848] 1854), p. 63.

[29]Roche, Ladies' Repository, p. 65.

[30]Her lack of a   able conversion experience is an oddity, given early nineteenth-century Methodism's belief in the necessity of a "heartwarming" experience of divine grace, and her parents' concern that their children be so converted. Her experience parallels much more closely the pattern Horace Bushnell advocated in the 1840s in Christian Nurture, the child never knowing himself or herself to be other than a Christian. This was troublesome to her. For Phoebe's thoughts on this see Phoebe Palmer, The Way of Holiness, With Notes by the Way (New York: W. C. Palmer, [1843] 1867), pp. 72-78. Cf. Faith and Its Effects, pp. 63-66, and Wheatley, pp. 29-30.

[31]Palmer, Faith, p. 62.

[32]Wheatley, p. 20.

[33]Wheatley, p. 18.

[34]The first was likely Oberlin College which admitted women from its founding in 1833, although it did not grant a bona fide B.A. degree to any until 1841. See Edward H. Madden and James E. Hamilton, Freedom and Grace: The Life of Asa Mahan (Metuchen, N.J. and London: The Scarecrow Press, Inc., 1982), pp. 89-94. The first women's college was, interestingly, Wesleyan College, Macon, Georgia. See Norwood, p. 219. For a lively account of the history of public education in New York City see Diane Ravitch, The Great School Wars (New York: Basic Books, 1975).

[35]It is moot as to how thoroughly she understood some of the sources, particularly Wesley's writings, but the familiarity is demonstrably   there. Two of the "classics" which influenced her most are the Memoirs of Mrs. Hester Ann Rogers, available in America as early as 1814, and the Life of William Carvosso, first published in 1835. See chapters IV and V on their significance.

[36]Wheatley, p. 479.

[37]Phoebe Palmer, The Promise of the Father; or, A Neglected Specialty of the Last Days (Boston: Henry V. Degen, 1859). See especially pp. 5-9, 24-28, 34-51, 96-110.

[38]This is the date given in Wheatley, p. 23 and Rev. George Hughes, The Beloved Physician, Dr. Walter C. Palmer, M.D., and His Sun-Lit Journey to the Celestial City (New York: Palmer and Hughes, 1884), p. 40. The date of Sept. 27 given in Roche, Ladies' Repository, appears to be erroneous.

[39]Wheatley, p. 23. This is dated Aug. 12, 1827.

[40]Wheatley, p. 22.

[41]Hughes, Beloved Physician, p. 18.

[42]See Bucke, vol. I, pp. 75-80; cf. Norwood, pp. 655-69 and Sweet, pp. 50-59.

[43]Albert C. Outler, editor, John Wesley (New York: Oxford University Press, 1964), "The Witness of the Spirit; Discourses II," pp. 209-220, p. 219.

[44]Hughes, Beloved Physician, pp. 18-20. Emphasis added.

[45]Hughes, Beloved Physician, p. 21.

[46]Hughes, Beloved Physician, p. 56.

[47]Hughes, Beloved Physician, pp. 62-63.

[48]Hughes, Beloved Physician, p. 58, lists long term involvements as member of the board of managers of the Missionary Society of the Methodist Episcopal Church, president of the Young Men's Total Abstinence Society, and superintendent to the Sabbath School.

[49]Roche, Ladies' Repository, p. 65.

[50]Wheatley, p. 139. This is dated Oct. 1, 1838.

[51]John Wesley, A Plain Account of Christian Perfection (Kansas City, MO: Beacon Hill Press of Kansas City, 1966. Reprinted from the text authorized by the Wesleyan Conference Office, London, 1872), p. 61.

[52]John Telford, editor, The Letters of the Rev. John Wesley, A.M., 8 volumes (London: The Epworth Press, 1931), volume 8, p. 238. Dated Sept. 15, 1790.

[53]Quoted in Bucke, p. 302.

[54]Bucke, pp. 488-523, gives an excellent overview of "Methodism on the Frontier." The theological implications of the "frontier experience" are noted by Leland Howard Scott, Methodist Theology in America in the Nineteenth Century (Unpublished Ph.D. dissertation, Yale University, 1954), pp. 104ff.

[55]Wheatley, p. 19. Emphasis added.

[56]Wheatley, p. 19.

[57]Palmer, Faith, pp. 63-64.

[58]Palmer, The Way, p. 73.

[59]Wheatley, p. 21. Dated Jan. 1, 1826.

[60]Wheatley, p. 24. Dated Nov. 24, 1827.

[61]Wheatley, p. 25. Dated April 28, 1832.

[62]Palmer, Faith, p. 65.

[63]Wheatley, pp. 25-26.

[64]Quoted in Peters, pp. 99-100.

[65]Quoted in Roche, The Life, pp. 103-104.

[66]Wheatley, p. 25. Dated April 28, 1832.

[67]Wheatley, p. 29.

[68]Palmer, The Way, p. 74.

[69]Wheatley, p. 26. Emphasis added.

[70]Palmer, The Way, p. 254.

[71]Palmer, The Way, p. 255.

[72]Palmer, The Way, p. 256.

[73]Palmer, The Way, p. 255.

[74]Palmer, The Way, p. 256.

[75]Wheatley, p. 27.

[76]Wheatley, pp. 30-31.

[77]Wheatley, pp. 30-32. Dated July 24, 1836.

[78]Palmer, Faith, p. 68.

[79]Cf. Palmer, The Way, p. 34; Palmer, Faith, pp. 68-69; Wheatley, p. 144.

[80]Wheatley, p. 314.

[81]Wheatley, p. 146.

[82]Wheatley, p. 238.

[83]Roche, The Life, p. 39. Cf. Hughes, Fragrant Memories, p. 11.

[84]Roche, The Life, pp. 19-20.

[85]Roche, The Life, pp. 21-35. Cf. Hughes, Fragrant Memories, pp. 5-10.

[86]Roche, The Life, pp. 32-33. Also see chapters IV and V for analysis of the significance of her influence on Phoebe Palmer's understanding of Christian perfection. This quotation appears on pp. 135-136 of An Account of the Experiences of Hester Ann Rogers (New York: Land and Scott, 1850) in only slightly different wording.

[87]Roche, The Life, p. 21. Emphasis added.

[88]Roche, The Life, p. 33.

[89]Roche, The Life, p. 33.

[90]Cf. Wheatley, pp. 29-30, 36-49, 65, 124-131; Palmer, The Way, passim.; Palmer, Faith pp. 61-74, 83-87, 311-312. One exception is Faith, pp. 147-149, where she appeals to Sarah's experience and notes that her "example and prayers have been very helpful in all my heavenward way."

[91]Hughes, Fragrant Memories, p. 14.

[92]Hughes, Fragrant Memories, p. 15.

[93]Palmer, The Way, pp. 37-38.

[94]Palmer, The Way, p. 38.

[95]Palmer, The Way, p. 55.

[96]See chapters IV and V of the present study for the derivation and implications of this term.

[97]The Guide to Holiness, February 1874, p. 46.

[98]Wheatley, pp. 36, 65. Cf. The Guide to Holiness, September 1873, p. 88.

[99]Palmer, Faith, pp. 311-312.

[100]Cf. Wheatley, p. 238; Roche, The Life, pp. 109-112; Hughes, Fragrant Memories, pp. 10-13; Hughes, Beloved Physician, pp. 90-92.

[101]This interpretation is in contrast to Roche, The Life, p. 109, which claims that Sarah "desired to help other souls that were earnestly seeking the entire sanctification of their moral nature, and for this reason she began the Tuesday meeting...." Dr. Palmer's claim to being "made holy" came in connection with a camp meeting sometime after Phoebe's experience according to Hughes, Beloved Physician, p. 41.

[102]Delbert Rose, A Theology of Christian Experience, p. 34, is in my estimation wrong in asserting that, "Possessing greater gifts of leadership than her sister Mrs. Lankford, Mrs. Phoebe Palmer soon became the recognized leader...." Cf. Hughes, Beloved Physician, p. 94: "Mrs. Palmer shrank from the responsibility [of leadership], but was delighted to aid her elder sister in the work." Cf. also Wheatley, pp. 77-79, 264, 272 for Phoebe's reticence.

[103]Extended analysis of the meeting is provided in chapter III.

[104]Wheatley, pp. 34-35, 90. In an interesting comment Phoebe notes in connection with her resignation that she has abused her health in laboring for religious ends: "I have sacrificed myself...and now, though my Father doth not chide, yet in love he assures me that I might have acted more wisely," Wheatley, p. 90. This is

written by one who ten years before saw clearly that God
desired greater effort and time invested in the
"religious activities demanded." The matter of Phoebe's
fragile health is important, though not altogether
clear, throughout her life. As will be seen she suffered
from periodic "attacks," sometimes claiming that these
left her near death. Her death in 1874 was due to
"Bright's Disease" or nephritis, a degenerative kidney
disease often associated with hypertension and arterio-
sclerosis (see The Guide to Holiness, December, 1874,
pp. 161-163). The layperson can only surmise that Phoebe
perhaps suffered from high blood pressure and kidney
related problems all of her adult life.

[105]Wheatley, pp. 133, 178.

[106]Wheatley, p. 178.

[107]Wheatley, p. 179. Dated December 5, 1839.

[108]Hughes, Fragrant Memories, pp. 162-175. Cf.
Hughes, Beloved Physician, pp. 226-227.

[109]Quoted in Peters, p. 101.

[110]A brief sketch of Upham is given in Warfield,
pp. 343-351.

[111]Phoebe Palmer thought it to be his "theological
work on the "will,'" Wheatley, p. 240. However,
Warfield, p. 358, argues quite convincingly that this
must have been his Outlines of Imperfect and Disordered
Mental Action, published by Harpers in 1840.

[112]Warfield, pp. 357-359.

[113]Wheatley, pp. 239-242. Cf. Warfield, pp. 353-359
and Hughes, Fragrant Memories, pp. 26-28.

[114]Wheatley, p. 242.

[115]Wheatley, p. 259.

[116]Wheatley, p. 83.

[117]Wheatley, p. 264.

[118]Wheatley, p. 259.

[119]On Böhler's influence see Peters, pp. 23-24, 48-50, 201-202; Outler, pp. 14-15, 17, 41, 52-58, 353ff.

[120]Wheatley, pp. 265-266.

[121]Wheatley, pp. 197-199.

[122]See Wheatley, pp. 259-281 for account of the travels between 1840-1850.

[123]Wheatley, p. 174. Cf. Roche, Ladies' Repository, pp. 69-70, and The Guide to Holiness, July 1874, p. 20, and December 1874, p. 170.

[124]These lines are among those entitled "Christian, To Arms" printed over Palmer's pseudonym, "Shepherdess," in The Christian Advocate, November 3, 1841, p. 48.

[125]See The Christian Advocate, Oct. 13, 1841, p. 33; Oct. 20, p. 37; Nov. 3, p. 45; Nov. 10, pp. 49-50; Nov. 24, pp. 56-58. Here one finds stress on the obligation to be holy, the singular instrumentality of faith in attaining Christian perfection, the disparagement of emotion, and even the "altar imagery" so prominent in Palmer's thought. Wheatley is surely in error, however, when he contends that these articles constituted a serial presentation of Palmer's then forthcoming book The Way of Holiness (see Wheatley, p. 480). Certain continuities there are, but The Way is altogether a personal narrative of Phoebe's religious struggle. Of all her books, The Advocate articles much more closely approximate Entire Devotion to God than they do any others. It is clear that in The Advocate pieces Phoebe has not yet found her "own" style.

[126]Wheatley, p. 483; Hughes, Fragrant Memories, p. 185.

[127]Hughes, Fragrant Memories, p. 182.

[128]Wheatley, p. 155.

[129]Wheatley, p. 482.

[130]Wheatley, pp. 484-485.

[131]Wheatley, p. 136.

[132]Wheatley, p. 135.

[133]Wheatley, p. 90.

[134]Wheatley, pp. 189-190.

[135]"The Christian man and woman that God has set unitedly at the head of a household must...say 'I and my house WILL serve the Lord!' No outward duties can supersede this one great all-commanding duty...in rearing a family for immortality and eternal life." Hughes, Beloved Physician, pp. 253-254.

[136]Interesting in this connection is an entry in her journal in which she describes a hectic day in which she had endeavored "to serve the Lord...in domestic orderings, and by attention to company," having a class meeting to lead that evening. She notes somewhat wryly: "I sometimes have occasion to observe, that the idea has obtained, that I have no domestic cares; such are usually incumbent on house-keepers and mothers. This idea can only have obtained from the want of observation, or due consideration." Wheatley, p. 157.

[137]Hughes, Beloved Physician, pp. 76-79. Cf. Wheatley, pp. 159-160.

[138]Wheatley, p. 630. Illustrative of this is the following journal entry dated Sept. 2, 1839: "Today has been very much taken up in seeing company, but I have reason to be very thankful that I do not have many trifling visitors. My friends seem to have learned what to expect from me, and if afraid of serious conversation, do not make long visits--unless they become interested in the subject which, in all companies, I feel it a duty to bring forward as most prominent." Wheatley, p. 165.

[139]Palmer, Faith, pp. 116-117. The reference is to the biblical book of 1 Samuel, chapter 2.

[140]Palmer, Faith, p. 117.

[141]Palmer, Faith, p. 121.

[142]Wheatley, p. 169.

[143]Wheatley, p. 282.

[144]Wheatley, p. 283.

[145]Wheatley, p. 288.

[146]Wheatley, p. 300.

[147]Wheatley, pp. 302-303, 308-309, 312-314, 316-331.

[148]Wheatley, p. 315; Smith, Revivalism and Social Reform, pp. 63-79.

[149]Smith argues most vigorously for understanding the revival as a major American awakening, representing the culmination of all pre-Civil War revivalism (see especially pp. 45-94). Cf. Dieter, pp. 37-42. Opposed is the assessment of William G. McLoughlin, Revivals, Awakenings, and Reform (Chicago: University of Chicago Press, 1978), pp. 142-143, where he questions whether the "Prayer Meeting Revival" ought to be considered part of a "great awakening" at all. This matter is addressed further in chapter III of the present study.

[150]Wheatley, p. 334.

[151]Wheatley, p. 335.

[152]Wheatley, pp. 315-347, passim.

[153]See The Christian Advocate and Journal, February 12, 1857, p. 25; February 19, p. 29; February 26, p. 33; March 12, p. 43.

[154]The Christian Advocate and Journal, Nov. 29, 1855, p. 189.

[155]See Norwood, pp. 212-215 or early serial publications.

[156]See the letter dated Jan. 25, 1852 in Wheatley, pp. 551-554.

[157]The Christian Advocate and Journal, August 2, 1855, p. 121.

[158]The Christian Advocate and Journal, Nov. 15, 1855, p. 181.

[159]The Christian Advocate and Journal, Nov. 29, 1855, p. 189.

[160]Wheatley, p. 94. The entire account is in a letter to her close friends Bishop and Mrs. Leonidas

Hamline, dated Nov. 19, 1855, the day the Mattison article appeared in The Advocate, pp. 93-95.

[161]Wheatley, p. 94.

[162]See "Incidental Illustrations of the Economy of Salvation" and "Mrs. Palmer and Her Works" in The Christian Advocate and Journal, Dec. 6, 1855, p. 195.

[163]See "Believe That Ye Have It And Ye Have It" in The Christian Advocate and Journal, December 20, 1855, pp. 201-202.

[164]See Mattison's "Dr. Perry and the New Theology" in The Christian Advocate and Journal, January 3, 1856, p. 3 and Perry's "Professor Mattison and His Eight Propositions" in the January 10 issue, pp. 5-6.

[165]The Christian Advocate and Journal, January 10, 1856, pp. 6-7. It is interesting to note that Phoebe and Walter Palmer had visited Bond the day the November Mattison article appeared and applied considerable pressure to suppress further articles of that kind. See Wheatley, pp. 94-95.

[166]Hughes, Beloved Physician, p. 189. Cf. Wheatley, p. 348.

[167]Hughes, Beloved Physician, pp. 191-192. Cf. Palmer, Four Years, pp. 26-28.

[168]Hughes, Beloved Physician, pp. 9, 169.

[169]For accounts of opposition see Palmer, Four Years, pp. 325-328, 339, 378ff, 397, and Carwardine, pp. 184-188.

[170]Palmer, Four Years, passim. Cf. Wheatley, pp. 350-395, passim.

[171]Carwardine, p. 185.

[172]Wheatley, p. 403.

[173]Wheatley, p. 409.

[174]Wheatley, p. 73.

[175]Wheatley, p. 442.

[176]The itineraries of these years and descriptions of her work at the various places are in Wheatley, pp. 403-478.

[177]Wheatley, p. 418.

[178]Wheatley, p. 452.

[179]Wheatley, p. 462.

[180]Wheatley, p. 475.

[181]The Guide to Holiness, July 1873, p. 26.

[182]Hughes, Fragrant Memories, p. 176.

[183]Hughes, Fragrant Memories, p. 176-177. For some reason there is considerable confusion concerning the date of the transaction in the sources. Jones, p. 3, says it occurred in 1858, a date for which there is no confirmation whatever. Deiter, p. 48, has the date as 1864, which is likewise erroneous. Rose, p. 39, claims 1865 is the proper date. In this Rose is on better grounds than either Jones or Deiter because he is following the date given by Hughes in Fragrant Memories, p. 175. It appears, however, that even Hughes, an associate of the Palmers in the publishing enterprise, is in error. It is stated specifically in the July, 1873 issue of The Guide in an editorial marking the commencement of a new volume that the Palmers purchased the paper in 1863, at which time its circulation was only about 7,000.

[184]Again the sources differ. This figure is given in The Guide to Holiness, July 1873, p. 26.

[185]Hughes, Fragrant Memories, p. 177. Cf. Hughes, Beloved Physician, p. 227.

[186]Wheatley, p. 469.

[187]Wheatley, p. 138.

[188]Wheatley, p. 621.

[189]Wheatley, p. 475.

[190]The Guide to Holiness, December 1874, p. 166.

[191]The Guide to Holiness, November 1874, p. 148.

[192]Hughes, Beloved Physician, pp. 223-224.

CHAPTER III

[1]Roche, The Life, pp. 223-224.

[2]In 1867 Phoebe had issued a new fiftieth edition of The Way of Holiness noting her intention to issue subsequent volumes of "Notes by the Way"--i.e. to expand and supplement the original scope of the book. The intended work was never carried out. George Hughes writes of new editions as late as 1886--Hughes, Fragrant Memories, p. 234. I have personally seen an undated fifty-second edition of The Way. The book has been in and out of print even in the twentieth century. A much abridged edition is currently available through joint publication by Beacon Hill Press of Kansas City, Missouri and Christian Outreach of Wilmore, Kentucky. Also in 1981 H. E. Schmul Publishers of Salem, Ohio, reissued an abridged edition of Palmer's Promise of the Father as part of their "Holiness Classics" series.

[3]Hughes, Fragrant Memories, pp. 180; 232-234. Cf. Hughes, Beloved Physician, p. 257. An interesting aspect of the post-Civil War direction of the holiness movement is the competition for support among the various agencies springing up, and in some cases the "devouring" of the "fathers and mothers" by the "sons and daughters" in the process. The Guide to Holiness notes in 1873 a drop off in subscriptions which it attributes to a rumor circulating "for reasons which we prefer not to state" that The Guide has been merged into another magazine-- The Guide to Holiness, July, 1873, p. 27. Cf. The Guide to Holiness, July 1874, p. 21. The reference is likely to be either the Christian Standard or the Advocate of Holiness, both papers being published by the 1870s by the newly formed National Campmeeting Association for the Promotion of Holiness. There is a sense of injury apparent in a further reference to the role of The Guide in helping to get the first "national" holiness camp meetings underway and publicizing their leadership.
    Concerning the final demise of The Guide, there is some confusion as to whether it came in 1901 or 1902-- cf. Jones, p. 4, and Dieter, p. 95. It was still operat- ing at least as late as the summer of 1901. See S. B. Shaw, editor, Echoes of the General Holiness Assembly (Chicago: S. B. Shaw, Publisher, 1901), p. 14.

[4]Roche, The Life, pp. 196-202.

[5]Palmer, Promise, p. 1.

[6]Palmer cites numerous commentators to the effect that in biblical terminology "preaching" signifies these functions along with "proclaiming the Gospel," "heralding the glad tidings," exhorting and instructing to the benefit of the Church, etc. Palmer, Promise, passim.

[7]Wheatley, p. 614.

[8]Palmer, Promise, p. 36.

[9]Palmer, Promise, pp. 37, 26, 4, 45 and passim.

[10]Wheatley, pp. 330-331.

[11]Wheatley, p. 256.

[12]General accounts of the form and content of the Tuesday Meeting are found in several places, some of these being identical with one another. The most complete is found inserted into Phoebe Palmer's Promise, pp. 225-240. Other accounts are found in Wheatley, pp. 250-254; Hughes, Fragrant Memories, pp. 38-42; Hughes, Beloved Physician, pp. 160-161; Roche, The Life, pp. 109-113. There is also a very brief description in Roche, The Ladies' Repository, p. 69.

[13]Palmer, Promise, p. 228. Cf. Wheatley, p. 252, and Hughes, Fragrant Memories, p. 39.

[14]One fascinating account is found in Abel Stevens, Life and Times of Nathan Bangs, D. D. (New York: Carlton and Porter, 1863), pp. 396-402. Bangs, a prominent Methodist editor and scholar and generally supportive of Phoebe Palmer, attended a Tuesday Meeting in March of 1857 with the express intention of repudiating certain theories taught there which he held were "not sound ...unscriptural, and anti-Wesleyan." These had to do with the relative roles of faith and the "witness of the Spirit" in the experience of "entire sanctification." There are also tantalizing, but incomplete, references elsewhere to other challenges to prevailing views which apparently were mounted from time to time--e.g. The Guide to Holiness, December 1874, p. 184, which refers to the "sovereignty" of Palmer's "presiding spirit" in the meetings as defusing fanaticism and heresy. In the

same context it is noted that Palmer was "naturally a presiding spirit" and that "though diffident" she could have "graced a throne or filled the office of a bishop...." p. 185. Cf. Hughes, Beloved Physician, p. 162.

[15]See Chapter II, pp. 40-42.

[16]Warfield, Perfectionism, pp. 337-373.

[17]Warfield, pp. 353-354.

[18]Wheatley, p. 240.

[19]Wheatley, p. 240.

[20]Wheatley, p. 240.

[21]Wheatley, p. 241; Warfield, pp. 353-354.

[22]Wheatley, pp. 241-242.

[23]Wheatley, p. 242.

[24]Wheatley, p. 241.

[25]Wheatley, p. 242.

[26]Wheatley, p. 242.

[27]Hughes, Beloved Physician, p. 104.

[28]Hughes, Beloved Physician, p. 109.

[29]Hughes, Beloved Physician, p. 115.

[30]Hughes, Beloved Physician, p. 119.

[31]Hughes, Beloved Physician, pp. 121-122.

[32]Hughes, Beloved Physician, p. 132.

[33]Hughes, Beloved Physician, pp. 129-130.

[34]Hughes, Beloved Physician, p. 133.

[35]Sydney E. Ahlstrom, "The Scottish Philosophy and American Theology," Church History, 24 (1955), pp. 257-272; James E. Hamilton, "Academic Orthodoxy and the Arminianizing of American Theology," Wesleyan Theo-

logical Journal, 9 (1974), pp. 52-59; William G. McLoughlin, The American Evangelicals, 1800-1900: An Anthology (New York: Harper and Row, 1968), pp. 1-27.

[36]Ralph H. Gabriel, "Evangelical Religion and Popular Romanticism in Early Nineteenth Century America," Church History, 19 (1950), pp. 34-47; McLoughlin, American Evangelicals, pp. 1-27.

[37]Timothy L. Smith, "Righteousness and Hope: Christian Holiness and the Millennial Vision in America, 1800-1900," American Quarterly, XXXI (1979), pp. 21-45; Smith, Revivalism and Social Reform; Whitney R. Cross, The Burned Over District: The Social and Intellectual History of Enthusiastic Religion in Western New York, 1800-1850 (New York: Harper and Row, 1950), pp. 238-251.

[38]Roche, The Ladies' Repository, p. 69.

[39]Palmer, Promise, pp. 232-233.

[40]Wheatley, p. 254; Palmer, Promise, p. 231; Hughes, Fragrant Memories, pp. 41-42.

[41]Roche, The Ladies' Repository, p. 69.

[42]The Tuesday Meeting had of course evolved from two women's Bible study and prayer groups. The interesting thing is that this original complexion was not wholly submerged by the inclusion of men--many of them men of influence and power--from 1839 on. Phoebe Palmer and then Sarah Lankford Palmer presided successively for over half a century and women always participated freely and significantly.

[43]This is dealt with in greater detail under "Sanctified Feminism" and in chapter IV.

[44]Palmer, Promise, p. 272.

[45]Palmer, Promise, p. 22.

[46]Palmer, Promise, p. 23. Emphasis added.

[47]Acts 2:17-18; cf. Joel 2:28-29.

[48]Palmer, Promise, p. 273.

[49]"A Laity for the Times," The Christian Advocate and Journal, February 26, 1857, p. 33.

[50]*Christian Advocate and Journal*, February 19, 1857, p. 29. Emphasis added. Cf. *The Guide to Holiness*, September 1864, pp. 60-61.

[51]Wheatley, pp. 197-199; 267; 578-579. See Henry Belden's account of his religious pilgrimage in *The Guide to Holiness*, April 1865, pp. 73-77.

[52]Wheatley, p. 244.

[53]Wheatley, p. 245.

[54]Roche, *The Ladies' Repository*, p. 69.

[55]Hughes, *Fragrant Memories*, *passim*.

[56]Wheatley, pp. 577-578.

[57]Phoebe Palmer, *Entire Devotion to God: A Present to a Christian Friend* (London: Salvationist Publishing and Supplies, Ltd., [1845] 1853), p. 4.

[58]Wheatley, p. 247.

[59]Wheatley, pp. 571-572.

[60]Wheatley, p. 57. Cf. *The Guide*, September 1864, pp. 60-61; Palmer, *Faith*, p. 256.

[61]On interdenominational cooperation and its decline in nineteenth-century American religion see Charles C. Cole, Jr., *The Social Ideas of the Northern Evangelists, 1826-1860* (New York: Octagon Books, Inc., 1966); Robert T. Handy, *A Christian America: Protestant Hopes and Historical Realities* (New York: Oxford University Press, 1971); Winthrop S. Hudson, *The Great Tradition of the American Churches* (New York: Harper and Brothers, 1953).

[62]Hudson, "The Methodist Age in America," pp. 3-15, especially pp. 9ff.

[63]F. Ernest Stoeffler, "Pietism, The Wesleys, and Methodist Beginnings in America" in F. Ernest Stoeffler, editor, *Continental Pietism and Early American Christianity* (Grand Rapids: William B. Eerdmans Publishing Company, 1976), pp. 184-221, especially pp. 185-206.

[64]Baker, p. 195.

[65]Bucke, pp. 115-117.

[66]Bucke, p. 116; 307-313.

[67]Peters, p. 94; Baker, pp. 195-196; Norwood, pp. 32-34.

[68]A. Kent, "The Work of Holiness in New York Some Years Ago," The Guide to Holiness, February 1858, pp. 20-21.

[69]Bucke, pp. 264-265; Norwood, pp. 24, 231; Baker, pp. 190-191.

[70]Norwood, p. 231.

[71]Interestingly, it was a love feast at the Mulberry Street Church of which Sarah Lankford was a member, which became the inspiration to Timothy Merritt to begin publishing The Guide to Christian Perfection (Later The Guide to Holiness) to give greater circulation to the kind of testimonies he had heard there. In this he was much encouraged by Sarah. See Hughes, Fragrant Memories, pp. 162-163.

[72]Wheatley, p. 243.

[73]Hughes, Fragrant Memories, pp. 142-143.

[74]E.g. I have personally seen an early handbill from the Church of the Nazarene, organized in Los Angeles, California in 1895, which advertises a "Tuesday Holiness Meeting" meeting at 2:30 p.m. This remains a regular feature of the congregation's life at least until 1916, according to materials in the Nazarene Archives, Kansas City, Missouri.

[75]Hughes, Beloved Physician, pp. 159-162.

[76]The notable exception here would of course be Smith's Revivalism and Social Reform. Also McLoughlin in his Revivals, Awakenings, and Reform briefly mentions Palmer, though she is not mentioned in his earlier Modern Revivalism: Charles Grandison Finney to Billy Graham (New York: The Ronald Press Company, 1959).

[77]McLoughlin, Revivals, pp. 10-11. Elsewhere he holds to a different set of dates; in Modern Revivalism he suggests 1795-1835.

[78]McLoughlin, Modern Revivalism, p. 166.

[79]The views are both McLoughlin's. The former is articulated in Modern Revivalism, pp. 165-277, while the latter is argued in Revivals, p. 141-145.

[80]Handy, A Christian America, pp. 29-30; McLoughlin, Revivals, p. 127. For stimulating analyses of the wide impact which revivalism made on American culture in the nineteenth-century, see Perry Miller, The Life of the Mind in America from the Revolution to the Civil War (New York: Harcourt and Brace, 1956), pp. 3-95, and H. Richard Niebuhr, The Kingdom of God in America (New York: Harper and Row), pp. 99-163.

[81]Whitney Cross, The Burned Over District, was one of the first to stress the large role of women in nineteenth century revivalism, though he provides little analysis or explanation. Among more recent studies which have examined the phenomenon in some detail are Martha Tomhave Blauvelt, "Women and Revivalism" in Ruether and Keller, pp. 1-45; Hardesty, in Thomas and Keller, pp. 88-101; Mary P. Ryan, "A Woman's Awakening: Evangelical Religion and The Families of Utica, New York, 1800-1840" in Janet Wilson James, editor, Women in American Religion (University of Pennsylvania Press, 1980), pp. 89-110; Barbara Welter, "She Hath Done What She Could: Protestant Women's Missionary Careers in Nineteenth Century America" in James, pp. 111-125.

[82]See Chapter IV.

[83]See Margaret Van Cott, The Harvest and the Reaper: Reminiscences of Revival Work of Mrs. Maggie N. Van Cott (New York: N. Tibbals and Sons, 1876); Amanda Berry Smith, An Autobiography: The Story of the Lord's Dealings With Mrs. Amanda Smith The Colored Evangelist Containing an Account of Her Life Work of Faith and Her Travels (Chicago: Meyer and Brother, 1893); Dayton and Dayton, pp. 67-92.

[84]Later she sometimes was available at informal gatherings at private homes, conducted "holiness meetings" as part of a camp meeting, or participated in Tuesday-Meeting-like groups, as well as headlining special meetings in churches and halls.

[85]Wheatley, p. 264.

[86]Wheatley, p. 263.

[87]Wheatley, p. 261.

[88]Wheatley, p. 272. This was written in December of 1844.

[89]Palmer, Entire Devotion, p. 113.

[90]Palmer, Entire Devotion, p. 83. Written in December of 1873.

[91]Wheatley, p. 157.

[92]Wheatley, p. 161.

[93]Blauvelt's contention that "Palmer may have broken sexual barriers by conducting revivals, but she always worked side by side with her husband" (Ruether and Skinner, p. 8) is quite wrong. There are numerous letters from Phoebe to Walter describing the progress of her meetings and lamenting their separation. Walter does not seem to have accompanied her much before the middle 1850s and they did not become full revival partners until the British trip, 1859-63. Her three children at the beginning of her public career were all under eight years of age, the two youngest under five.

[94]E.g. in a letter to a camp meeting organizer she urges that Rev. Nathan Bangs, an invited speaker, be fairly remunerated. Concerning herself she writes: "Permit me to say here that the Lord has blessed us with all things needful for life and godliness; and when we fly about on errands of His grace, it is not needful that our expenses be paid; as we have 'the needful' for such emergencies, and even feel that our all belongs to God, and we are not accustomed to have our expenses met,-- though such is sometimes proffered." Wheatley, p. 110. Cf. Palmer, Four Years, p. 250.

[95]Wheatley, p. 260.

[96]Wheatley, p. 144.

[97]The term "social religion" is used to describe a complex of religious practices emerging out of nineteenth-century revivalism which led to the creation of a "community of feeling" centering upon an intense personal conversion experience. See Sandra S. Sizer, Gospel Hymns and Social Religion: The Rhetoric of Nineteenth Century Revivalism (Philadelphia: Temple University Press, 1978), especially pp. 50-110.

[98]Wheatley, pp. 273-274.

[99]Wheatley, p. 283.

[100]Wheatley, p. 288.

[101]See Hughes, Beloved Physician, pp. 189-221; Wheatley, pp. 348-393; Palmer, Four Years, passim.

[102]On the camp meeting, its origin and function see John B. Boles, The Great Revival, 1787-1805: The Origins of the Southern Evangelical Mind (Lexington: The University Press of Kentucky, 1972); Dickson Bruce, Jr., And They All Sang Hallelujah: Plain-Folk Campmeeting Religion, 1800-1845 (Knoxville: The University of Tennessee Press, 1974); Charles A. Johnson, The Frontier Campmeeting: Religion's Harvest Time (Dallas: Southern Methodist University Press, 1955); For Methodist development of the camp meeting see Bucke, pp. 494-523.

[103]Wheatley, p. 466.

[104]Wheatley, p. 341.

[105]Wheatley, p. 269.

[106]Wheatley, p. 271.

[107]For a first hand account of the origins of the holiness camp meeting movement and description of the first three "National Campmeetings" see A. McLean and J. W. Eaton, editors, Penuel, or Face to Face With God (New York: W. C. Palmer, Jr., Publisher, 1870). The story of later meetings is chronicled in George Hughes, Days of Power in the Forest Temple (Boston: John Bent and Company, 1873), and Rev. Adam Wallace, A Modern Pentecost: Embracing A Record of The Sixteenth National Campmeeting for the Promotion of Holiness (Philadelphia: Methodist Home Journal Publishing Company, 1873). The biography of one who spearheaded the movement is W. McDonald and John E. Searles, The Life of Rev. John S. Inskip (Boston: McDonald and Gill, 1885). See especially pp. 185ff.

[108]This was part of an intense generalized revival climate in Canada which paralleled the Laymen's or "Prayer Meeting Revival" in the United States at this time. See J. Edwin Orr, The Second Evangelical Awakening in Britain (London: Marshall, Morgan, and Scott, Ltd., 1949), pp. 14-15.

[109]Wheatley, pp. 342-343. Cf. Palmer, Promise, pp. 292-293.

[110]Palmer, Four Years, p. 57; 127.

[111]See Sizer, pp. 50-55; Frank Baker, Methodism and The Love Feast (London: The Epworth Press, 1957).

[112]Hughes, Beloved Physician, p. 200.

[113]Palmer, Faith, p. 296.

[114]Palmer, Faith, p. 113.

[115]Palmer, Faith, p. 113.

[116]On the controversy see "Deceived Professors of Sanctification," The Christian Advocate and Journal, Aug. 2, 1855, p. 121; "Believe That Ye Have It and Ye Have It," Nov. 29, 1855, p. 189 and Dec. 20, 1855, pp. 201-202.

[117]McLoughlin, Revivals, pp. 127-128.

[118]Clearly many of these elements were present in the camp meeting "holiness meetings" as well, yet I contend that the church setting and the use of the pulpit resulted in a significantly different psychological impact.

[119] See Wheatley, pp. 316-344, passim.

[120]Wheatley, p. 323.

[121]Palmer, Four Years, pp. 93-120; cf. Wheatley, pp. 354-355. Wheatley also gives the number as 2,000, p. 357.

[122]Palmer, Four Years, p. 120-147, cf. Wheatley, p. 355.

[123]Roche, Ladies' Repository, pp. 67-68. This was written in 1866, by which time Phoebe and Walter constituted a "team." Both participated in public services in contrast to the earlier period (pre-1857) when Phoebe generally traveled alone. On the magazine see Norwood, pp. 214-215.

[124]Wheatley, p. 634.

[125]Quoted in Palmer, Four Years, pp. 114-115.

[126]Palmer, Four Years, p. 180. On the controversy over revivalism see Carwardine, pp. 104-107, 126-133, 184-185.

[127]Palmer, Four Years, p. 216.

[128]Palmer, Four Years, p. 294.

[129]The Guide to Holiness, December 1874, p. 171.

[130]Wheatley, p. 300. Whether or not this is true is difficult to judge. Students of the camp meeting in Canada do see an upsurge in activity and popularity in the 1850s, but interpret this as the culmination of a long period of development dating back to the first camp meetings in Canada in 1805 (Canadian camp meetings began only slightly later than U.S. meetings). They also date decline of such meetings to the middle of the century due to increasing urbanization, institutionalization of the camp meeting, and "denominationalizing" of it--i.e. forsaking a long tradition of interdenominational participation to turn the camp meeting into a Methodist recruiting tool. See Arthur A. Kewley, "Camp meetings in Early Canadian Methodism," and Neil Semple, "The Decline of Revival in Nineteenth Century Central-Canadian Methodism: The Extraordinary Means of Grace," Canadian Methodist Historical Society Papers, Volume 2, 1980.

[131]Wheatley, p. 300. See Bruce A. Woods, The Great Hamilton Revival of 1857 (Hamilton, Ontario: Stanley Avenue Baptist Church, n.d.), pp. 4-5.

[132]Palmer, Promise, pp. 251-265; cf. Wheatley, pp. 329 ff.

[133]Wheatley, p. 331; Palmer, Promise, pp. 262-263.

[134]Palmer, Promise, p. 259.

[135]Woods, pp. 15-16.

[136]Woods argues that U.S. "Laymen's Revival" in fact began with the Hamilton revival rather than the later New York City and Boston prayer meetings; cf. Orr, p. 8 ff. This is overstated in my view.

[137]This revival still awaits definitive treatment. The best study is still Smith, Revivalism and Social

Reform, especially pp. 63-79. Contemporary accounts include William C. Conant, Narratives of Remarkable Conversions and Revival Incidents (New York: Derby and Jackson, 1858) and Samuel Irenaeus Prime, The Power of Prayer, Illustrated in The Wonderful Displays of Divine Grace at the Fulton Street and Other Meetings (New York: Charles Scribner, 1859). Cf. Samuel Irenaeus Prime, Five Years of Prayer, With The Answers (New York: Harper and Brothers, 1864). Some bit of analysis is provided by Russell E. Francis, Pentecost 1858: A Study in Religious Revivalism (Unpublished Ph.D. thesis, University of Pennsylvania, 1948) and Carl L. Spicer, The Great Awakening of 1857 and 1859 (unpublished Ph.D. thesis, Ohio State University, 1935). Helpful recent critical treatment is supplied by Carwardine, pp. 159-169. See also Sandra Sizer, "Politics and Apolitical Religion: The Great Urban Revivals of the Late Nineteenth Century," Church History, 48 (1979), pp. 81-98, and Miller, Life of the Mind, pp. 88-95.

[138]Conant, pp. 354-444. Cf. Prime, The Power, p. 171.

[139]Conant, pp. 358, 360, 413; cf. Prime, The Power, pp. 21-22.

[140]Smith, p. 66.

[141]Palmer, Promise, p. 255.

[142]See Carwardine, pp. 162-164. Carwardine offers evidence that new converts were drawn disproportionately from northern urban areas hit hardest by the recession. Smith, pp. 67-68, disputes this.

[143]Carwardine, pp. 164-167. The revival, of course, did not heal sectional differences or ease political and social tensions. In fact it may have done quite the opposite by solidifying the urban north in a heightened, but ultimately self-righteous, piety. So argues McLoughlin, Revivals, pp. 142-143.

[144]Carwardine, pp. 167-168. Smith, p. 64, also notes the "penny press" and the national telegraph system as two new vehicles used to giving unprecedented publicity to the revival.

[145]Wheatley, p. 335.

[146]Palmer, Promise, p. 269.

[147]Wheatley, p. 338.

[148]Wheatley, p. 341; Palmer, Promise, p. 290.

[149]As with the parallel American revival, the British movement has not been thoroughly examined. Helpful for details, but short on analysis is Orr, The Second Evangelical Awakening. Providing helpful analysis is Carwardine, pp. 169 ff.

[150]It was in this context that Charles haddon Spurgeon was beginning his work in London. Phoebe Palmer heard him there in the Surrey Music Hall in 1859 and was moderately impressed, judging him as not "distinguished for his eloquence or intellectual ability," yet having "much good common sense"--Palmer, Four Years, p. 32.

[151]Carwardine, p. 169.

[152]Quoted in Carwardine, p. 174.

[153]Carwardine, pp. 28-155, explores this in detail. Of course the influence did not all flow eastward across the Atlantic. North American Christianity had deep roots in British Christianity and there was always considerable interaction between the two. Methodism provided an especially strong conduit for British input into American religious life. However, by the-mid nineteenth century the unusual vitality of American Christianity seems to have cast it as the "stronger partner," so that "earthquakes" in America were almost always felt in Britain as well.

[154]Wheatley, p. 348; Hughes, Beloved Physician, p. 189.

[155]Wheatley, p. 348.

[156]Hughes, Beloved Physician, p. 189. What circumstances these were we are not told.

[157]Palmer, Four Years, pp. 20-23.

[158]Palmer, Four Years, pp. 15-16; 23-24.

[159]Palmer, Four Years, pp. 17-18; Hughes, pp. 190-191.

[160]Palmer, Four Years, pp. 28-44 and passim.

[161]Palmer, Four Years, p. 28. She generally found England "decadent" compared to the United States.

[162]Palmer, Four Years, pp. 35, 43, 403 and passim. She is thankful that America is free from the "incubus" of a national church, and she is amazed that English Wesleyans should want to identify with Anglicanism, betraying a very American and revivalistic perception of the English religious situation. Around Oxford she encountered "Puseyism" or the "Oxford Movement" which sought to renew Anglicanism by recapturing its historic Catholic roots. This she denounced as a "return to the practice and principles of Romanism!", "Romanism in disguise," and "Jesuitism," pp. 392-393, 406. Also, though she exalted Queen Victoria as an example of a woman called by God to serve in a generally male preserve in Promise of the Father, on closer examination Phoebe found her lacking as an "experimental Christian" because of her attendance at the theater and horse racing, and her proclivity to yacht on the Sabbath. While in England, she wrote her a letter of exhortation and reprimand. She did receive a "respectful note" from the Queen's secretary acknowledging receipt of the letter, but no reply from Victoria. See Four Years, pp. 285, 411-413, and Wheatley, pp. 368-369.

[163]Palmer, Four Years, p. 40.

[164]Palmer, Four Years, p. 120 and passim.

[165]Wheatley, pp. 349-350. See Carwardine, p. 183.

[166]Young had even preached to his congregation on the importance of women in ministry. See Palmer, Four Years, p. 92.

[167]Palmer, Four Years, p. 93.

[168]Palmer, Four Years, p. 108.

[169]Palmer, Four Years, pp. 93-120; Wheatley, pp. 354-355; Hughes, Beloved Physician, p. 197. The careful taking of names becomes an integral part of the revival methodology of the Palmers in Britain. This first appeared in connection with Phoebe's travels in Canada, but does not then seem the preoccupation it later becomes. Phoebe's justification is that it furnishes work for visiting ministers and "newly baptized disciples" in visitation and "follow up." It may be also noted that

she regularly quotes the recorded statistics with obvious relish.

[170]Palmer, _Four Years_, p. 120.

[171]Palmer, _Four Years_, pp. 120-147; Wheatley, pp. 355-357; Hughes, _Beloved Physician_, pp. 197-199. One coal owner claimed four hundred of his miners had been "brought to Christ" while a sea captain credited the Palmers with the salvation of his entire crew.

[172]Palmer, _Four Years_, pp. 121-122. It is not clear whether this was original with the Palmers or not. The record indicates that the technique had not been used much, if at all, in Phoebe's career to this point. Whatever the case, it became an honored method in revivalism generally, and especially in those groups which grew from the "holiness movement" Palmer helped to create. The "theatrical" element observable in this incident was a contribution Walter made to Phoebe's ministry in those years they worked together. Freer than his no nonsense wife, Walter was quick to use "gimmicks." E.g. at the close of the Sunderland revival, noting that he could not expect many of his "Sunderland friends" to visit him at his New York home, he invited them all to visit him in his "heavenly mansion." He then asked all who would accept his invitation (thereby indicating their resolve to persevere on the "way of holiness") to stand, bringing the entire congregation to its feet. See Palmer, _Four Years_, p. 147, and Hughes, _Beloved Physician_, p. 199.

[173]Palmer, _Four Years_, pp. 175-177; Hughes, _Beloved Physician_, pp. 199-200. The new arrangement continued after the Palmers left. On the use of "altar invitations" in English religion see Carwardine, p. 120.

[174]Palmer, _Four Years_, pp. 170-171; Wheatley, p. 361.

[175]Palmer, _Four Years_, p. 184. It is in connection with the visit to Scotland that I find the only hint of humor anywhere in Phoebe's writings. Professing herself in favor of "cheerful Christians," yet always cautious lest cheerfulness "degenerate into levity," she is markedly devoid of humor. In this instance, however, a bit somehow slips through. Commenting on a visit to St. Giles Church in Edinburgh, she recounts a story from its history concerning one Jennet Geddes who threw a stool at the officiating minister the first time she heard a

new Church of England liturgy prepared by Archbishop William Laud (1573-1645) read in the church. The liturgy was from The Book of Common Prayer which, under Land's influence, was strongly "Anglo-Catholic" and hence anti-Puritan and anti-Calvinist, both of the latter strong strains in the Scottish church. The Scots resisted such efforts as Laud's to "Anglicize" Scottish religion. Of the Geddes incident Palmer notes: "This curious way of settling theological difficulties, though questionable, seems to have been effective; for though the stool missed the head of the dean, it appears to have struck a deathblow to the system"--Four Years, p. 197.

[176]Palmer, Four Years, p. 363. Her embarrassment had clearly lessened since the initial appearance of "show bills" some years earlier in Canada.

[177]Wheatley, p. 377.

[178]Carwardine, pp. 187-188. He notes two critical pamphlets circulating: P. J. Jarbo, A Letter to Mrs. Palmer, in Reference To Women Speaking in Public, and A. A. Rees, Reasons for not Co-operating in the Alleged "Sunderland Revivals". On Catherine Booth see Dayton and Dayton, "Your Daughters Shall Prophesy," pp. 74-77. Also see Catherine Booth, Female Ministry; or, Women's Right to Preach the Gospel (New York: Salvation Army Supplies Printing and Publishing Department, 1975. Reprint of the first edition, London, 1859).

[179]Carwardine, pp. 187-188.

[180]Carwardine, pp. 102-133.

[181]Carwardine, pp. 128-131. See Caughey's account of matters in Rev. Daniel Wise, editor, Methodism in Earnest: Being the History of a Great Revival in Great Britain; in Which Twenty Thousand Souls Professed Faith in Christ, and Ten Thousand Professed Sanctification, in About Six Years in Connection With The Labors of Rev. James Caughey (Boston: Charles H. Pierce, 1850).

[182]Palmer, Four Years, pp. 146; 335. Emphasis added.

[183]Wheatley, p. 369.

[184]Carwardine, pp. 184-185.

[185]Palmer, Four Years, p. 601; cf. Wheatley, p. 388, 393. Phoebe does refer implicitly to the Conference's stand in connection with meeting an "outlawed" English itinerant, Richard Weaver--see Palmer, Four Years, pp. 425-430.

[186]Carwardine, p. 185. As usual the Wesleyans did not uniformly abide by the Conference's decision, so that pockets of support for the Palmers remained even there.

[187]For American developments see Bucke, Vol I, pp. 256-258 and Vol. III, pp. 329-343. For English developments see Carwardine, pp. 79-80, 119-120, 135-136.

[188]Carwardine, pp. 119-120. On the Palmers' connections with Caughey see Wheatley, pp. 191-192.

[189]Palmer, Four Years, pp. 327-328.

[190]Palmer, Four Years, p. 326. The reference is to the biblical book of Joshua, chapter 7.

[191]Palmer, Four Years, p. 327.

[192]Palmer, Four Years, p. 328.

[193]Palmer, Four Years, p. 328.

[194]Palmer, Four Years, p. 327.

[195]Palmer, Four Years, p. 380.

[196]Palmer, Four Years, pp. 381-383.

[197]Palmer, Four Years, p. 398.

[198]Palmer, Four Years, pp. 408-410. The secret came to light when, during an address by Phoebe, an intoxicated deliveryman dropped several kegs down a ramp causing a loud commotion.

[199]Wheatley, p. 391.

[200]Wheatley, p. 403.

[201]See chapter II, pp. 86-88.

[202]See chapter II, pp. 85-86.

[203]For analysis of the issues see Bucke, Volume II, pp. 339-360. Cf. Marston, From Age to Age a Living Witness, especially pp. 134-142 and 273-290, on the holiness issue.

[204]Benjamin Titus Roberts, Why Another Sect (Rochester: Earnest Christian Publishing House, 1879), p. 54. Cf. Hughes, Fragrant Memories, where the date is given as 1849. Roberts' wife had also been a member of Walter Palmer's Methodist class before her marriage.

[205]I.e. The "Wesleyan Methodist Connection" withdrew in 1844 over the issues of slavery and episcopacy; the Methodist Episcopal Church, South formed in 1845 over slavery; the Free Methodist Church formed in 1860.

[206]Wheatley, p. 452.

[207]Wheatley, p. 452.

[208]See Marston, pp. 227-232.

[209]Wheatley, p. 452.

[210]Wheatley, pp. 448, 450.

[211]Wheatley, p. 450.

[212]See reference and note on p. 132. Good secondary treatments are in Rose, pp. 48-78; Dieter, pp. 96-147; and Jones, p. 16 ff.

[213]McDonald and Searles, pp. 146-184; Wheatley, pp. 66-69.

[214]Rev. W. H. Boole in The Guide to Holiness, December 1874, p. 179.

[215]Rev. J. Parker, The Guide to Holiness, December 1874, p. 182.

[216]Quoted in Dieter, pp. 210-211.

[217]See Robert E. Chiles, Theological Transition in American Methodism: 1790-1935 (Nashville: Abingdon Press, 1965); Thomas A. Langford, Practical Divinity: Theology in the Wesleyan Tradition (Nashville: Abingdon Press, 1983), pp. 100-130; and Peters, pp. 133 ff.

CHAPTER IV

[1]This is a common Moody anecdote perpetuated in many sources, apparently originating from a story Moody told on himself. One of the most recent studies of Moody, Stanley N. Gundry, Love Them In: The Life and Theology of Dwight L. Moody (Grand Rapids: Baker Book House, 1976), pp. 62-86, contests quite convincingly, however, the usual interpretation placed on it. Gundry argues that Moody was not indifferent to creeds, doctrine, or theology as this story would suggest. A good account of some of the forces discouraging critical reflection in revivalistic Protestantism is in Sidney E. Mead, The Lively Experiment: The Shaping of Christianity in America (New York: Harper and Row, 1963), pp. 103-133.

[2]This is in contrast to the process often at work in revivalism. E.g. see the analysis of the modification of New England Calvinism by Nathaniel William Taylor in Sidney E. Mead, Nathaniel William Taylor, 1786-1858: S Connecticut Liberal (Chicago: University of Chicago Press, 1942), especially pp. 95-127.

[3]Charles G. Finney, Lectures on Systematic Theology, ed. James H. Fairchild (Oberlin, Ohio: E. J. Goodrich, 1878). All but two "lectures" out of fifty-one deal with moral obligation or human salvation through the work of Jesus Christ. One lecture (number 45) concerns "Divine Sovereignty" and one (number 46) the "Purposes of God."

[4]T. L. Smith, Revivalism and Social Reform, represents the first tendency. He is, with reason, enormously impressed with her many activities. John L. Peters' Christian Perfection and American Methodism notices peculiarities in Palmer's thought, but quickly concludes that these are not "major emphases in Mrs. Palmer's teachings," p. 112.

[5]Palmer, Entire Devotion, pp. 13-14. Emphasis added.

[6]The Christian Advocate and Journal, Oct. 13, 1841, p. 33.

[7]Christian Advocate, Oct. 13, 1841, p. 33.

[8]Christian Advocate, Oct. 13, 1841, p. 33. This is
of course interesting, given that the installment
dealing with "How may we enter into the enjoyment of
[holiness]" will not appear for two more weeks.

[9]This is typical of Palmer's methodology. Cf. The
Way of Holiness, p. 20: "My chief endeavors shall be
centered in the aim to be an humble Bible Christian...
[taking] the Bible as the rule of life, instead of the
opinions and experience of professors...." On the surface this is a significant departure from Wesley, but in
fact Palmer gives greater authority to experience than
she either recognizes or admits.

[10]The Christian Advocate and Journal, Oct. 20,
1841, p. 37. Cf. Palmer, Entire Devotion, p. 15.

[11]Christian Advocate, Oct. 20, 1841, p. 37.

[12]Christian Advocate, Oct. 20, 1841, p. 37.

[13]See the accounts in Charles G. Finney, Memoirs of
Rev. Charles G. Finney (New York: A. S. Barnes and
Company, 1876), pp. 339-351, where Finney declares himself "satisfied that the doctrine of sanctification in
this life, and entire sanctification, in the sense that
it [is] a doctrine taught in the Bible, and that abundant means [are] provided for the securing of that attainment" and Asa Mahan, Autobiography, Intellectual,
Moral, and Spiritual (London: Published for the author,
1882), pp. 365 ff. Mahan soon published Scripture Doctrine of Christian Perfection; With Other Kindred Subjects, Illustrated and Confirmed in a Series of
Discourses Designed to Throw Light on the Way of Holiness (Boston: D. S. King, 1839), copies of which Phoebe
Palmer gave to acquaintances prior to the publication of
her own first book, The Way of Holiness, in 1843
(Hughes, Beloved Physician, p. 372). Finney expressed
his emerging views in his Lectures to Professing Christians which he delivered in the winter of 1836-37 and
later published. See Charles G. Finney, Lectures to
Professing Christians (New York: Fleming H. Revell Company, 1878) and Charles G. Finney, The Promise of the
Spirit, ed. by Timothy L. Smith (Minneapolis: Bethany
House Publishers, 1980). Finney also published Views on
Sanctification (Oberlin, Ohio: James Steele, 1840). It
should be noted that Mahan's views are, on close inspec-
tion, the more "Wesleyan" of the two even though the
same Methodist sources figured largely in their joint
conversion to perfectionism.

[14]Christian Advocate and Journal, Nov. 3, 1841, p.
45. Cf. George O. Peck, The Scripture Doctrine of Christian Perfection Stated and Defended (New York: Carlton
and Porter, 1842), pp. 397-404. Peck, a contemporary of
Palmer's and a respected editor and educator, suggests
that, among other things, the seeker after holiness
anxiously pursue the blessing, expecting that "A deep
and ... godly sorrow" which will "arise from a conviction of hidden corruptions and inward unlikeness to God"
will "take possession of [the] heart."

[15]Christian Advocate, Nov. 3, 1841, p. 45.

[16]The "evangelical Arminians," such as Wesley
was, never underestimated the role of God's grace in
salvation, though they were not willing to allow humans
to be passive objects in the process. There was always,
however, in this camp the tendency to resolve the
tension between the human and divine elements in the
direction of the human, a movement from a doctrine of
"free grace" to one of "free will." See Chiles,
especially pp. 144 ff. Palmer in the mid-nineteenth
century illustrates the transition in progress. Her view
is also consistent with the general "Arminianizing" of
religious thought in America in this period; see
McLoughlin, Revivals, pp. 98-140, especially pp. 113-
119.

[17]Christian Advocate, Nov. 3, 1841, p. 45. Emphasis
added.

[18]In other places Palmer is even plainer. Hesitancy
to believe at this crucial juncture is "sin." E.g.
Palmer, Faith, p. 36; Wheatley, p. 574, and passim.

[19]All Arminians have struggled at the same point,
given their attempt to hold to both the necessity of
divine grace and human freedom. Palmer's trouble is in
her tendency to minimize the difficulty--and her drive
to make all elements of Christian conversion "simple."

[20]Christian Advocate, Nov. 3, 1841, p. 45. Emphasis
added. Cf. Palmer's own religious pilgrimage outlined on
pp. 18-34, particularly her reflection on the lack of
"ecstasies" in her own life: "It has often been suggested that I gave myself up so fully to live a life of
faith, that God has taken me at my word. And will you
believe, the enemy sometimes tries to tempt me to be
sorry for it...." Palmer, Faith, p. 311.

[21]E.g. the Rev. W. H. Boole, writing in The Guide to Holiness, December 1874, pp. 177-178: "[Mrs. Palmer's] presentation of entire sanctification under the type of 'the altar' and its sacrifice, was entirely original with her...Certain it is, no writer or teacher before her had presented this special truth of entire sanctification under that figure."

[22]Here, as elsewhere, she has little regard for the context of the words cited. The passage actually has nothing at all to do with the subject under consideration.

[23]The emphasis is Palmer's, and is crucial.

[24]Christian Advocate, Nov. 3, 1841, p. 45. For the use of typology in America see Sacvan Bercovitch, "Introduction," and Thomas M. Davis, "The Traditions of American Typology," in Typology and Early American Literature (Amherst: University of Massachusetts Press, 1972), and Conrad Cherry, Nature and Religious Imagination: From Edwards to Bushnell (Philadelphia: Fortress Press, 1980), pp. 14-25.

[25]Christian Advocate, Nov. 3, 1841, p. 45.

[26]E.g. Palmer, Entire Devotion, pp. 40-41, 186-193; Palmer, The Way, pp. 62-68; Wheatley, passim.

[27]Christian Advocate, Nov. 10, 1841, pp. 49-50 and Nov. 24, pp. 57-58.

[28]Very interesting, and significant, in this connection is the biographical root of her concern revealed in The Way of Holiness, pp. 22 ff.

[29]See section on "Holiness in Action" in the present study.

[30]Christian Advocate, Nov. 24, 1841, pp. 57-58. It is true that the Palmers published Mrs. T. C. Upham's Letters of Madame Guyon and her husband's Divine Union, both works reflective of the mystical tradition in Christianity. Phoebe herself, however, was quite uncomfortable with this strain in the holiness movement, as her periodic warnings against "mysticism" and her insistence on specific biblical foundations for religious experience make clear.

[31]Christian Advocate, Nov. 24, 1841, pp. 57-58.

[32]See sections of the present study on "pentecostal" terminology and imagery.

[33]See pp. 47 and 91 of the present study on this.

[34]There was also a considerable tradition of spiritual autobiography in America which may have influenced Palmer, although, given her Methodist roots, it is doubtful she knew this well or drew much inspiration from it, since it was essentially Puritan-Calvinist. See Daniel B. Shea, Jr., Spiritual Autobiography in Early America (Princeton, N.J.: Princeton University Press, 1968).

[35]Wheatley, pp. 155, 482.

[36]Though Romanticism was a lively leaven, it was not alone in Palmer's day. Countervailing forces were also well represented. See Theodore Dwight Bozeman, Protestants in An Age of Science: The Baconian Ideal and Antebellum American Religious Thought (Chapel Hill: The University of North Carolina Press, 1977).

[37]Palmer, The Way, pp. 17-18.

[38]Palmer, The Way, pp. 20 and 54-55. Her turn to "biblicism" is quite typical of nineteenth-century American Christianity. See Nathan O. Hatch and Mark A. Noll, editors. The Bible in America: Essays in Cultural History (New York: Oxford University Press, 1982), especially Nathan O. Hatch, "Sola Scriptura and Novus Ordo Seclorum," pp. 59-78. Hatch's contention that the appeal to the Bible provided a new ground of certainty for a generation perplexed by sectarian rivalry may apply equally to the individual perplexed by the ambiguities of religious experience. Palmer's tradition gave considerable authority to experience. Cf. Mead, Lively Experiment, pp. 108-113.

[39]Palmer, The Way, p. 74. Elsewhere she refers to lacking "those high-wrought feelings, or that distress of spirit, which I have heard some speak of, as given preparatory to receiving purity...." See Faith and Its Effects, P. 66.

[40]This appears in some form in numerous places including Leviticus 11:44-45, 19:22, 20:7, 20:26; Deuteronomy 26:19; Matthew 5:48; 1 Peter 1:15-16.

[41]Palmer, The Way, p. 19.

[42]Palmer, The Way, p. 19.

[43]Reflecting Palmer's view is the letter to a "Mrs. R--," teaching that hesitation is actually sin. Palmer writes, "If you delay in presenting the sacrifice [i.e. entirely devoting oneself to the service of God] from any cause whatever, you make food for repentance. God demands present holiness." Palmer, Faith, p. 104.

[44]Palmer, The Way, p. 19.

[45]Palmer, The Way, p. 19.

[46]See pp. 190-191.

[47]Palmer, The Way, p. 28.

[48]Palmer, The Way, p. 32. This discovery, so liberating to Palmer, was not always as obvious to everyone else. There is a fascinating account in one of her books of a conversation between her and "Father M--," who though unexcelled in "devotedness of life" made no public claim to having attained Christian Perfection. Seeing this as a detriment to the cause she championed, Phoebe undertook to persuade him that he was indeed enjoying a state of holiness if he only understood holiness as she did. Not convinced at first, he finally succumbed to her lengthy argument, declaring, "Is that all? Why, that is what I have been doing for years," whereupon he shouted, "O praise the Lord! Praise the Lord!" Thus instructed, Palmer recounts that he became a witness "before hundreds," testifying "in an unequivocal manner" to the "enjoyment of perfect love." See Phoebe Palmer, Incidental Illustrations of the Economy of Salvation (Boston: Henry V. Degen, [1855] 1859), pp. 355-362.

[49]Palmer, The Way, p. 68.

[50]Palmer, The Way, p. 60.

[51]Palmer, The Way, pp. 60-61.

[52]Palmer, The Way, p. 62.

[53]Palmer, The Way, p. 61.

[54]Palmer, The Way, p. 61. Emphasis added.

[55]Matthew 23:19 (KJV). The statement echoes the
teaching of the Old Testament that "whatever touches the
altar shall be holy" (Exodus 29:37).

[56]Palmer, The Way, p. 65. Illuminating here is
Phoebe's childhood reflections on the "superiority" of
the ancient Hebrews' relationship to God, dependent as
it was upon outward rites of animal sacrifice: "Had I
lived in that day, how gladly would I have parted with
everything...and have purchased the best possible offering. All I would have to do, would be to lay it upon the
altar and know that it was accepted," Wheatley, p. 19.
By contrast she found the nineteenth-century Methodist
path to God fraught with subjectivity and ambiguity.
Palmer is even more explicit about her discovery of
the "altar principle" in a letter dated November 15,
1849. Here she recounts how it came to her first in the
form of several Bible verses impressed upon her mind
while she ate, following a long session of praying and
writing. Returning to her room, she tracked the verses
down with the help of a concordance and found that,
taken together, they seemed to give grounds for assurance
of her sanctification, an insight she "knew to be of the
Holy Spirit's inspiration." In view of the new insight
she reflected: "I remembered seasons, since I had laid
all upon the altar, when I had but just retained my
hold, that the offering I presented was sanctified; when
in view of the infinite and inherent holiness of the
ALTAR upon which my offering was laid, I ought to have
believed myself abundantly saved. O, I indeed blushed at
the narrowness of my perceptions and the lightness of my
faith," Wheatley, pp. 532-535.
It may also be noted that there is an inconsistency
in Palmer's use of the imagery of altar and sacrifice in
this connection. On the one hand spiritual rebirth and
holiness come through the sacrifice of Jesus (he "suf-
fers without the gate" that he might "sanctify the
people with his own blood" and it is "the blood of
Jesus" which can "sanctify and cleanse"), yet on the
other hand Jesus is the altar upon which the sacrifice
of entire consecration is to be made. Jesus is thus both
sacrifice and altar, according to Palmer's view. What
she of course means to convey is that because of his own
sacrifice, Jesus becomes the "Christian's altar"--i.e.
the mediator between holy God and sinful humanity.

[57]Palmer, Faith, p. 31; Palmer, Entire Devotion, p.
40.

[58]Palmer, Faith, p. 38.

[59]Wheatley, pp. 516, 158.

[60]Palmer, Faith, p. 142.

[61]Palmer, Faith, p. 343. Yet in other places she refers to faith as a "holy violence" which seizes the "promises" of God--see The Christian Advocate and Journal, November 15, 1855, p. 181.

[62]Palmer, The Way, p. 67.

[63]Wheatley, p. 516.

[64]Palmer, Faith, p. 113.

[65]Palmer, Faith, p. 296. The text of this letter is also in Wheatley, pp. 548-551, where its recipient is identified as Leonidas Hamline. Hamline and his wife, close friends of the Palmers, were staying with them during the momentous General Conference of the Methodist Episcopal Church in 1844. Hamline was elected bishop that year and Phoebe left this letter in his room censuring him for his failure to more openly espouse holiness and identify with the cause. In it she suggests that, as a bishop, his establishment in holiness and unambiguous testimony to it would be of immense value to the church.

[66]Palmer, Faith, p. 328.

[67]Palmer, The Way, p. 48. This seems a rather grandiose vision for a self-professed "retiring" young woman. It may be that her developing writing and preaching career colored her recollection of the event.

[68]Palmer, The Way, pp. 48-49.

[69]Palmer, The Way, p. 49; Palmer, Faith and Its Effects, p. 76.

[70]Palmer, The Way, p. 49.

[71]Palmer, The Way, p. 51.

[72]Wheatley, p. 547. Dated January 9, 1841.

[73]Testimonials included in the second and subsequent editions of The Way, pp. 8-10.

[74]Wheatley, p. 488.

[75]See Wheatley, pp. 494-499, for a sampling of published notices of her books abroad.

[76]Charles Jones is quite right when he observes that elements in Palmer's thought are similar to the role of covenant in Puritan theology. See Jones, pp. 5-6.

[77]Palmer, Entire Devotion, p. 150.

[78]Palmer, Entire Devotion, p. 146. The form of her "covenent" resembles somewhat the "covenent service" developed by John Wesley and first published in 1780 for use by Methodists. For a slightly abridged recent version see Wesley Hymns (Kansas City, MO: Lillenas Publishing Company, 1982), pp. A-1 to A-10.

[79]Palmer, Entire Devotion, pp. 146-152.

[80]Palmer, Entire Devotion, p. 8.

[81]Palmer, The Way, p. 57.

[82]Palmer, Entire Devotion, p. 16. Cf. definition of "holiness" on p. 15 and The Christian Advocate, Oct. 20, 1841, p. 37.

[83]Palmer, Entire Devotion, p. 109.

[84]Palmer, Entire Devotion, p. 21.

[85]Palmer, Entire Devotion, p. 154.

[86]Palmer, Entire Devotion, p. 155.

[87]Palmer, Entire Devotion, p. 156. Emphasis added.

[88]Palmer, Entire Devotion, pp. 146-152.

[89]Palmer, Entire Devotion, pp. 108-116.

[90]Palmer, Entire Devotion, p. 156.

[91]Palmer, Entire Devotion, p. 158.

[92]Edmund Storer Janes (1807-1876) was elected bishop of the Methodist Episcopal Church in 1844 along with Leonidas Hamline. Both men were important ecclesiastical confidants and supporters of Mrs. Palmer. Janes' wife was Charlotte Thibou Janes (1808-1876).

[93]Wheatley, p. 485. Emphasis added.

[94]Palmer, Faith, p. 67.

[95]Palmer, Faith, p. 244.

[96]Palmer, Faith, p. 107.

[97]Palmer, Faith, p. 106.

[98]Palmer, Faith, p. 29.

[99]Palmer, Faith, p. 132.

[100]In support she quotes John 3:18, "He that believeth not is condemned already."

[101]Palmer, Faith, p. 98.

[102]Palmer, Faith, pp. 348-349.

[103]Palmer, Faith, p. 342.

[104]Palmer's "biblicism" of course severely circumscribes the role of the latter.

[105]Palmer, Faith, p. 99. Emphasis added.

[106]Palmer, Faith, p. 40.

[107]Palmer, Faith, p. 190.

[108]Palmer, Faith, p. 47. Emphasis added.

[109]Palmer, Faith, p. 191.

[110]Palmer, Faith, p. 185.

[111]Palmer, Faith, p. 104. Emphasis added.

[112]Christian Advocate, October 20, 1841, p. 37.

[113]Outler, John Wesley, "The Witness of the Spirit; Discourse II," pp. 209-220, p. 219. An excellent analysis of Wesley's doctrine is Lycurgus M. Starkey, Jr., The Work of the Holy Spirit: A Study in Wesleyan Theology (Nashville: Abingdon Press, 1962), pp. 63-78.

[114]E.g. Hester Ann Rogers (1756-1794), one of Palmer's spiritual models, who confesses, "I have not

always had so clear a witness of perfect love (i.e.
holiness)." She notes, "At other times I have had that
witness full and clear," adding, "I must feel [the
witness of the Spirit], or I cannot be happy." An
Account of the Experiences of Hester Ann Rogers (New
York: Lane and Scott, 1850), pp. 74-75. Wesley himself
recognized the variability of the "witness." See E. H.
Sugden, editor, The Standard Sermons of John Wesley, 2
volumes (London: The Epworth Press, 1921), 2, pp. 358-
59; Telford, 2, pp. 89-90, 103, 138, and 6, p. 93.

[115]Palmer, The Way, p. 44.

[116]Palmer, The Way, p. 26.

[117]Palmer, Faith, pp. 61-62.

[118]Palmer, Faith, pp. 61-74.

[119]Palmer, Faith, p. 135.

[120]Palmer, Faith, pp. 135-136.

[121]Palmer, Faith, p. 239.

[122]Palmer, Faith, p. 242.

[123]Palmer, Faith, p. 242.

[124]Palmer, Faith, p. 245.

[125]Palmer, Faith, pp. 269-273. She refers to this
elsewhere as a "special state of grace" which is characterized by "a divine conviction inwrought in the heart
of our ultimate steadfastness and final salvation"--a
kind of "eternal security," though not unconditional--and
"holy endeavors for the salvation of man," Wheatley, pp.
544-545. On Wesley's use of the term see Starkey, pp.
68-69, 97-98, and Wesley, Plain Account, pp. 90-91.

[126]Palmer, Faith, p. 338.

[127]Palmer, Faith, p. 146.

[128]Palmer, Faith, p. 203.

[129]Palmer, Faith, pp. 254-256.

[130]Palmer, Faith, p. 208.

[131]Palmer, Faith, p. 212.

[132]Palmer, Faith, pp. 252-253.

[133]Palmer, Faith, pp. 225-234.

[134]It is important to note that Palmer's own "entire sanctification" involved a "conversion to terminology." As she recounts, "Though I have ever been a firm believer in the doctrine of Christian holiness, embracing the entire sanctification of body, soul, and spirit, as taught from the Scriptures by the apostolic Wesleys, and their contemporaries; yet the terms made use of, in speaking of this attainment, were objectionable to my mind....Though from early life I had felt that I needed just the blessing comprehended, yet the terms made use of I seldom used." This changed when she finally entered a state of holiness: "Now there seemed such a glorious propriety in the words "HOLINESS," "SANCTIFICATION," that I thought nothing less than infinite Wisdom could have devised words so infinitely proper," Palmer, Faith, pp. 73-74. Cf. The Way of Holiness, pp. 43-45, where she finds "holiness," "sanctification," and "perfect love" to be "most significantly expressive of a state of soul in which every believer should live." No words "of mere earthly origin" are able to "imbody to her own perceptions, or convey to the understanding of others, half the comprehensiveness of meaning contained in them." She "well remembered how often her heart had risen against these expressions, as objectionable...."

[135]Palmer, Faith, p. 255.

[136]Palmer, Faith, p. 251.

[137]Palmer, Faith, pp. 251-252.

[138]Her boldness sometimes troubled even her friends and supporters, however, e.g. her encounter with a merchant who occasionally sold liquor, pp. 246-250. She tells him at one point that he will be eternally damned if he sells or allows to be sold another drop. Sensing the disapproval of her "severity" by others present, she defends herself on the grounds that she "feared that the blood of his soul might be found on her skirts, did she not faithfully declare the whole counsel of God." Needless to say, the merchant, with his whole family, heeding Phoebe's advice, was fully sanctified. Of her con-

frontations with British Methodists over teetotalism, see chapter III of the present study.

[139]See Hughes, Beloved Physician, p. 188.

[140]Palmer, Incidental Illustrations, pp. 208-210.

[141]Palmer, Incidental Illustrations, p. 277.

[142]Palmer, Incidental Illustrations, p. 349.

[143]Palmer, Incidental Illustrations, p. 347.

[144]Palmer, Incidental Illustrations, pp. 75-77.

[145]Palmer, Incidental Illustrations, pp. 36-43.

[146]Palmer, Incidental Illustrations, pp. 53-55. An interesting element of Palmer's comments on the need for missionaries is a muted anti-intellectualism. She warns against "too much ado" over formal training for missionaries. This, coupled with her views on "younger or less pious" ministers, suggests some uneasiness with Methodism's growing stress on formal training for ministry, represented by the standardization of the Course of Study for ministers in 1848, the founding of numerous colleges in the 1830s and '40s, and seminaries in the 1840s and '50s. Palmer was by no means alone in her concern. See History of American Methodism, volume I, pp. 546-571, and Norwood, pp. 217-222, 302-308. Also Frederick A. Norwood, editor, Sourcebook of American Methodism (Nashville: Abingdon Press, 1982), pp. 297-300.

[147]Palmer, Incidental Illustrations, pp. 87-91.

[148]Palmer, Incidental Illustrations, pp. 202-203.

[149]Palmer, Incidental Illustrations, pp. 223-225. Note that the "family" is made up of holiness proponents. Those not firmly behind the cause are presumably not "family" in the same sense. The seeds of division are quite obvious here.

[150]E.g. pp. 13-25, 45-51, 319-323, and passim.

[151]E.g. pp. vi, 105-107, 121-123, 128-133, and passim.

[152]E.g. pp. 39-40, 182, 241, 325-334, and passim.

[153]E.g. pp. 45-47, 53, 105, 264-265, and passim.

[154]E.g. pp. 107, 148-154, 307-312, and passim.

[155]E.g. pp. 40-42, 92, 319-323, 353-355, and passim.

[156]Palmer, Incidental Illustrations, p. 140.

[157]Palmer, Incidental Illustrations, pp. 141-143.

[158]Palmer, Incidental Illustrations, p. 227.

[159]Palmer, Incidental Illustrations, pp. 328-334.

[160]Notably Ruether and Keller, Women and Religion in America; Rosemary Ruether and Eleanor McLaughlin, editors, Women of Spirit; Female Leadership in the Jewish and Christian Traditions (New York: Simon and Schuster, 1979); James, Women in American Religion; Alice Rossi, editor, The Feminist Papers: From Adams to de Beauvoir (New York: Columbia University Press, 1973).

[161]See Thomas and Keller, Women in New Worlds; Dayton and Dayton, "'Your Daughters Shall Prophesy': Feminism in the Holiness Movement"; Nancy Hardesty, Lucille Sider Dayton and Donald Dayton, "Women in the Holiness Movement: Feminism in the Evangelical Tradition" in Ruether and McLaughlin, pp. 225-254; Rosemary Skinner Keller, "Women and The Nature of Ministry in the United Methodist Tradition," Methodist History, January, 1984, pp. 99-114; Dayton, Discovering An Evangelical Heritage, pp. 85-98.

[162]Dayton, Discovering an Evangelical History, p. 96. Also on Palmer see Ruether and Keller, pp. 1-9, 193-206, 217-218; Hardesty, "Minister as Prophet? or as Mother?" in Thomas and Keller, pp. 88-101; Theodore Hovet, "Phoebe Palmer's 'Altar Phraseology' and the Spiritual Dimension of Woman's Sphere," The Journal of Religion, 63 (1983), pp. 264-280.

[163]It does not appear that Phoebe faced as much opposition on account of her sex as one might suppose. It is, of course, always possible that some of the opposition which expressed itself under other guises was in reality "sexist." Hiram Mattison, her chief doctrinal antagonist, while usually keeping his controversy with her in the realm of religious ideas, did at least once reveal his opposition to more than ideas. Criticizing

her widespread travel to promote her "new measures" brand of holiness, he asks, "...are we so ignorant [of holiness] as to require a <u>sister</u> to travel from conference to conference to instruct us on this subject?" He then adds, "Is the course pursued by some of our sisters in perfect accordance with the apostolic rule, 1 Timothy 2:12, 'But I suffer not a woman to teach, nor to usurp authority over the man, but to be in silence'?", <u>The Christian Advocate and Journal</u>, Nov. 29, 1855, p. 189. Emphasis added. There was also the one who wondered upon publication of <u>The Way of Holiness</u> if its author might not have been better engaged in washing dishes than in writing. See Wheatley, p. 488. Similar opposition is hinted at by the Methodist "patriarch," Nathan Bangs, in whose Methodist class Phoebe had been as a child, when he writes, "And why should any one oppose another, <u>even though a female</u>, so eminently owned by the Head of the Church, in the conversion of sinners and the sanctification of believers?" See Stevens, <u>Life and Times of Nathan Bangs</u>, p. 351. Emphasis added. Cf. <u>The Guide to Holiness</u>, February 1875, pp. 42-44, where Rev. William Reddy characterizes the doctrinal controversies in which Palmer was involved as "degenerating into an attack upon her womanly and wifely character." The most overt attack against Palmer's right as a woman to minister seems to have been launched in Britain rather than the U.S. On this see chapter III of the present study.

On opposition to other women, see Wheatley, p. 613, and Palmer, <u>Promise of the Father</u>, <u>passim</u>. Palmer also seems to have been inspired by the example of the Quakers. See her 1850 comments on female Quaker "ministers" in Wheatley, pp. 601-602.

[164]Wheatley, pp. 496-497.

[165]Palmer, <u>Promise</u>, p. 37.

[166]Palmer, <u>Promise</u>, pp. 14, 23. Cf. the subtitle of the book, "A Neglected Specialty of the Last Days."

[167]Palmer, <u>Promise</u>, pp. 18-19.

[168]Palmer, <u>Promise</u>, p. 22. Emphasis added. In the book Palmer equates "preaching" and "prophesying." See pp. 34-51, 329-338 and the present study, chapter III.

[169]Palmer, <u>Promise</u>, p. 70.

[170]Palmer, <u>Promise</u>, p. 70.

171Palmer, Promise, pp. 49-51. This is a most
interesting comment in light of Phoebe's heavy reliance
in her other doctrinal tracts on the very sort of "proof
texting" here condemned. Those works were all published
prior to 1859.

172Palmer, Promise, p. 6. The "irregularities," she
thinks, were "disorderly debates" prompted by impious
questioners at public worship. Women, lacking instruction and "devoid of spirituality," were entering into
these, prompting St. Paul's exhortation. He was not
forbidding "the ordinary speaking of women in prophesying."

173Palmer, Promise, pp. 48-49.

174See Robert Bruce Mullin, "Biblical Critics and
the Battle Over Slavery," Journal of Presbyterian History, 61 (1983) pp. 70-85. It is not surprising that
Palmer should cite Albert Barnes' Notes on the New
Testament frequently in Promise of the Father, as Barnes
was a major shaper of the "abolitionist hermeneutic."
See Albert Barnes, An Inquiry Into the Scriptural Views
of Slavery (Philadelphia: Perry and McMillan, 1846). Cf.
the arguments of James Blanchard in Rev. J. Blanchard
and N. C. Rice, A Debate on Slavery Held in The City of
Cincinnati.... (Cincinnati: H. Moore and Company, 1846).

175Palmer, Promise, pp. 54-59, 107-109, 115-118.
Several of these women's stories are recounted by Palmer
in the book. A recent treatment of women in Wesley's
movement is Earl Kent Brown, "Women of the Word: Select
Leadership Roles of Women in Mr. Wesley's Methodism" in
Thomas and Keller, pp. 69-87.

176Palmer, Promise, pp. 5-6. It is interesting to
note here that The Promise was dedicated to an
Episcopalian, Philadelphia pastor Dudley A. Tyng.

177Palmer, Promise, passim.

178Palmer, Promise, p. 71.

179Palmer, Promise, p. 1. There are several references in The Promise to the superiority of women, from
the view of the Rev. H. Woodruff that Christian women
are "more eloquent, winning, and persuasive, in propor-
tion to their educational advantages, than the other
sex," to Adam Clarke's amazing calculation that the

influence of one woman is equal to that of seven and one half men. See pp. 96-100 and passim.

[180]Palmer, Promise, p. 1.

[181]Palmer, Promise, p. 12.

[182]Palmer, Promise, pp. 1-2. Palmer reflects to a large degree the concept of "woman's sphere" as a number of recent scholars have described this. The term refers to the religiously sanctioned role of nineteenth-century woman as foot soldier for religion through various voluntary female religious associations, but in the wider social context confined to home and family as "domestic overseer," and subject to men. Palmer believes home and family represent woman's "normal" place of responsibility even though she also advocates engaging in religious activities outside the home. She was herself a member of "female associations" for evangelistic and charitable work.

As several have noticed, this circumscribed role of women had a dual thrust which was at the same time conservative (women as "domestic overseers" and women as subordinate religious foot soldiers) and progressive (women bonded in a self-conscious female community of religious activism which provided identity outside the home and a political training ground). Palmer's views evidence this ambiguity. She skirts the issue of women taking positions of leadership in church or state, pronounces herself satisfied with women's lot generally, counsels female subordination, but also introduces a destabilizing influence into the "cult of domesticity" which, it can be argued, has even greater potential for overthrowing the status quo than the usual encouragements to women to band together in female religious support groups. This is her insistence on an equalitarian "Spirit baptized" religious activism embracing women and men alike. The demands of this may well take a woman largely out of the home, as they did Palmer herself. Interesting in this regard is a note she recorded fairly early in her career (1849) in which she criticized a talented wealthy lady acquaintance for carrying "unaided the cares of her family" when by hiring domestic help she could do much religious work. She considered this a "misappropriation of talents." See Wheatley, pp. 597-598. Also important is Palmer's concept of "entire consecration" which may well involve for the woman seeking sanctification a "giving up" to God of spouse and family, attachments which may distract her from "religious duties" God may require. In this Palmer is wedding the

activism engendered by American revivalism generally to
her own brand of "perfectionism."
The essential studies of women in nineteenth-
century America are Nancy F. Cott, The Bonds of Woman-
hood: Woman's Sphere" in New England, 1780-1835 (New
Haven and London: Yale University Press, 1977); Ann
Douglas, The Feminization of American Culture (New York:
Alfred A. Knopf, 1977); Barbara Welter, Dimity Convic-
tions: The American Woman in the Nineteenth Century
(Athens, Ohio: Ohio University Press, 1976).

[183]Palmer, Promise, pp. 1-13. For the Women's
Rights Movement which provided an important backdrop for
Palmer's book, see Aileen S. Kraditor, Up from the
Pedestal: Selected Writings in the History of American
Feminism (Chicago: Quadrangle Books, 1968).

[184]Palmer, Promise, p. 4.

[185]See the Christian Advocate, Oct. 20, 1841, p.
37.

[186]Wheatley, pp. 406, 374, 470; Palmer, Faith, p.
256; The Guide to Holiness, May 1873, pp. 169-171.

[187]Wheatley, pp. 230-323.

[188]Wheatley, pp. 233-234.

[189]Wheatley, pp. 231-232.

[190]Wheatley, pp. 222-230.

[191]Wheatley, pp. 188-190.

[192]Wheatley, pp. 227-230. Palmer's views of the
second advent do not fit neatly into the categories of
pre- or postmillennialism or the like. She did believe
that certain "signs of the times" suggested by the Bible
could be discerned, pointing to the approach of the end
of the age, but she was adamant that no "timetable"
could or should be constructed, cautioning that adventist speculations could easily become an unhealthy preoccupation. Fascinating in this connection is a letter
she wrote to William Miller, whose views sparked the
"Adventist" movement in America, in 1844, two days after
the "Great Disappointment" (October 22, 1844) at which
time Miller's precise predictions of Christ's visible
return had not been fulfilled. Adding insult to his
already considerable injury, she scolds him for present-

ing Adventist views as "The faith," and charges him to acknowledge his errors and "sound a retreat," so that the people misled by him can get back to the real business of working in the churches. See Wheatley, pp. 512-513. Another undated letter to Miller is even stronger, Phoebe suggesting that his erroneous calculations are a deception of Satan. See Faith, pp. 319-324. Though Palmer believed the second advent was near, she was neither markedly optimistic nor pessimistic in her evaluation of the events of her time which might signal its approach. For her views see Wheatley, pp. 513-514 and The Guide to Holiness, April, 1873, p. 122. For general treatments of adventist and millennial views in America see Ernest R. Sandeen, The Roots of Fundamentalism: British and American Millennarianism, 1800-1930 (Chicago: University of Chicago Press, 1970) and Timothy P. Weber, Living in the Shadow of the Second Coming: American Pre-millennialism 1875-1925 (New York: Oxford University Press, 1979).

[193]Hughes, Beloved Physician, p. 84. Cf. Palmer, Incidental Illustrations, pp. 77-78.

[194]Wheatley, pp. 213-214. The terms of the "adoption" are not clear. The boy had been jailed by his parents, according to Phoebe, for "embracing the Christian faith." The Palmers were then given custody and the boy's "indenture" by city authorities, a kind of "foster care" arrangement it would appear.

[195]Wheatley, pp. 224-227; The Old Brewery and the New Mission House at the Five Points. By Ladies of the Mission (New York: Stringer and Townsend, 1854); Smith, Revivalism and Social Reform, pp. 170-171. The circumstances of Phoebe's initial interest in Five Points are most interesting. It was while passing through the area on the way to Greenwood Cemetery to bury her father in the spring of 1847 that she first conceived the idea. One wonders if this is mere coincidence since there is clearly a strong link for her between the death of those close to her and efforts to please God through religious activity. The deaths of her three children, her mother, and father are all accompanied by resolutions to make their deaths the occasion for more vigorous service to God.

[196]Wheatley, pp. 205-210.

[197]Wheatley, pp. 211-213, 218-220. The accounts make plain that her main interest was conversions, as

with the boy who is provided with a coat in exchange for a promise to attend Sabbath school.

[198]Wheatley, p. 223.

[199]Wheatley, p. 600.

[200]Wheatley, p. 601.

[201]Palmer, Faith, p. 222.

[202]Wheatley, p. 600.

[203]Wheatley, pp. 214-218.

[204]Wheatley, pp. 220-222.

[205]Wheatley, p. 221.

[206]E.g. her surprise at the sudden entire sanctification of a missionary: "I had not thought her so near the reception of the blessing, as she was more conformed in outward manner to the world, than earnest seekers after holiness generally are." See Wheatley, p. 246. Cf. Palmer, Incidental Illustrations, pp. 79-80, where Palmer confronts a seeker after holiness about her "relics of worldliness" which keep her from the blessing. Finally giving up her "last needless ornament," she was able to "appropriate the promises [of God], and was cleansed from all filthiness of the flesh and spirit."

[207]The Guide to Holiness, February 1875, pp. 49-50.

[208]The Guide to Holiness, October 1874, pp. 117-119.

[209]Wheatley, pp. 117-118.

[210]Wheatley, pp. 327-328. See her somewhat playful, but stinging attack on earrings as "relics of heathendom" in "She Is an Ishmaelite," The Guide to Holiness, July 1874, pp. 21-23. Phoebe was in this, as always, an exemplar of her own views. Wheatley considered her very close to the Shakers on dress. Some referred to her and Sarah as "the drab sisters." See Roche, The Life, p. 261. Interesting is Phoebe's commendation of an English "Women's Dress Association" to promote moderate, inexpensive, healthy dress in The Guide to Holiness, November 1873, p. 153.

[211]Wheatley, pp. 608-610.

[212]Wheatley, pp. 606-607, 450-451.

[213]See chapter III of the present study. On the temperance/abstinence movement see Ian R. Tyrell, Sobering Up: From Temperance to Prohibition in Antebellum America, 1800-1860 (Westport, CT: Greenwood Press, 1979).

[214]See The Guide to Holiness, July 1874, pp. 23-24 and June 1873, pp. 188-189.

[215]Palmer, Incidental Illustrations, pp. 271-278. Interesting is the fact that these all seem to relate to upper-middle-class life and the "temptations" of upwardly mobile persons seeking wealth, social acceptance, and status. Many mid-nineteenth-century Methodists fit into this category.

[216]John Wesley, Advice to the People Called Methodists With Regard to Dress (London: John Parmore, 1780).

[217]Hiram Mattison, Popular Amusements: An Appeal to Methodists in Regard to the Evils of Card-Playing, Billiards, Dancing, Theatre-Going, Etc. (New York: Carlton and Porter, 1867).

[218]Wheatley, pp. 60-61.

[219]Smith, pp. 211-212.

[220]See William A. Clebsch, "Christian Interpretations of the Civil War," Church History, 30 (1961), pp. 212-222; William J. Wolf, Lincoln's Religion (Philadelphia: Pilgrim Press, 1970).

[221]Wheatley, pp. 599-600; cf. Palmer, Four Years, pp. 498-502, 647-650.

[222]Wheatley, p. 162.

[223]Wheatley, pp. 61-63; 548-551; 561-565.

[224]Wheatley, pp. 607-608.

CHAPTER V

[1]Wesley, _Plain_ _Account_, p. 20.

[2]Wesley, _Plain_ _Account_, pp. 11, 9-10.

[3]Wesley, _Plain_ _Account_, p. 60.

[4]Quoted in Norwood, _Story_, p. 130.

[5]Especially helpful in describing this "American style" and analyzing the forces which contributed to it is Winthrop S. Hudson, _American_ _Protestantism_ (Chicago: University of Chicago Press, 1961).

[6]Langford, pp. 11-12.

[7]Dieter, p. 3.

[8]Among others, Lindström, _Wesley_ _and_ _Sanctification_, Peters, _Christian_ _Perfection_ _and_ _American_ _Methodism_, and, more recently, Langford, _Practical_ _Divinity_.

[9]Thomas Jackson, editor, _The_ _Works_ _of_ _The_ _Rev._ _John_ _Wesley_, _A.M._ 14 volumes (Kansas City, MO: Nazarene Publishing House. Reprint of the 1872 edition), vol. 8, p. 300; Telford, _Letters_, vol. 8, p. 238.

[10]Wesley, _Plain_ _Account_, p. 50.

[11]The crisis "is constantly both preceded and followed by a gradual work," and the one "perfected in love may grow in grace far swifter than he did before," Wesley, _Plain_ _Account_ , p. 114.

[12]Wesley, _Plain_ _Account_, p. 116.

[13]Wesley, _Plain_ _Account_, p. 30.

[14]Outler, "The Scripture Way of Salvation," p. 278.

[15]Outler, pp. 275-276.

[16]Outler, pp. 279-280.

[17]Outler, pp. 279-280.

[18]Peters, pp. 56-57.

[19]Peters, pp. 56-57.

[20]It is hard to disagree with Peters' view that "Wesley's choice and use of terms was unfortunate." He is also correct in asserting that, because of this, "It is quite possible to quote Wesley at length against Wesley," Peters, pp. 63-64.

[21]Wesley, Plain Account, p. 104.

[22]Wesley, Works, III, p. 449.

[23]Joseph Benson, The Life of The Rev. John W. De La Flechere (New York: The Methodist Book Concern, n.d.).

[24]See David C. Shipley, Methodist Arminianism in the Theology of John Fletcher (Unpublished Ph.D. Dissertation, Yale University, 1942).

[25]Luke Tyerman, Wesley's Designated Successor (New York: A. C. Armstrong and Son, 1886), p. 346. In fact, as early as the 1790s it was said of the typical American Methodism preacher that he "read himself full of Fletcher's Checks and Wesley's Sermons, which, besides his Bible, were the only books within his reach." Quoted in Bucke, History of American Methodism, Vol. I, p. 332.

[26]See The Works of the Rev. John Fletcher. 4 Volumes (New York: Carlton and Phillips, 1854), Vol. 2, pp. 483-669.

[27]Fletcher, Works, 2, p. 492.

[28]See Benson, p. 203; Fletcher, Works, 2, pp. 627-657; John Allen Knight, John William Fletcher and The Early Methodist Tradition (Unpublished Ph.D. Dissertation, Vanderbilt University, 1966), especially pp. 306-325; John Allen Knight, "John Fletcher's Influence on the Development of Wesleyan Theology in America," Wesleyan Theological Journal, 13 (1978), pp. 13-33.

[29]A fascinating recent study is Blake J. Neff, John Wesley and John Fletcher on Entire Sanctification: A Metaphoric Cluster Analysis (Unpublished Ph.D. Dissertation, Bowling Green State University, 1982). Neff finds a considerable difference in emphasis. Among other things he demonstrates that Christ is central to sanctification for Wesley, the Holy Spirit for Fletcher; sanctification is a "preventitive cleansing" for Wesley to prevent an onset of actual sinning, while for Fletcher

it is the healing of already present "disease," or sin;
Fletcher is more concerned with the "external evidences"
of sanctification in the life of the believer than is
Wesley.

[30]Fletcher, Works, 2, pp. 632-633. Different interpreters have made different claims about Fletcher--as
with Wesley--by focusing on different aspects of his
thought. Thus, Peters finds Fletcher to stress the
gradualness of sanctification and to give only "qualified" endorsement to Wesley's "second blessing schemati-
zation" by noting his statements about "growth in grace"
and multiple "baptisms of the Spirit," while Langford,
noting Fletcher's identification of sanctification with
Pentecost, concludes he introduced a new "emphasis on
the instantaneous event of sanctification." See Peters,
pp. 71-80, and Langford, pp. 50-53.

[31]Fletcher, Works, 2, pp. 259ff. Knight concludes
that Fletcher came very close to asserting that one is
not a true Christian until he or she is "filled with the
Holy Spirit." See Knight, John William Fletcher and the
Early Methodist Tradition, p. 306.

[32]Benson, p. 80.

[33]Benson, p. 154.

[34]Chiles, pp. 144-183.

[35]Knight, John William Fletcher and The Early
Methodist Tradition, pp. 381-397. Cf. Knight, "John
Fletcher's Influence on the Development of Wesleyan
Theology in America," pp. 16-22.

[36]An Account of the Experience of Hester Ann
Rogers, pp. 132-135. Emphasis added.

[37]The Life of Faith Exemplified; or, Extracts from
the Journal of Mrs. Hester Ann Rogers (New York: Carlton
and Porter, 1861), pp. 137-138. Emphasis added. The text
here differs slightly from that in An Account, cited
above.

[38]An Account, p. 137. This supports Knight's
contention that Fletcher held that one is not a true
Christian until "filled with the Holy Spirit."

[39]Adam Clarke, Christian Theology, edited by Samuel
Dunn (New York: T. Mason and G. Lane, [1835] 1840).

[40]Clarke, pp. 207-208.

[41]Wesley, Works, XI, p. 390.

[42]Clarke, pp. 191-192.

[43]Clarke, pp. 129-132.

[44]Clarke, p. 130.

[45]Clarke, pp. 130, 133.

[46]Clarke, p. 206.

[47]Clarke, pp. 184-185.

[48]Clarke, pp. 400-401.

[49]Clarke, pp. 404-410.

[50]Clarke, pp. 401-403. His thoughts on dress are interesting in light of his opposition to clergy wearing black, because the color does not express the "beauty of holiness." "Is it emblematical of anything that is good, glorious, or excellent?" he asks.

[51]An Account, p. 95. As for pioneering, in her day the Wesleyan movement was quite revolutionary and disturbing to many. Methodist preachers were sometimes attacked or even marked for assassination. See her account of an attempt on her husband's life while preaching in Dublin, pp. 151-153. Though the details are not given, Catholic-Protestant and Anglo-Irish tensions were probably involved.

[52]For example, in one place she recommends first to one seeking entire sanctification "Mr. Fletcher's Polemical Essay," and only secondarily Wesley's Plain Account. In another place she refers to meditating on "those beautiful ideas of Mr. Fletcher on the millennium." Rogers also adopted Fletcher's "pentecostal language" to describe Christian Perfection, his views of the nature of faith, and perpetuated his remarks about losing holiness by not publicly testifying to it. See An Account, pp. 228-229; 164; and passim.

[53]An Account, pp. 43, 99.

[54]An Account, pp. 253-254.

[55]An Account, pp. 201, 233. The statement on faith as "the act of man" reflects Fletcher's view, and is also almost a direct quote of Adam Clarke, although, interestingly, Rogers was apparently in print on this topic before Clarke.

[56]An Account, p. 218.

[57]An Account, pp. 40, 131. Emphasis added.

[58]An Account, p. 224. Emphasis added.

[59]An Account, p. 188. Emphasis added.

[60]An Account, pp. 47, 100.

[61]An Account, p. 148.

[62]See Chapter II of the present study. She is, of course, drawing on biblical imagery, notably Matthew 6:21 and Luke 12:34--"For where your treasure is, there will your heart be also"--though the twist she gives it is suggested by Rogers.

[63]An Account, p. 121.

[64]Cf. Wheatley, pp. 305-307 and An Account, pp. 154-155.

[65]Life of William Carvosso, Sixty years A Class Leader, edited by Benjamin Carvosso (Cincinnati: Jennings and Pye, n.d.). This was first published in 1835.

[66]Carvosso, p. 5.

[67]Carvosso, p. 18.

[68]Very likely Carvosso was introduced to Fletcher's ideas by Hester Ann Rogers. In one place he notes, "For some of my best thoughts on faith, I am indebted to the excellent Memoirs and Letters of Hester Ann Rogers." Elsewhere he describes leading one into entire sanctification by reading an exhortation of Fletcher's from the pages of Rogers' Memoirs. Only later does he refer to having read Fletcher's Letters and quotes at some length from them on "naked faith." See Carvosso, pp. 130; 196-1917; 201-202; 246-248.

[69]Carvosso, p. 147. Emphasis added. Cf. Rogers, Memoir, pp. 201, 233 and Clarke, pp. 129-132.

[70]Carvosso, pp. 74, 214. Emphasis added.

[71]Carvosso, p. 154. Cf. Palmer's insistence that faith is one's "reasonable" obligation, and her statement that belief in divine promises for salvation "is hardly of faith, but rather of knowledge; it is so easy." See chapter IV of the present study and Palmer, Faith, p. 343.

[72]Carvosso, p. 8.

[73]Carvosso, p. 12. Note faith, not God or Christ, did this.

[74]Carvosso, p. 146.

[75]Carvosso, p. 119.

[76]Carvosso, p. 101.

[77]Carvosso, p. 210.

[78]Carvosso, p. 6. Emphasis added.

[79]Carvosso, p. 139.

[80]Carvosso, pp. 37-38. Emphasis added.

[81]Carvosso, p. 68. Emphasis added. Cf. the many places Phoebe Palmer instructs seekers similarly, as well as the role this concept plays in her own, and her sister Sarah's, religious pilgrimage.

[82]Carvosso, pp. 246-248, 136.

[83]Carvosso, p. 230.

[84]Carvosso, pp. 33-34; 192; 214. Even Palmer's use of Romans 10:10 is anticipated by Carvosso.

[85]E.g. pp. 80-82.

[86]Carvosso, p. 82.

[87]Carvosso, p. 8.

[88]Palmer, Incidental Illustrations, pp. v-vi.

[89]Cf. Incidental Illustrations, pp. 355-362, and Carvosso, pp. 10-12.

[90]Carvosso, pp. 242-244.

[91]See Bucke, I, pp. 440-452, on the schism centering around James O'Kelley. See also Ahlstrom, Religious History, pp. 445-454.

[92]See Scott, Methodist Theology in the Nineteenth Century; Bucke, I, pp. 346-357; Norwood, The Story, pp. 223-229.

[93]See chapter II, pp. 21-22; Peters, pp. 90 ff. Cf. Allan Coppedge, "Entire Sanctification in Early American Methodism: 1812-1835," Wesleyan Theological Journal, 13 (1978), pp. 34-50, which argues, quite alone, that there was no "neglect" of Christian Perfection in this period and hence no cause for concern. Nevertheless, concern there was.

[94]See Timothy Merritt, The Christian's Manual: A Treatise on Christian Perfection (New York: N. Bangs and J. Emory, 1825) and Aaron Lummus, Essays on Holiness (Boston: Timothy Ashley, 1826).

[95]See Johnson, Frontier Campmeeting; Bucke, I, pp. 494-523.

[96]It may be argued that the Wesleyan movement was "revivalistic" from its inception, being generated out of religious "awakenings" in Britain and America, and building itself through "revivalistic" techniques like field preaching, itinerant preachers, etc. This must be granted, but it must also be remembered that the revivalism of the nineteenth century was a "different beast" from that of the eighteenth century awakenings. Also, the new stress on Christian Perfection as neglected and in need of special promotion created a new climate for its presentation. On the new elements in nineteenth-century revivalism see McLoughlin, Modern Revivalism, and McLoughlin, Revivals, especially pp. 98-140.

[97]It is interesting and instructive to look at Palmer's concern with the methodology of attaining Christian Perfection in comparison with her contemporaries. Peck's Scripture Doctrine of Christian Perfection, published in 1842, after Palmer's Advocate articles, but before The Way of Holiness, gives only twenty pages out of 470 to the means of attaining holiness. And

even then his advice is quite general, listing the
following five steps: 1) "Endeavour to have a definite
idea of the thing"--i.e. aim at a specific goal, which
he identifies as "the destruction of sin, and the
renewing of the soul in the image of God" (pp.
397-398); 2) "A certain amount of feeling upon the subject is
necessary"--i.e. one must <u>anxiously</u> pursue the goal (p.
400); "We must exercise feelings of contrition....A deep
and. . .godly sorrow must take possession of our hearts.
This feeling will arise from a conviction of hidden
corruptions and inward unlikeness to God...." 4) "The
grand condition upon which our entire sanctification is
suspended, and which must be met and discharged, is
faith in the Lord Jesus Christ" (p. 405); 5) "I would
urge the necessity of attendance upon all the means of
grace," including the reading of the Bible, prayer,
corporate worship, and all "the great duties of piety,
charity, and mortification prescribed in the gospel"
(pp. 409-413).

[98]Peters, p. 89.

[99]Finney, <u>Lectures on Systematic Theology</u>, pp. 378,
373, 374.

[100]Outler, p. 49.

[101]Outler, p. 29. Emphasis added.

[102]E.g. see Chiles' discussion of Richard Watson in
this connection, pp. 87-95.

[103]For Wesley "perfect love" was much <u>more</u> than an
emotion, or feeling, but it would be <u>felt</u> and would
reorient all human affections away from self and sin
toward God and others. For an analysis of the motif of
"perfect love" in Wesley which includes both historical
analysis and contemporary application, see Mildred Bangs
Wynkoop, <u>A Theology of Love</u> (Kansas City, MO: Beacon
Hill Press, 1972).

[104]There were the occasional outbreaks of "enthusiasm" within Methodist ranks which provided critics
with ammunition. See Outler, pp. 298-305, and Peters,
pp. 67-68.

[105]<u>An Account</u>, p. 124.

[106]<u>Carvosso</u>, pp. 70 , 150.

[107]Bucke, I, p. 514-515.

[108]For this debate in the first Great Awakening see Jonathan Edwards, Religious Affections, edited by John E. Smith (New Haven: Yale University Press, 1959) and Charles Chauncy, Seasonable Thoughts on the State of Religion (Hicksville, New York: The Regina Press, 1975. Reprint of 1743 edition). John Wesley abridged and circulated Edwards' treatise as part of his Christian Library for Methodists.

[109]Scott, Methodist Theology in America in the Nineteenth Century, p. 104 ff., describes the "exaggeration of the experiential dimension of religion" among Methodists which occurred due to the influence of frontier revivalism.

[110]The "biblicism" which marks her thought has some parallels in Adam Clarke, but it is quite unlike anything in Wesley, Fletcher, Rogers or Carvosso.

[111]Most interesting in this regard is the gradually enlarging gap which grew between Palmer and her early convert, Thomas Upham, as the latter became ever more "mystical" in his understanding of holiness, teaching a "third state" beyond entire sanctification in which the human will is utterly annihilated and replaced by the will of God. Upham grounded his teaching upon experience and the immediate inspiration of the Holy Spirit. Some of Palmer's other converts began adopting Upham's views. In response to an article Upham published on the topic, Phoebe wrote a letter in April of 1851, warning him that his dependence upon experience left him open to the "subtilety of Satan," and urging him to cleave to the "written Word" of God as his guide. It was her opinion that his views were not backed by "an explicit 'Thus saith the Lord'" and thus must have "originated in error." See Wheatley, pp. 518-523.

[112]See chapter II of the present study.

[113]Christian Advocate, August 2, 1855, p. 121.

[114]Christian Advocate, August 2, 1855, p. 121.

[115]Christian Advocate, November 15, 1855, p. 181.

[116]Christian Advocate, November 29, 1855, p. 189.

[117]Christian Advocate, December 6, 1855, p. 195.

[118]*Christian* *Advocate*, December 20, 1855, pp. 201-202.

[119]Finney, *Lectures* *on* *Systematic* *Theology*, p. 405. On the "New Divinity" see Mead, Nathaniel William Taylor; Cherry, *Nature* *and* *Religious* *Imagination*, pp. 113-133; George M. Marsden, *The* *Evangelical* *Mind* *and* *the* *New* *School* *Presbyterian* *Experience* (New Haven: Yale University Press, 1970). On Oberlin perfectionism see Warfield, II, pp. 3-215; Madden and Hamilton, *Freedom* *and* *Grace*; Donald W. Dayton, "Asa Mahan and the Development of American Holiness Theology," *Wesleyan* *Theological* *Journal*, 9 (1974), pp. 60-69; Timothy L. Smith, "The Doctrine of the Sanctifying Spirit: Charles G. Finney's Synthesis of Wesleyan and Covenant Theology," *Wesleyan* *Theological* *Journal*, 13 (1978), pp. 92-113.

[120]*Christian* *Advocate*, January 3, 1856, p. 3.

[121]*Christian* *Advocate*, January 10, 1856, pp. 5-7.

[122]Stevens, *Nathan* *Bangs*, pp. 350-353, 396-402.

[123]Stevens, p. 398. Notice that Bangs argues not only for an "internal conviction" of sanctification, but for external evidence ("any change in our disposition") as well. Palmer would have agreed with him that such external expression of holiness is necessary, but she would not--and did not--agree that such is necessary before one has a right to believe oneself entirely sanctified.

[124]Stevens, p. 402. Bangs was so concerned that his views be accurately conveyed that he left written instructions for the public use of the relevant portion of his journal after his death.

[125]The matter of the emergence of "Pentecostal" themes in American religious thought is a badly tangled thicket at best. Several students have tried to untangle it. Among these are Smith, "The Doctrine of The Sanctifying Spirit," Donald W. Dayton in several articles including "Asa Mahan and the Development of American Holiness Theology," "The Doctrine of the Baptism of the Holy Spirit: Its Emergence and Significance," and "From Christian Perfection to the 'Baptism of the Holy Ghost,'" in Vinson Synan, editor, *Aspects* *of* *Pentecostal-Charismatic* *Origins* (Plainfield, New Jersey: Logos International, 1975), pp. 41-54; and Melvin E. Dieter, "Wesleyan-Holiness Aspects of Pentecostal Origins: As

Mediated through the Nineteenth Century Holiness Revival" in Aspects of Pentecostal-Charismatic Origins, pp. 57-80. Palmer clearly plays an important role in this story, contributing to the development of "Pentecostal" vocabulary and conceptions, but what is not so clear is the process by which she developed her ideas. Smith thinks Finney pioneered the process, directly influencing Methodists like Palmer. Dayton tends to see Oberlin and Methodist ideas developing along separate, but parallel tracks. Prominent in both he thinks is British Methodist William Arthur's book, The Tongue of Fire; or, the True Power of Christianity (New York: Harper and Brothers, Publishers, 1857). Dieter's view is similar. Though all acknowledge Fletcher's contribution of "Pentecostal" themes to the Wesleyan tradition, little is made of the survival of these themes in the Wesleyan "popularizers" like Rogers and Carvosso and even early American holiness exponents like Timothy Merritt.

My own view is that Palmer was guided more by her Methodist sources than anything else. This would be consistent with the development of her thought generally. She was not unaware of Oberlin, and may have taken some cues from Mahan and Finney, but this cannot be documented. Mahan and Finney may well have learned their Pentecostal doctrine from Fletcher. As for Arthur, Palmer nowhere cites him, even in her Promise of the Father where one might expect to find him alongside other quoted authorities. However, even if she had not read him, she might have heard him. The Christian Advocate and Journal of both November 1 and December 6, 1855 carried news items on a tour of the U.S. made by Arthur which included New York. Even so, his "pentecostal language" was not tied explicitly to the idea of sanctification, but was used more generally in connection with a hoped for "Pentecostal outpouring" upon the Christian Church to empower it for faithful service to God and humankind. Also, Palmer was evidencing considerable "spirit concern" prior to 1855.

[126]See Elizabeth Flower and Murray G. Murphey, A History of Philosophy in America, 2 volumes (New York: G. P. Putnam's Sons, 1977), Vol. I, pp. 203ff.; Henry F. May, The Enlightenment in America (New York: Oxford University Press, 1976), pp. 307-362; Ahlstrom, "The Scottish Philosophy and American Theology," pp. 257-272.

[127]As Ahlstrom aptly puts it, "It came to exist in America...as a vast subterranean influence, a sort of water-table nourishing dogmatics in an age of increasing

doubt." See "The Scottish Philososphy and American Theology," p. 268.

[128]Cherry, Nature and Religious Imagination, p.
104. Emphasis added.

[129]See Frederick Dreyer, "Faith and Experience in
the Thought of John Wesley," The American Historical
Review, 88 (February, 1983), pp. 12-30.

[130]Cf. The hymn of Charles Wesley, the brother of
John, "My God, I Know, I Feel Thee Mine."

[131]The Guide to Holiness, July 1867. This was to be
a "general" camp meeting in contrast to the usual district or conference camp meetings.

[132]The story of the "sectarian holiness movement"
has been well told. Overviews are Dieter, The Holiness
Revival of the Nineteenth Century; Jones, Perfectionist
Persuasion; Rose, A Theology of Christian Experience;
Bucke, II, pp. 608-627; E. Dale Dunlap, "Tuesday Meet-
ings, Camp Meetings, and Cabinet Meetings: A Perspective
on the Holiness Movement in the Methodist Church in the
United States in the Nineteenth Century," Methodist
History, 13 (1974), pp. 85-106. Also see such denomina-
tional histories as Timothy L. Smith, Called Unto Holi-
ness, The Story of the Nazarenes: The Formative Years
(Kansas City, MO: Nazarene Publishing House, 1962); Paul
Westphal Thomas and Paul William Thomas, The Days of Our
Pilgrimage: The History of The Pilgrim Holiness Church
(Marion, Indiana: John Wesley Press, 1976); John W. V.
Smith, Quest for Holiness and Unity: A Centennial
History of the Church of God (Anderson, Indiana:
Warner Press, 1980).

[133]Rev. W. H. Boole in The Guide to Holiness,
December 1874, p. 179.

[134]Hughes, Beloved Physician, p. 169.

[135]Cited in Peters, pp. 137-138. Emphasis added.

[136]W. E. Shephard, How to Get Sanctified: An Illustrated Sermon on Practical Consecration (Cincinnati: The
Revivalist Press, 1916), pp. 1-2.

[137]Shephard, pp. 7-11.

[138]Shephard, p. 14.

[139]Shephard, pp. 15-17.

[140]Shephard, pp. 18-19.

[141]Shephard, pp. 34-36.

[142]Shephard, pp. 36-37.

[143]Not unusual is the experience of one turn of the century holiness evangelist who, seeking entire sanctification but finding "there is no feeling," "took it" on "naked faith." This was followed, however, by "spiritual ecstasy" which lasted all night, and which confirmed his faith. See Merle McClurkan Heath, A Man Sent of God: The Life of J. O. McClurkan (Kansas City: MO: Beacon Hill Press, 1947), pp. 34-35.

[144]J. G. Morrison. Achieving Faith (Kansas City, MO: Nazarene Publishing House, 1926), pp. 16-17, 23.

[145]Morrison, pp. 17-19, 25-26.

[146]Morrison, pp. 74-75.

[147]Fannie McDowell Hunter, Women Preachers (Dallas: Berachah Printing Company, 1905).

[148] Hunter, p. 23.

[149]See Hunter, pp. 43-93, for these stories. Interesting is Hunter's inclusion of Anne Hutchinson in her list of important women ministers of the past. Palmer would have found her too emotional and "subjective." See also Mary Lee Cagle, Life and Work of Mary Lee Cagle (Kansas City, MO: Nazarene Publishing House, 1928), pp. 160-176, a sermon entitled "Woman's Right to Preach" which parallels Hunter's--and Palmer's--argument.

CHAPTER VI

[1]Guide to Holiness, January 1875, p. 6. Cf. p. 1 of the present study.

[2]Guide to Holiness, December 1874, p. 184.

[3]Guide to Holiness, December 1874, p. 181.

[4]Smith, Revivalism, pp. 124-125.

[5]George M. Marsden, Fundamentalism and American Culture: The Shaping of Twentieth Century Evangelicalism (New York: Oxford Univrsity Press, 1980), p. 75.

[6]Alice Felt Tyler, Freedom's Ferment: Phases of American Social History from the Colonial Period to the Outbreak of the Civil War (Minneapolis: University of Minnesota Press, 1944).

[7]See James F. Findlay, Jr., Dwight L. Moody: American Evangelist, 1837-1899 (Chicago: University of Chicago Press, 1969), pp. 113, 121, 131-133, 219-222 and Gundry, pp. 153-160.

[8]See J. C. Pollock, The Keswick Story (Chicago: Moody Press, 1964), esspecially pp. 11-37 on the Smiths. Cf. Dieter, pp. 156-189.

[9]See especially Asa Mahan, Baptism of the Holy Ghost (New York: Walter C. Palmer, Jr., 1870). On Phoebe Palmer's views see the present study, passim.

[10]E.g. Marsden, Fundamentalism and American Culture, pp. 72-101; Sandeen, pp. 132-161; Weber, pp. 13-42.

[11]See Vinson Synan, The Holiness-Pentecostal Movement in the United States (Grand Rapids: William B. Erdmans Publishing Company, 1971), pp. 141-153, for this aspect of Pentecostal doctrinal development. Synan strongly emphasizes the Wesleyan influence on Pentecostalism. See also Robert Mapes Anderson, Vision of the Disinherited: The Making of American Pentecostalism (New York: Oxford University Press, 1979), pp. 28-46. Anderson strongly emphasizes the Keswick influence on Pentecostalism. Cf. Synan, Aspects of Pentecostal-Charismatic Origins, pp. 39-98, for assessments of both views.
It should be noted that even the "finished work" Pentecostals--those combining forgiveness and purification from sin in one work of grace--and usually designated "non-Wesleyan," still seek to maintain a "two works of grace" schema, a "Wesleyan" concern, even though their "second work" is quite different from what Wesley envisioned. The "three works of grace" Pentecostals--usually deemed the more "Wesleyan," on the other hand, have more faithfully preserved Wesley's understanding of the "second blessing," but have appended a subsequent, distinct "work of grace," a hardly "Wesleyan" move, though not incompatible with the thrust of Phoebe Palmer's thought, as has been seen.

INDEX

Ecumenism, 94ff., 192f., 291
Education, Palmer's, 28f.
Edwards, Jonathan, 64, 380
Egalitarianism in Palmer's
  Teaching, 91ff., 298
Entire Consecration, 155ff.,
  169ff., 178ff., 184, 197,
  211, 227, 259, 263, 282,
  283f., 356
Entire Devotion to God, 3, 57,
  59, 130, 178ff., 220
Episcopal Church (Protestant
  Episcopal Church), 1, 63, 87,
  96, 108, 125, 207, 291, 315,
  366
Ethics, and Palmer, 11, 27,
  162f., 180f., 211ff., 218ff.,
  244, 370f.

Faith and Its Effects, 3, 57,
  60, 159, 182ff., 194
Faith and Feeling in Palmer's
  Thought, 35f., 44f., 167f.,
  174f., 182ff., 250ff.,
  259ff., 263ff., 267f., 271f.,
  267f., 284, 353, 360f., 384
Family Life, of Palmer, 61f.,
  329
Finney, Charles G., 3, 6, 10,
  70, 115, 118, 123, 127, 150,
  155, 223, 257, 270, 292, 294,
  295, 382
Five Points Mission, 213, 215,
  369
Fletcher, John, 163, 235ff.,
  250, 254, 259, 261, 296,
  373f.
Foster, Rev. Elon, 71
Four Years in the Old World,
  69, 129, 200, 273
Free Methodist Church, 4, 97,
  143ff., 294, 350
Friends, Society of (See
  Quakers)
Fundamentalism, and Palmer, 16,
  294f.
Funeral, of Palmer, 1

Gaddis, Merrill E., 5, 6, 7, 8
German Reformed Church, 314
Gladden, Washington, 10
Grace of God, Palmer's Views
  of, 157ff., 170f., 183ff.
Great Awakenings, 102, 265, 291
Guide to Christian
  Perfection/Holiness, The, 3,
  7, 8, 13, 52, 57, 71, 75,
  130, 142f., 145, 257, 332f.
  338

Hamline, Leonidas, 79, 225,
  330f., 358, 359
Hamline, Melinda Truesdell, 73,
  224, 330f.
Hammond, Edward Payson, 127
Hardesty, Nancy, 17
Hibbard, Rev. Billy, 21f.
Hill, Rev. William, 94
Holiness Church of Christ, 286
Holiness, Palmer's Definitions
  of, 153ff., 169
Holiness Denominations, 2, 3,
  4, 5, 101, 147, 200, 293f.,
  383f.
Holiness Revival (Holiness
  Movement), 2, 4, 5, 9, 12,
  13, 14, 15, 16, 110, 147,
  191ff., 195ff., 200, 277ff.,
  290ff., 316f.
Holiness, Terminology of,
  192f., 234f., 243f., 282f.
  362, 373
Holiness, and Testimony,
  113ff., 162f., 175ff., 197,
  239ff., 247f., 252, 282f.,
  284
Holy Spirit, Doctrine of in
  Palmer, 92f., 187ff., 197f.,
  200, 202ff., 273f., 294f.,
  296f., 380
Howard, Ivan, 14
Hudson, Winthrop S., 5, 315
Hughes, George, 75, 101, 113,
  280f.
Hume, David, 89, 274
Hunter, Rev. Fannie McDowell,
  286f.
Hutcheson, Francis, 89
Hutchinson, Anne, 384

Illinois Wesleyan University,
  70
Illnesses, of Palmer, 59, 72f.,
  137, 165, 326f.
Incidental Illustrations of the
  Economy of Salvation, 64,
  194ff., 253, 273
Inskip, Rev. John, 146

Janes, Charlotte Thibou, 359
Janes, Edmund, 120, 225, 359
Jefferson, Thomas, 21
Jewish Mission, and Palmer,
  213ff., 369
Jones, Charles E., 14f., 332,
  333
Jones, Humphrey Rowland, 127

Keswick Movement, 294ff., 297
Kirk, Edward Norris, 10, 127

STUDIES IN WOMEN AND RELIGION